A Sailor's Logbook

A Sailor's Logbook

A Season Aboard Great Lakes Freighters

Mark L. Thompson

Wayne State University Press   Detroit

Great Lakes Books

*A complete listing of the books in this series can be found
at the back of this volume.*

Philip P. Mason, Editor
Department of History, Wayne State University

Dr. Charles K. Hyde, Associate Editor
Department of History, Wayne State University

Library of Congress Cataloging-in-Publication Data

Thompson, Mark L., 1945–
    A sailor's logbook : a season aboard Great Lakes freighters /
Mark L. Thompson
        p.   cm. — (Great Lakes books)
    ISBN 0-8143-2827-X (alk. paper) —
    ISBN 0-8143-2844-X (pbk. : alk. paper)
    1. Thompson, Mark L., 1945–   . 2. Merchant mariners—
Great Lakes—Biography.   3. Cooks—Great Lakes—Biography.
4. Seafaring life—Great Lakes.   I. Title.   II. Series.
VK140.T495A3   1999
386'.544'0977—dc21   98-45995

To my shipmates on
the *Calcite II, Edgar B. Speer, John G. Munson*
and *Roger Blough* during the 1996 season . . .
and to Julie, who has added so much
happiness to my life.

Introduction

There are few firsthand accounts of life aboard ships on the Great Lakes. For the most part, all we have are snippets, a few worn threads that survive from the thick bolt of rich fabric that is the story of the sailors who have crewed the passenger ships and freight vessels on the inland seas of North America for more than three hundred years. On the other hand, we know a lot about the shipping companies, the ships, the cargoes they carried, and the navigational system that gradually developed on the lakes. These aspects of the industry were carefully documented by government bureaucrats, company bean-counters, and the business-oriented maritime press. Museums, archival collections, and the dusty file cabinets in dozens of company and government offices bulge with all sorts of data about these aspects of the industry. There's even a fair amount of statistical information on the number of sailors who worked on the lakes, how much they were paid, how many days they worked during a particular season, how much was spent on their food, and so on. It's interesting data, and obviously valuable, but it appears sterile when compared to the few in-depth accounts of shipboard life that have survived.

The best firsthand accounts I've come across are Fred W. Dutton's *Life on the Great Lakes: A Wheelsman's Story* (William Donohue Ellis, ed., Detroit: Wayne State University Press, 1991) and Horace L. Beaton's *From the Wheelhouse: The Story of a Great Lakes Captain* (Cheltenham, Ont.: Boston Mills Press, 1991). Dutton began sailing in 1916 when he was only sixteen years old. The son of an ore company official, Dutton went on to earn a law degree and work for the Chesapeake & Ohio Railway Company's legal department. At heart, though, Fred Dutton was always a diehard sailor. He worked summers on the boats while in college; later, he wrangled relief jobs as a wheelsman during his yearly vacations from the railroad. Dutton continued this practice into the 1950s. His book touches on virtually every aspect of life aboard freighters during the five decades he worked on the lakes.

Captain Beaton sailed on passenger and freight ships of the Canada Steamship Lines at about the same time that Fred Dutton was working on American bulk freighters. His memoir doesn't deal as completely as Dutton's with the day-to-day aspects of shipboard life, but it does an excellent job of documenting major events that took place within the Canadian shipping community during his career, as well as the dramatic changes that occurred in the operation of ships.

Both Dutton and Beaton began sailing at a time when the only navigational equipment aboard a ship were a magnetic compass, taffrail log, and lead line—rudimentary equipment familiar to Christopher Columbus. Both began on ships that were less than 400 feet long, capable of carrying less than four thousand tons of cargo. The first steamers they worked on communicated by whistle signals, or, if that wasn't adequate, the captain used a megaphone to bellow across the water. The boats Dutton and Beaton sailed on during most of their careers were pushed along by coal-fired reciprocating steam engines that were generally rated between 1,500 and 2,500 horsepower.

From those humble beginnings, the careers of Dutton and Beaton spanned the introduction of the gyrocompass, radio direction-finder, and radar, sophisticated navigational equipment that allowed captains to navigate with almost pinpoint accuracy. The coal-fired, "up-and-down" steam engines they were familiar with eventually gave way to oil-fired steam turbines producing up to 7,700 horsepower. Captains conversed back and forth across the water, and to their offices in Cleveland, Duluth, and Buffalo, on radiotelephones. Dutton and Beaton also both lived to see the launching of the first 1,000-foot freighters on the lakes, churning along under the power of diesel engines with almost 20,000 horsepower, their cavernous holds filled with over 60,000 tons of cargo. In fact, the only things that didn't change appreciably during their years on and around the lakes were the sailors—and Dutton and Beaton describe the sailors better than any of the dozens of landlubber authors who have written about shipping on the lakes . . . *because they were sailors.*

One day as I lamented the fact there were so few first-hand accounts of life on the lakes, I began to think that I should keep a journal so that I could eventually write a book about my sailing days. Just before leaving home at the beginning of the 1996 season, I mentioned the idea to Arthur Evans, director of Wayne State University Press, which had published my two books about the lakes—*Steamboats and Sailors of the Great Lakes* (Detroit: Wayne State University Press, 1991) and *Queen of the Lakes* (Detroit: Wayne State University Press, 1994). Arthur was interested in the idea, partly because Wayne had published Dutton's book. Dutton wrote about sailing during the first half of the century; I would write about sailing during the 1990s at the end of the century. With Arthur's modest encouragement, I began keeping my "logbook" a few days after I reported aboard the *Calcite II* at Fraser Shipyard in Superior, Wisconsin, at the start of the 1996 shipping season.

Logbooks were kept aboard ships long before Christopher Columbus and his little flotilla made their epic crossing of the Atlantic in 1492. Captains like Columbus recorded the courses steered, weather conditions, landmarks passed, ports called at, cargo loaded or unloaded, the numbers of crew and passengers aboard, drafts, and the like. In addition, they commonly included entries in their logbooks about ship's business, their evaluations of various crew-members, disciplinary actions, deaths aboard the ships and burials at sea, and their personal reflections. Logs kept by many early maritime explorers, like Columbus, Magellan, and Drake, are highly prized documents, not only because they record their voyages, but because they give us so many insights into the men themselves. Unfortunately, the nature of logbooks changed dramatically over time, at least on cargo ships like those that operate on the lakes. Shipping became routine and mundane—businesslike—and the logbooks reflected that.

The logbooks kept in the pilothouses of Great Lakes boats eventually became what are called "smooth logs." They contain only basic information required by the Coast Guard for each trip the vessel makes—cargo tonnage, drafts, courses steered, speeds run, landmarks passed, weather conditions, and the signature of the deck officer on watch. Brief notations are also made whenever a required fire and boat drill is held, or whenever the vessel is involved in a casualty. Today's abbreviated logs are only skeletons of the meaty logbooks kept by earlier mariners, logs that gave you many insights into life aboard their ships, and often a peek into the soul and sinew of the sailors themselves.

For those today and in the future, who have an interest in learning what it was like to live and work on a Great Lakes freighter in the final years of the twentieth century, I offer *A Sailor's Logbook*—my record of the 1996 shipping season as I saw it and lived it. In this logbook you will also be exposed to a cross section of the various ships that operated on the Great Lakes in 1996. I started the season on the *Calcite II*, built in 1929 and one of the oldest ships operating on the lakes. Its 605-foot length makes it one of the smallest freighters around. During the season I served twice on the 1,000-foot *Edgar B. Speer,* one of the largest and most modern ships on the lakes. In September I also completed a short stint on the 768-foot *John G. Munson,* built in 1951 and typical of the vessels built by Great Lakes shipyards between World War II and the introduction of thousand-footers in the 1970s. After the *Calcite II* laid up in early November, I made a couple of trips on the unique *Roger Blough,* which in many respects represents the transition between traditional freighters and the more modern thousand-footers.

During the season, the four ships I sailed on hauled just about every type of dry bulk cargo that's moved on the lakes—iron ore pellets, coal, stone, sand, salt, and a dirty, evil-smelling substance called coke breeze. By my calculations, the boats I was on hauled a combined total of approximately 1.2 million tons of cargo.

Operating twenty four hours a day, seven days a week, the four boats also traveled something in excess of forty-five thousand miles—nearly far enough to make two complete trips around the world. The boats called at dozens of ports, from Port Colbourne in the east to Green Bay in the west, from smokestack cities like Cleveland, Detroit, and Gary in the south to Duluth, Two Harbors, and Silver Bay along Minnesota's iron-rich northern shores.

The crewmembers I sailed with were just as diverse as the cargoes the ships hauled and the ports they called at. The stereotypical merchant seaman, a poorly educated, heavy-drinking, free-spending, foul-mouthed womanizer, is hard to find on the ships that ply the Great Lakes today. It's just as impossible to describe a typical sailor as it is to describe a typical Republican, a typical rock-and-roll fan or a typical Chevy owner. If nothing else, I hope this logbook accurately portrays the character and diversity of today's sailors.

The entries in this logbook reflect my thoughts, my feelings, my biases, and my interpretations of events, including some undoubtedly erroneous interpretations. It is, after all, *my* logbook. It's just as personal a record as any carefully guarded diary or journal. As the 1996 shipping season progressed, though, this logbook became more than just my record of a year on the lakes. Crewmembers I sailed with, particularly those on the *Calcite II,* became partners in the project. They willingly shared sea stories with me, answered hundreds of questions I asked, told me personal things about themselves, tolerated me as I followed them around with a camera, and almost universally expressed their support for what I was doing. The 1996 season described here was theirs, too. It's only fitting that this book be dedicated to them, with my deepest appreciation and respect. More than anything, I hope they enjoy this logbook and I hope you will, too.

In the process of editing my logbook I thought it would be valuable to add explanatory notes in a number of places. Those notes appear as footnotes.

Sunday, April 28, 1996

M/V *Calcite II*

Fraser Shipyard
Superior, Wisconsin

My intention of keeping a daily journal during the sailing season has gone the way of most New Year's resolutions and many people's marriage vows. At about 4:00 P.M. last Tuesday afternoon, Bob Jackson, the personnel supervisor with the USS Great Lakes Fleet, called me in Rogers City, Michigan, and asked if I could get to Superior, Wisconsin, by the next morning to fit out the *Calcite II*. The steward who had been assigned to the boat got drunk the second day he was on the job and got into trouble with the shipyard people. It seems he drove his van through the yard at about thirty-five miles per hour and then tried to hide aboard one of our other boats. When he was found, the company sent him home. I hurriedly packed and caught the 8:20 P.M. bus heading north. After a miserable twelve-hour ride on bumpy, deer-infested, and sometimes snow-slick roads, I managed to reach the boat during the middle of the breakfast hour and took over from Gene "Geno" Schaedig, the second cook, who had been ably holding down the fort in the absence of a steward. I stumbled through lunch and dinner without poisoning anyone or completely destroying my reputation as a cook. Fortunately, a couple of day workers were assigned to us from our fleet's port services crew; one of them cleaned my room—which was a pigsty—and made my bed. After dinner, I unpacked, took a badly needed shower, and kept my eyes propped open with toothpicks until 8:00 P.M., at which time I crawled into bed between crisp, clean sheets.[1]

---

[1]The *Calcite II* is a 605-foot self-unloading freighter built at American Ship Building in Lorain, Ohio, in 1929 for U.S. Steel's Pittsburgh Steamship Division. Originally christened the *S.S. William G. Clyde,* the traditional straight-deck bulk freighter was designed for the trade between the iron ore ranges around Lake Superior and the steel mills on the lower lakes. In 1961 U.S. Steel transferred the *Clyde* to its Bradley Transportation Line subsidiary and converted it to a self-unloader at Manitowac, Wisconsin. The ship was rechristened as the *Calcite II*. In 1964 the boat's original 2,200-horsepower, triple-expansion steam engine was

After going to bed early after my first day on the *Calcite II*, I was up on Thursday at 3:30 A.M. I brewed a pot of coffee, planned some menus, and put together a grocery order before Geno showed up for work at 6:00 A.M. It, too, was a long day, but I stayed up to watch *E.R.* at 9:00 P.M. (We're on Central Standard Time for now.) I managed to sleep in until 5:30 A.M. Friday.

Friday was a wretched day. At about 9:00 A.M., a truck arrived from the USS Great Lakes Fleet warehouse in Sault Ste. Marie with our "fit out order," about ten thousand dollars' worth of groceries. We had lots of help getting the groceries hoisted aboard the ship and carried into the officers' dining room; after that, it was up to Geno and me to stow everything in the storeroom, coolers, freezers, and assorted nooks and crannies, while at the same time preparing and serving lunch and dinner. All but a few non-perishables had been put away by suppertime . . . and I still got out of bed the next morning!

Gene Schaedig, the second cook, is from Rogers City, and an old friend of my brother's. With more than twenty years on the boats, Gene doesn't require a lot of direction. He's always helpful, and doesn't seem to get upset when I ask him a hundred times a day where to find things.

In addition to Gene and me, only eight other crewmembers are aboard; they all work in the engine room. The captain, the other people in the deck department, and the porter will arrive tomorrow afternoon or evening to start work Tuesday morning. The plan right now is for the boat to sail on Wednesday to begin the season with a load of pellets at Two Harbors, Minnesota, for delivery to Gary, Indiana, and then probably travel around to Rogers City for a load of stone.

---

also removed and replaced with a 12-cylinder, 3,240-horsepower Nordberg diesel engine. Today, the *Calcite II* is part of the USS Great Lakes Fleet, a subsidiary of Transtar. Transtar, apparently short for "transportation star," operates seven railroads, including the Bessemer and Lake Erie, Birmingham Southern, and Duluth Missabe and Iron Range, which delivers ore to the company docks at Duluth and Two Harbors, Minnesota. Transtar also operates Warrior & Gulf Navigation, a tug fleet headquartered in Birmingham, Alabama. Since her conversion to a self-unloader in 1961, the ship's home port has been Rogers City, Michigan, the site of Michigan Limestone's Calcite Plant, for which the vessel is named.

The old and new, long and short. The 605-foot *Calcite II*, built in 1929, is dwarfed by the 1,000-foot *Oglebay Norton*, launched in 1977, as the two vessels pass in the St. Clair River. The *Oglebay Norton* can carry more than four times as much cargo as the *C-2*. (Gary C. Thompson, *M/V Columbia Star*)

Two other ships in the fleet that are crewed mainly by Rogers City men also wintered here in Superior. The *George A. Sloan* left the day before I got here, and the *Myron C. Taylor* will probably head out tomorrow. We'll be the last of the fleet to begin the 1996 season. Given the fact that only a month ago the office said the *Calcite II* might not sail until late in the season, getting her out on May 1 is a positive sign.

I'm not going to be here for the season, though. One steward who was out on the winter run until late February is on vacation right now, but as soon as he comes back I'll head home again. His return will set off a round of personnel transfers that involve stewards on four different boats. Eventually, it will trickle down to me, probably about the time we get to Rogers City. At that time I'll go home, reopen my unemployment claim, and wait until the regular vacation schedule kicks in before I get another relief job. This is work I hadn't counted on, so I'm a bit ahead of the game. I look forward to a good season this year. I'm glad to be sailing again, or will be once we throw off the mooring lines and head across Lake Superior's icy blue waters.

Monday, April 29
Superior, Wisconsin

The hardest part of sailing relief is to be assigned to a boat you haven't been on with a crew you don't know. Crewmembers are often a little standoffish until they get to know you, especially on boats like the *Calcite II* where almost all the crewmembers are from Rogers City or nearby communities in Presque Isle County that view Rogers as an urban center. Aboard the *Calcite II* I think one engineer is from Posen and an oiler is from Onaway, both in Presque Isle County; all the rest of the crewmembers are from Rogers City. I don't think the crew here is any different from the crews of any of the other boats I've been on, where the hometowns of crewmembers are scattered around the lakes and beyond, except possibly in how the crew reacts to new-comers they consider outsiders. They usually warm up to new crewmembers fairly quickly, but an outsider probably will always feel a bit like a square peg in a round hole on a boat like this. It's not anything intentional on the crew's part, but they talk about people and places back home us-ing a verbal shorthand that doesn't make much sense to someone not from the area. They also eat a little differently. For example, Kielbasa, a garlicky type of smoked sausage, is a staple on the menu. Around the holidays the crew also wants liver paste, a concoction made with chicken livers and lots of garlic, and raw chopped beef, the Rogers City version of steak tartar. The crew is not interested in eating low-fat or low-cholesterol foods, which are growing in popularity on other boats I've been on. Boiled ring bologna is always more popular here than salads or stir-frys—at least that's my impression.

Another impression I have is that the *Calcite II* is an old tub. Built in 1929, she is approaching the ripe old age of seventy. It's apparent the old girl is nearing the end of her career. She's hauled quite a bit of salt in recent years, which is usually a death sentence for a ship. The corrosive salt eats up the cargo hold and the unloading machinery, so it's not something you want to haul on a boat you're planning to continue operating for any length of time.

This is only the second boat I've sailed on that's older

16

than I am. (The other was the *Kinsman Enterprise,* built in 1927.) Interestingly, the *Calcite II* was the first boat I ever worked on. When I came back from the army in 1968, I sailed on her briefly as a deckhand during the summer. Much water has passed under her keel and mine since then.

Wednesday, May 1
Superior, Wisconsin

Word is we'll finish fitting out and leave the shipyard sometime this afternoon. I'm ready. Being here at the shipyard is starting to wear thin. We served about forty-five people for lunch yesterday in a feeding frenzy that was unparalleled in my experience as a steward. In addition to our entire crew, we had all the big shots from the company's office in Duluth, some Coast Guard inspectors, several technicians working on our generators, and the port gang that has been helping us ready the boat to sail. It seemed that all our guests had big appetites. Free food tends to bring that out in people. Today may well be a repeat performance. Argh!

Several old friends and acquaintances were among the deck crew that arrived by bus from Rogers City Monday night. Butch Kierzek and I went through school together in Rogers City, and our fathers both worked for the city for many years. I've also known Jerry Macks most of my life, though he's a little older than I am. Interestingly, Jerry was my roommate when I sailed on the *Calcite II* back in 1968. He was a wheelsman then, and I was a lowly deckhand. Twenty-eight years later, here we are again. He's the first mate now, and I'm the steward.

Several other crewmembers, including the captain, were high school classmates of my brother Gary. It's good to see some familiar faces on the boat, and it's helped break the ice with the rest of the crew.

The rumor is that we're going to Two Harbors, Minnesota, to load iron ore pellets and deliver them to the U.S. Steel mill at Gary, Indiana. A small boat like the *Calcite II* normally wouldn't carry taconite, because its carrying capacity is so limited, but it makes sense to haul a load of pellets down the lakes, instead of running light.

The "revolving stewards" scenario has apparently been set in motion. The steward who was on vacation supposedly returned to work yesterday, so the guy he bumped will be on his way to catch the *Myron C. Taylor*. The steward now aboard the *Taylor* will go to his regular boat, the *Roger Blough*, and the cook presently working on the *Blough* will come here and bump me. I don't know when that will happen. It could come as early as the Soo on Friday, or it might not occur until we arrive in Gary on Sunday, or Rogers City sometime Tuesday. I'm hoping the steward holds off until Rogers City, because it would make my life easier. I wouldn't have to travel to get home, and I would have worked two full weeks on the boat. I'll have to go back in and file for unemployment when I get off, which is a pain. Two full weeks of work would make it a little more palatable.

We don't know exactly where we're going when we leave Superior, Wisconsin, and I don't know how long I'll be on the boat. This ambiguity is common in the shipping industry.

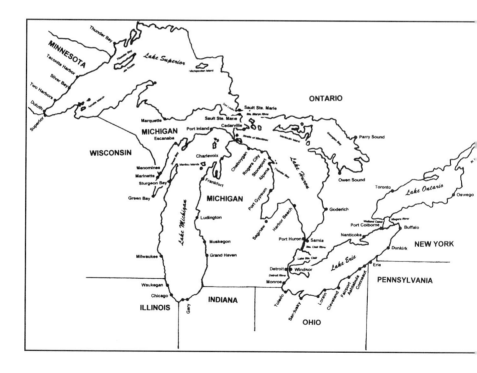

We function in what is often a fluid situation, and orders are changed frequently. You can imagine the logistics involved in transferring four stewards between ships scattered all over the Great Lakes. If the boats are in the right places, the transfers may be accomplished in as little as one day, but that's unlikely. Usually each transfer takes a couple days, due to travel time and the need to wait for boats to arrive in port.

The same factors also affect the ship's orders. For example, if several boats are waiting to load at Two Harbors, the company may have us load at Duluth, or they could decide to send us down the lake empty instead of risking a big delay up here. I remember when I was on the *Kaye E. Barker* and we were supposed to load at the Calcite plant at Rogers City. When we left Detroit and headed north, we thought we would arrive at Calcite about suppertime, when many crewmembers would be done working for the day, so a lot of the guys called their wives and girlfriends and asked them to meet the boat. Unfortunately, several boats were loading when we got to Calcite, so we anchored outside the harbor. The crewmembers with people waiting on the dock paced the deck and hoped for a short delay. The anchor was barely in the water when the dispatcher in the office called and changed our orders. He told us to go to Marquette for a load of ore. That's what we did, leaving the wives and girl-friends waiting on the dock. It was a great disappointment for everyone involved. That's part of being a sailor . . . or the loved one of a sailor.

Saturday, May 4
Rogers City, Michigan

Speaking of ambiguity, I was bumped from the *Calcite II* yesterday on about fifteen minutes' notice. We were in the MacArthur Lock at the Soo early in the afternoon when the supply boat at the Soo Warehouse called the captain and told him that they were bringing out the regular cook.

After sitting out on the last hatch to enjoy one of the first warm days of spring, I returned to the galley to start supper as the *Calcite II* made her way into the lock. No sooner had I started my preparations than the second cook ran in to tell me that I was getting off on the supply boat. I was forced to drop what I was doing and frantically pack my bags.[2] What's annoying is that the cook who was coming aboard had been at the Soo since the prior evening, but the office hadn't bothered to call the boat and let us know. Our captain was apparently upset by that, because the following day one of the guys in personnel called me to apologize.

Disembarking at the Soo wasn't so bad, except for the haste with which I had to pack. I managed to convince a cab driver to take me to Rogers City for $150; I was home by early evening. Traveling would have been much more of a pain if I'd gotten bumped off somewhere along the lower lakes, like Ashtabula, Ohio, or Gary, Indiana.

It sounds as though I'm going to be working relief from June through the end of August, so I'm glad to have these three to four weeks to tie up the loose ends of the shipwreck book I'm writing. I went back to the Soo the Monday after I left the *Calcite II* and met with Captain Tom Trosvig and Lieutenant Tom Cafferty to get answers to some of my questions about when various Coast Guard regulations took effect. They were helpful and I cleared up all but two points. I still don't know if ships were required to install radio direction finders, or when they were ordered to carry ship-to-shore radios. I've got some leads for that information, so perhaps I'll wrap up the research phase of the book within a few days.

I've also made tentative plans to go to Saginaw early next week to look through Ralph Roberts's collection of ship photos. He sent me several lists of wreck photos in his collection, which have been most helpful in pinpointing what I'll use in the book. It looks as though I may be able to get almost everything I need from his private collection.

---

[2]The Soo Locks compensate for the difference in the levels of Lake Huron and Lake Superior, allowing ships to bypass a series of turbulent rapids in the St. Marys River that blocked vessel navigation between the lower lakes and Lake Superior for several centuries. The locks at the Soo raise or lower ships about 21 feet. There are four locks at the Soo, although only two—the MacArthur and the Poe—accommodate large freighters.

I also had a letter from Arthur Evans, the Wayne State University Press director, asking about my progress with the book. I haven't talked to him about it in two years, so I was pleased to write him that the manuscript is nearly done. If I don't get called back to work until June 1, I may have the book completed before I ship out again.

Monday, May 27

Memorial Day

M/V Calcite II
Northern Lake Huron, Upbound

I returned to the *Calcite II* last Thursday night at Calcite; word is that I will be here for two months this time. It was nice to board the boat virtually in my back yard. When the office first called to tell me that I was going to relieve the steward here, they thought I would have to catch the boat at Menominee or Port Inland in Michigan's Upper Peninsula. Neither is easy to reach from Rogers City, so it was a relief when they called last Wednesday to tell me that I could get on when the boat got to Calcite.

When the call came from the office, I was actually in Saginaw, selecting photographs to illustrate *Graveyard of the Lakes*. I had to make a late-night trip home, but I was in particularly good humor. I was glad to return to work and pleased I no longer had to worry about how to get to some out-of-the-way dock in the Upper Peninsula's remote wilderness.

Despite my commitment to make entries in this journal every day, this is the first time since I've been back aboard that I've had the energy to sit down at the computer. Whenever I return to work, it takes about a week before my feet, legs, and back adjust to long hours standing on an unyielding steel deck. I actually took a hour-long break this afternoon, which was a real luxury. Up until today, I worked from 6:00 A.M. until about 5:30 P.M., with only an occasional break to sit in the messroom for a few minutes and smoke a cigarette.

Yesterday was particularly long. After supper last night,

21

I mixed up a batch of pizza dough and sauce to use today, and then worked until 9:30 P.M. on a grocery order to fax into the USS Great Lakes Fleet warehouse at Sault Ste Marie, where we receive most of our groceries. They'll deliver the stuff to us by truck on Wednesday when we load at Cedarville, Michigan, about an hour's drive from the Soo.

Ordering supplies is often a real problem on little boats like the *Calcite II*. Unlike boats in the iron ore trade, we seldom, if ever, travel through the Soo. Ships in our fleet that regularly go through the Soo have their groceries delivered by the *M/V Ojibway*, the Great Lakes Fleet's small supply boat that operates out of the warehouse complex just below the Soo Locks. Groceries and other supplies, such as parts and lubricants for the engine room, are stacked on skips, or large pallets. The *Ojibway* maneuvers alongside the passing freighter and a small crane lifts the skips onto the ship's deck. The freighter slows down, but doesn't stop, while it's being supplied, so it's a highly efficient system.[3]

There are also chandlers, or "grocery men," at most of the major ports around the lakes, including Cleveland, Toledo, Detroit, Chicago, Milwaukee, Escanaba, Duluth-Superior, and Taconite Harbor. Unfortunately, the *Calcite II* doesn't call at many of those ports. Our current orders are sending us to northern Michigan ports like Menominee, Port Inland, Brevort, and Boyne City, none of which are served by chandlers. With infrequent opportunities to get groceries, we must load up whenever we get the chance. We try to fill all our freezers and coolers right to the rafters whenever we can get supplies and then cross our fingers that we won't run out of anything crucial before we can take on more groceries. Milk, fresh fruits, and vegetables are the most difficult to make last from one "victualling" to the next. The last of our two-percent milk soured today, so we're now making our own by mixing whole and skim milk to

---

[3] At one time, the fleet operated a much larger supply boat that was outfitted like a warehouse and butcher shop. The steward on a passing ship actually climbed over and onto the supply boat to handpick the meats and vegetables he wanted.

get us through until Wednesday. The only fresh vegetables left are onions, celery, and carrots. Fortunately, our freezers are full of frozen vegetables; they'll do just fine until we get our groceries.

We go through $2,000 to $2,500 in groceries *each week* to feed a crew of 26. That's a sizable grocery bill, and reflects the quality of food available to crewmembers on Great Lakes ships. In my experience stewards spend $10–13 per man per day on groceries. Cooks of school lunch programs and other institutional food-service facilities will appreciate how generous that amount is. Unfortunately, many sailors still complain about the lousy food on their boats. Some stewards are unable to consistently turn out good meals, no matter how much they spend on groceries.

By the way, *Graveyard of the Lakes* isn't quite finished. If I'd been able to stay home until June 1 I would have completed it, but at this point it still needs a little more work. I've reviewed the manuscript once, doing some serious editing, but there are still a few odds and ends I must work on. Perhaps I'll have enough energy to get back to work on it sometime during the next few days.[4]

Arthur Evans, the director of Wayne State University Press, is expecting to see the manuscript on his desk around June 1, but since I returned to work a week earlier than planned, he'll have to tread water for awhile.[5]

Tuesday, May 28
Menominee, Michigan

It's 5:30 P.M., and I just finished another long day in the galley. We arrived here at Menominee at about 2:00 this afternoon to unload coal at a paper mill near the mouth of the river. We should be unloaded and on our way to Cedarville to load stone by about 7:00 or 7:30 this evening.

---

[4]To be honest, I never opened the book's computer file during the entire season. My hands were full with my job and making regular entries in this logbook.

[5]About a year, as it turned out.

It's my first trip into Menominee, located at the far southwestern corner of Michigan's Upper Peninsula, just across the river from Marinette, Wisconsin. Both Menominee and Marinette look like nice towns, but I'll pass up the opportunity to go up the street. The water isn't deep enough here for us to moor alongside the dock, so the *Calcite II*'s sitting in the middle of the river with her unloading boom swung out over the shore. To reach the dock you must make the short trip in our workboat, a beat-up aluminum fishing boat with an outboard motor that has seen better days. The dock is in poor condition, with rubble and holes that must be negotiated before you reach the paper mill property where the going is easier. If we were going to be here longer I might make the effort to go uptown, but not just for an hour or two. I'm not much of an up-the-street sailor anyway. I seldom leave the boat unless I'm running short of deodorant or toothpaste, and I'm well stocked up right now.

There are some guys, though, who will go uptown virtually every time we're in port if they're not working. Some are drinkers, or gamblers heading for a casino or an outlet where they can buy lottery tickets. Others merely want a little exercise and the chance to get away from the confines of the boat. Living in a world that is 605 feet long and 62 feet wide is definitely claustrophobic.

Over the years, many writers who enjoyed the opportunity to make a trip on a freighter commented on the luxurious quarters, often comparing them favorably with accommodations found in fine hotels. They were describing the passenger quarters, though, and not the crewmembers' rooms, which they either didn't see or were embarrassed to mention.

Our rooms are spartan, similar to the rooms in an old dormitory, I suppose. My room, for example, is ten feet by ten feet, with an attached bathroom that is a little over six feet by six feet. Two of the walls are lapped-and-rivetted steel plates. The other two walls are tongue-and-groove wooden boards; the ceiling is made of wood panels with decorative moldings. All the wiring is exposed, running across the walls and ceiling, and the light fixtures are heavy-duty and industrial in appearance. This room has some aging brown carpeting, while the walls are painted a reasonably attractive but outdated canary yellow. There are three portholes, one door that opens out to the main deck, and a second that leads directly into the officers' dining room and galley. I have a double bed with a tan metal footboard and headboard, a decrepit five-drawer brown dresser that students in a dorm would never tolerate, and a two-drawer file cabinet that serves as my office and computer desk.

Attached to the ceiling are two racks that hold my survival suit and life jacket. Over the head of my bed is a general alarm bell, assuring I will probably die of a fright-induced heart attack if an emergency occurs that necessitates sounding the earsplitting general alarm.

For relaxation, a recliner occupies one corner of the room. Given the limited space, the room would be more functional without it.

This is the worst room I've ever had on a boat. I suppose this is due in part to the fact that the previous regular stewards weren't interested in making any improvements to their quarters. The steward's room on the *George A. Sloan* is similar in size and layout, but the cook there made wise use of every inch of space. He built in a small desk unit and lots of handy shelving that help keep things organized and convenient.

By comparison, the steward's room on the *Edwin H. Gott,* one of the fleet's thousand-footers, is at least four times this size. The decor is fairly institutional, but the room is well equipped. Inside is a full-size desk and desk chair in the office area of the stateroom; a love seat, recliner, and a low dresser that doubles as a stand for the television occupy another area. The bedroom area features a double bed, a nightstand, and a second dresser. The bathroom is, unfortunately, similar to the one here, but lacks any outside light source.

One of the best features of the rooms on the thousand-footers is that they are air-conditioned. My room here isn't. While the weather has been cool and the room comfortable, I know it's going to be a sauna as soon as the hot summer weather sets in. Many crewmembers have gerry-rigged a porthole to accept a home-type air-conditioning unit, but the guy I relieved was here only three weeks and didn't face the reality that stifling hot weather lurks in the near future. He doesn't want to return to this boat anyway, because he lives in Duluth, Minnesota, and the *Calcite II* never goes there. I suspect he'll try to relieve on some of the larger boats that regularly load at Two Harbors and Duluth, and leave me here in his stead. That's fine with me, but if so, I will quickly invest in an air-conditioner.

Wednesday, May 29

Port Dolomite

Cedarville, Michigan

We just finished supper. The captain is swinging the boat around to back into the dock at Cedarville, along the Lake Huron shore of Michigan's Upper Peninsula, between the Mackinac Bridge and the village of DeTour. There's a stone quarry here that started as an offshoot of U.S. Steel's mine at Rogers City. The stone here at Port Dolomite is dolomitic limestone, or magnesium carbonate; the Rogers City limestone is calcium carbonate. The stone looks like little white rocks to me, though, and we're going to load about fifteen thousand tons of them in the next four to five hours.

It's now two hours later, and all the groceries have been stored. My back is sore from carrying the heavy boxes. Some stewards stand by and supervise the stowing of groceries, but I don't feel right unless I pitch in and do my share.

Some of the crew went up to the casino in nearby Hessel for a little gambling. The wives of several other crewmembers were waiting when the boat docked. Other crewmembers walked up to the pay telephone located near the plant gate to call home. Charlie Brege, one of the oilers in the engine room, rode his bicycle into Cedarville to do a little shopping. It's all part of the typical routine when we're at a dock.

Thursday, May 30

Lake Michigan, Downbound

It's a gorgeous day and there's hardly a ripple on the lake. This morning we passed by many verdant green islands that dot the northern portion of Lake Michigan and set a course south along the Michigan shoreline. The shoreline is a mix of forested bluffs and towering sand dunes. It's a beautiful sight, one I never tire of.

The lake surface was littered with logs this afternoon, flotsam from a barge that spilled much of its load of logs about a week ago. The wind and waves scattered the logs over a wide area between Frankfort and Ludington, Michigan. They pose no threat to a steel-hulled ship like ours, but do represent a serious hazard for pleasure boaters, who will probably be turning out in force this coming weekend.

The galley was a disaster area when I walked in at about 5:45 this morning. The dock and the ship's deck were both covered with pale dolomite mud last night, and a lot of it got tracked into the galley by guys ducking in for a cup of coffee or a snack. In addition, everything I touched felt gritty from the stone dust that floated in during the hours we were loading. It could have been worse, though—we could have been loading coal! We took care of the worst dirt before breakfast, and then finished restoring the galley to its pristine condition by mid-morning. Tomorrow morning we'll unload stone at U.S. Steel's Gary, Indiana, mill and then make a short trip across lower Lake Michigan to load coal at a dock on the Calumet River, just south of Chicago. The whole boat will be filthy by the time we leave the coal dock, and we'll start cleaning again.

The deckhands have it even worse. After each load or unload, they hose the boat down from stem to stern. It's not a bad job this time of the year, when we're blessed with nice weather, but you can imagine how unpleasant it can be in the fall and winter. During cold weather, the deckhands often come in covered with ice from the spray that blows back over them and freezes. Like many of the jobs aboard the boat, hosing is also repetitious. If the weather is nice, hosing might be rather fun the first few times you do it. Before long, it has become mindless drudgery.

The report from the gamblers who visited the casino last night is that they all lost money. This is not unusual. Score one for the American Indians who run the growing number of casinos around the Great Lakes. I wonder if they ever feel they are now extracting some measure of justice for the years of mistreatment by Americans of European extraction. I hope the proceeds from the casinos are doing some good in the American Indian communities and the towns and villages such as Hessel, where the casinos are located. Legalizing gambling hasn't benefited most of the people who frequent the establishments. It seems to me that gambling is another of those self-defeating compulsions that takes a toll on humanity.

Our first assistant engineer left for his vacation last night. He's been replaced by Bob Robertson, from Houghton, Michigan. Bob spent a couple of years as the chief engineer on the *Kinsman Independent,* but finally tired of the low pay, endless hours, and constant nickel-and-diming by those in the Kinsman office, and quit. I sailed on the *Kinsman Enterprise* for about six weeks at the end of the season last year, and found it to be quite an experience. The fleet's two ships owned by George Steinbrenner, more infamous as the owner of the New York Yankees, are poorly maintained. The company doesn't want to spend money on anything that isn't essential, so the boats deteriorate rapidly. They also pay less than other fleets, and they have problems attracting good personnel, especially officers. Both the captain and chief engineer on the *Enterprise* had drinking problems that clearly affected both their ability to do their jobs and their relations with others on the boat. We often joked that the boat had a screw loose at both ends.

The chief, married and probably in his early sixties, had much younger girlfriends at both ends of the lakes. He was always one of the first down the ladder when we docked at Duluth-Superior or Buffalo, and he seldom returned to the boat until it was ready to sail. He always appeared so agonizingly hungover that it was hard not to feel sorry for him. Aboard the boat, the chief spent most of his time in his cabin, probably recovering from his antics in port. During the entire time I was on the boat, I never exchanged more than a few words with him. When we did talk, he mumbled so badly I usually couldn't understand him.

While the chief's time was taken up by his lady friends, the captain seemed to be consumed by the fact that he didn't have a woman in his life. One of the deckhands on the boat moved in with a woman whom the captain apparently thought was *his* girlfriend, and most conversations of any length with the captain eventually included this fact. He even began discussing it with dock workers and other visitors to the boat, seeming to assume that they were aware of all the details (even though they weren't). He often generated strange looks from visitors to the boat, who were caught off guard when the captain switched the conversation from the weather, our schedule, or how long it was going to take to load the boat to a deckhand's love life. He also mumbled a lot, especially if he'd been drinking, so his ramblings were usually unintelligible. Most visitors to the boat seemed to leave less than impressed with our captain.

When we were in port, the captain made the rounds of the bars, and then often returned to the boat to fall sound asleep at the messroom table, oblivious to the steady stream of crewmembers and dock workers who came in for coffee or something to eat.

The captain was fairly unimpressed with my cooking. The only things he wanted to eat were fried or roasted beef or pork and potatoes. He constantly asked me, "Where's the beef?" He was good-natured about it, but I clearly got the message that he wasn't happy with the meals I prepared. The rest of the crew liked my cooking, so I ignored the captain as best I could. He was also offended, even downright indignant, whenever I served rice or pasta instead of potatoes, which was a frequent occurrence. When I found a few pounds of rice left in a bag at the end of the season, I taped it up and gave it to a wheelsman who frequented the same bar in West Duluth that the captain did. I drew a caricature of the captain on the bag and included a note stating I didn't want him to go all winter without any rice. I'll bump into him someday, and when I do I'm sure I'll hear about that rice . . . and the girlfriend he lost to a deckhand.

Saturday, June 1

Lake Michigan, Upbound

We unloaded yesterday morning at Gary, and then loaded coal last night at the KCBX terminal along the Calumet River south of Chicago. The train carrying our coal arrived late, so we didn't clear the dock until after 2:00 A.M. At about 3:00 A.M. tomorrow, we should be at the power plant on Lake Charlevoix at Advance, Michigan, inland from Charlevoix. We've encountered some fog, though, and we're supposed to get some heavy rain for the next twenty-four hours. That could force us to anchor somewhere en route. To reach Lake Charlevoix from "the big lake" you must go through a channel that's slightly wider than the boat. The captain probably won't attempt that unless weather conditions are good. We've got one guy leaving at Advance, and three others scheduled to go on vacation when we reach the sand dock at Brevort the following day, so they're all concerned about the possibility of a delay. As we say on the boats, they've got a dose of "channel fever." Now that they're close to getting off, that's all they can think about. They often have trouble sleeping and they become real cranky if the boat suffers any delays.

One of those leaving is Gene Schaedig, our second cook. Ron Bredow, now the porter, will take over as second cook and Jimmy Atkins, a deckhand, will come into the galley as porter. Neither Ron nor Jimmy are very experienced, so I'll have to keep an eye on them to make sure their jobs are done properly. That's something I haven't had to worry about when Gene was here.

Fog is depressing. There are times when I feel trapped on the boat. When you add the loud blare of the fog whistle every couple of minutes, it's enough to drive you loony.

The lake and shoreline were so beautiful when we were downbound. Now all we can see are the boat and a gray void beyond. I can't even imagine what it must have been like on boats in the days before radar and other sophisticated navigational aids. One minute they were feeling their way along in a fog, the next they had run aground or collided with another ship. That makes our present situation seem pretty trivial.

Wednesday, June 5

Buffalo, New York

We're on our way up the creek at Buffalo to deliver a load of sand we took on at Brevort, Michigan, just west of the Straits of Mackinac. The dock we're headed to is what's referred to diplomatically as "an unimproved dock," which means there's really no dock at all. We'll secure a couple of cables around something on the shore and just hang off in the center of the river when we unload. To get ashore we'll have to use the workboat, and since it's going to be about 8:00 P.M. before we get tied up, it's not worth the bother for an hour or two up the street. There's really nothing I need anyway.

We have two new deckhands, one of whom has never sailed before, and food consumption is up in the galley. Last night I made fourteen large pizzas, and they were totally gone by this morning. With only twenty-six crewmembers, that means each man ate more than half a large pizza!

New sailors tend to overeat when they first come aboard. They can't believe their good luck: free food, and two or three entrees to choose from at each meal. The eating binge usually only lasts a week or two before they realize they're having a hard time getting their pants buttoned and pull back a little. I know one young sailor who gained 65 pounds on the boats during a summer. When he returned home in late August to get ready to go back to college, his mother barely recognized him.

It's not just the young sailors who overeat, though. It's a widespread problem on the boats and many of us are seriously overweight. Many sailors seem to think of the food as part of their pay, and they want all they can get. Most don't eat particularly gluttonous quantities at meal hours, but they make numerous trips into the galley throughout the day to munch on whatever's available. All of the boats have a "night lunch," usually a typical home-type refrigerator stocked with milk, juices, and a wide variety of lunch meats, cheeses, frozen pizzas, ice cream, and ice cream bars. The night lunch was originally intended for crewmembers going on or getting off watch during the night, but everyone seems to raid it now. In fact, our union contract requires the shipping companies to provide a night lunch. In the old days, until the 1960s, some boats actually carried a night cook who prepared food for those going on or off watch.

It's always painful to watch new or inexperienced crewmembers. The boat is such a foreign environment and there's so much to learn, even for the lowest-rated ordinary seaman. The industry also has its own jargon, which is about as unintelligible to a new sailor as Swahili. It's easy

The tug *Mississippi* tows the *Calcite II* up the Buffalo River at Buffalo, New York, and past two decommissioned naval vessels now permanently moored along the riverfront as floating museums. (Author's collection)

to get hurt when you're a new sailor stumbling around out on deck or down in the engine room. You can easily end up with a broken leg if you step in the bight of a mooring cable when the operator takes up slack. You can fall from the ladders used to get on and off the boat, or, God forbid, you can fall into an open hatch.

In the fall of 1994 a new deckhand on the *Kinsman Enterprise* went up the street with some shipmates, consumed a few drinks, and then went back to the boat to close the hatch covers. He somehow fell into an open hatch, plummeted twenty-five or thirty feet below head first to the cargo hold's steel floor, and was killed. Unfortunately, the shipmates who allowed him to work after he had been drinking weren't disciplined by the Coast Guard.

Technically, Coast Guard regulations prohibit merchant seamen from drinking within four hours of the time they go on watch. Anyone who is intoxicated isn't supposed to do any work aboard ship. Sadly, enforcement of the regulations is weak and officers aboard the ships tend to look the other way if someone's had too much to drink, even though they could lose their licenses if the Coast Guard came aboard and administered breath tests. That only happens if someone is seriously injured or the ship is damaged to the extent that the Coast Guard must be notified. Everyone involved is usually forced to submit to alcohol and drug tests. That's the policy throughout the entire transportation industry since the *Exxon Valdez* oil spill in Alaska. The captain of the *Valdez* reportedly drank several bottles of beer before taking the ship out. At about the same time, several major train accidents occurred after the engineers drank or used drugs.

Regardless of the regulations and the zero-tolerance policies of most shipping companies, drinking is still a problem on the Great Lakes. It's likely to remain so until the Coast Guard or the shipping companies crack down on the offenders. Today's boats are often only in port four to eight hours, to load or unload, so any sailor who goes up the street to drink will probably violate Coast Guard regulations. Most gamble that they won't get caught. Recent history bears them out—the probability of getting caught by the Coast Guard for drinking is about the same as that for me getting appointed Pope . . . and I'm a Protestant.

We just got a new itinerary this afternoon that includes two trips into our home port at Rogers City. Those trips had better not get cancelled, or the crew is likely to mutiny. The other small boats in the fleet, particularly the *George A. Sloan* and the *Myron C. Taylor,* have visited Rogers City regularly, but the *Calcite II* has only been there once since leaving the shipyard on May 2. Most of the crewmembers have families and are eager to get home. I'm just eager to have a chance to take on another hefty supply of groceries—the cupboards are growing bare.

Friday, June 7

Cleveland, Ohio

We spent yesterday loading at Ontario Stone in the Welland Canal. It was the dustiest stone load I've ever seen. The wind blew from bow to stern and the galley was totally trashed by lunchtime, even though we buttoned it up as tight as we could. Everything sports a gritty coating of stone dust, including my computer keyboard.

We enjoyed a bird's eye view of shipping traffic in the Welland while we loaded. All of the boats we saw were either Canadian or foreign flag, not a single U.S. ship. One of the most noticeable and alarming things was the number of tug-barge units we saw. The liquid bulk (gasoline, fuel oil, tar, etc.) and cement trades are quickly being dominated by tugs and barges instead of ships, and three of them operate in the ore, coal, and stone trades on the lakes. It takes about ten fewer crewmembers to operate a tug-barge, which saves the shipping companies lots of money—at least one hundred thousand dollars for each crew billet eliminated. In addition, the Coast Guard's inspection standards are far less stringent for tugs, which also saves the companies money. It's a trend that's most distressing to those of us who work on ships. Pay, working conditions, and living conditions on the tugs are poor, perhaps a throwback to what the shipping industry was like at the turn of the century, or at least before sailors unionized during the 1950s and 1960s. Crewmembers, for example, work twelve hours a day, compared to the eight-hour days on conventional ships. That's simply too much. It burns people out and results in accidents and injuries due to fatigue.

Working conditions on many of the tugs resemble the sweatshop conditions in the garment industry. Living conditions are often slightly poorer than those found at the local hoosegow.

It's also become apparent to me that if being a second cook was against the law, few in this fleet would ever be convicted. Most second cooks in the fleet simply can't or won't cook. The second cook is responsible for preparing baked goods, desserts, and salads on the boat. All five of the second cooks I've worked with in this fleet relied almost totally on frozen pies, cakes, and bread doughs. I've only been here two weeks and I'm already tired of the stuff. Usually they only put out one major dessert a day, such as a cake or pie, and offer canned fruit, canned pudding, or ice cream as a second choice. You have the identical choices at lunch and dinner. So far, the only cookies baked by the second cook are chocolate chip, and they supplement those with store-bought varieties.

When I was a second cook with Interlake Steamship, we made virtually everything from scratch—bread, dinner

LaFarge Corporation's tug *Jaclyn M.* and barge *Integrity* made their debut in the cement trade on the lakes during the 1996 season. Before the tug and barge went into service, the multinational cement producer depended on conventional freighters to transport cement from its manufacturing plant at Alpena, Michigan, to distribution terminals around the lakes. Exempt from the Coast Guard crewing standards that apply to ships, the tug-barge can be operated by fewer than ten crewmembers. Operation of a conventional freighter requires at least twenty-six personnel. Launching of the tug-barge, combined with a change in management of the Alpena-based cement fleet, led officers aboard the fleet's ships to go on strike in what proved to be an unsuccessful attempt to gain union representation. (Author's collection)

rolls, sweet rolls, cakes, pies, cookies, and so on. I always had at least two desserts at lunch, and two new desserts at dinner, along with anything left from lunch. Many times the crew had their choice of five or six desserts at one meal. If variety is the spice of life, the crew's lives were pretty spicy, at least in the dessert department.

At this moment I have absolutely the worst second cook I've ever worked with. He's ordinarily the porter, but took the second cook's job when Gene Schaedig went on vacation because it pays a little more. If my cooking skills were as bad as his, I'd be too embarrassed to try to pass myself off as a second cook. As a cook, he's an imposter. I keep one eye on him at all times.

On boats in this fleet, the second cook prepares breakfast for the crew. One morning, while I was working in the back room during breakfast, I noticed smoke billowing through the doorway. I dashed into the galley and found the second cook trying to fry a pancake on a grill so hot and grease-coated it was ready to burst into flames. This lethal combination incinerated the pancake batter the instant he dropped it onto the grill. Yesterday, he burned a pan of sidepork that he was preparing in the oven. The second pan he attempted was removed from the oven about ten minutes before it was done, limp, greasy, and largely inedible. The postmortem for yesterday's batch of chocolate chip cookies isn't in yet, but early indications suggest he left something out (like the baking soda) because they were flat and hard.

When it gets busy during mealtime, most second cooks and many porters help dish up food, but this second cook can't even do that. He does serve soup, but usually manages to slop it over the edge of the bowl. I've asked him a hundred times to carry a paper towel in his pocket to wipe the rims of bowls and plates, but after a spill he conceals the bowl with his body and dashes for the dining room, convinced I can't see it. I'm not blind, my friend, and not dumb, either. I don't miss much that goes on in the galley, though I don't always say something when I see him doing things wrong. If I did I'd be hoarse by the end of the day . . . or by noon. He does try my patience. If I was the permanent cook on this boat, I'm afraid he'd be heading down the ladder with his seabag over his shoulder. He doesn't belong in food service.

We arrived at Cleveland at suppertime with our dusty load of Canadian stone. Thankfully, there's a light rain falling, which keeps the dust down as we unload. When we're finished unloading in four or five hours, we'll move farther up the Cuyahoga River to load petroleum coke, another dirty, nasty cargo. We'll probably be at that dock for at least thirty-six hours, so I hope that I'll be able to talk to my brother Gary on the ship's radio during that time. His boat, the *Earl W. Oglebay*, is supposedly running between Cleveland and Lorain this week. If they go as far as the LTV Steel mill, I may even get a chance to see him when his boat passes ours.

Tomorrow, my former wife and my daughter Meredith are throwing a surprise high school graduation party for my son Scott. When Meredith graduated three years ago, I prepared all the food and decorations for her party, and it was a big hit. I wish I could do the same for Scott, but when you sail relief you can't afford to give up a job, even for something as important as a high school graduation party for your son. There's a possibility that I may be on this boat until the end of the season. If I get off, however, there's a possibility some other relief cook will be here until the boat lays up. I'd end up bouncing around from boat to boat, picking up whatever relief jobs are available. Scott understands, but it still tears my heart out that I'll miss his party. Tomorrow will *not* be a good day for me. At least we'll be at a dock and I'll be able to call him and extend my congratulations.

Before the labor unions came in, sailors received no time off during the season. They sailed from fitout in the spring until lay-up, usually just before Christmas. While I grew up in Rogers City, I had many friends whose fathers sailed and were never home for elementary school programs, birthday parties, little league games, scout activities, football and basketball games, and the like. The fathers missed many important events in their children's lives. I'm sure that many of the children resented it, though they might not have said anything at the time.

Today, those of us who are officers are entitled to thirty days of paid vacation for every sixty days we work. Many officers take all the vacation time they have coming. Actually, our contract doesn't refer to it as vacation, but as family leave. When the union bargained the contract that gave us "60–30," they argued that we needed to be off the boats more, not to vacation, but to spend time with our families.

Unlicensed crewmembers get from one to twelve weeks of vacation, depending on how long they've been with the company. There are a lot of old-timers over here, with twenty or more years on the boats, and they have almost as much time off as we officers do, and deservedly so.

Sunday, June 9

Lake Erie, Eastbound

We just cleared Cleveland after spending over thirty-six hours to take on about ten thousand tons of petroleum coke. The loading rig they used looked like something they picked up during a blue-light special at K-Mart. It was not very efficient.

The first twenty-four hours we were tied up in the Cuyahoga just off downtown Cleveland was fascinating for me. In all the years I've sailed, I had never been up the Cuyahoga before, which has been the main artery of the Great Lakes shipping industry for over a hundred years. Old timers wouldn't recognize it now. The flats, the riverfront area that runs along the city's edge, was devoted to maritime activities almost from the time Cleveland was first settled by Mose Cleaveland two hundred years ago.[6] The riverfront was a hodgepodge of docks, chandlers, shipping company offices, tug berths, and typical waterfront bars until about fifteen years ago, when yuppies discovered the area. Since then, the flats has experienced a rebirth, transformed into an upscale playground of restaurants and trendy bars. The riverbanks are lined now with expensive pleasure boats as their owners sit on the decks of the bars and restaurants to watch freighters travel up and down the Cuyahoga. Occasionally, a freighter tangles with a pleasure boat while maneuvering through the narrow confines of the river. Guess who loses?

Quite a number of ships passed us while we were loading, including my brother's boat, the *M/V Earl W. Oglebay*. The *Oglebay*'s been making a number of shuttle runs from the iron ore transshipment dock at Lorain, Ohio, up the Cuyahoga to LTV Steel. She passed us at suppertime on Saturday, and I waved to Gary. Around midnight last night, they passed us a second time on their way back down the river after unloading. Early this afternoon, just as we finished loading, the *Oglebay* was heading back up the river again just as we were preparing to leave the dock. They tied up until we got around them. During the hour or so they waited for us to get everything battened down, their bow was only about fifty feet from our stern. Gary was stationed on the bow, so I went out and talked with him for a few minutes. In just three days on the shuttle run, he has worked sixteen hours of overtime. Whenever the boat

---

[6]The city was named after one of the region's early settlers of African American heritage, but they spelled Cleaveland's name wrong.

is docking or transiting the river, an extra mate is called out to assist. One mate is stationed at the stern and the other at the bow, and they use portable radios to inform the captain how close the boat is to buoys, docks, other ships, the riverbank, and other obstacles. From the pilothouse, it's often hard to judge what the situation is at the other end of the ship six hundred feet away (which is equivalent to two football fields laid end-to-end).

One reason for all the activity along the riverfront today is that the Olympic torch is scheduled to arrive early this evening. Appropriately, it will be aboard a lake freighter during its trip from Detroit to Cleveland, a point of pride for all of us in the industry, and fitting recognition of the critical role ships and sailors played in the development of the Great Lakes region and the entire country. The torch will be brought to Cleveland aboard American Steamship's *American Republic,* reportedly selected for the honor because of its name. All of us on the *Calcite II* feel a special attachment to the festivities. The captain of the *American Republic* is Ed Derry from Rogers City. A friend of many on our boat, Ed started his sailing career with this fleet. He's even a shirttail relation of mine. His uncle, Frank "Dutch" Derry, married my dad's sister Francis.

I also called my son Scott from Cleveland on the costly cellular pay phone located aboard the boat. At $3.50 a minute, I usually talk quite fast! I got through to him about an hour after his surprise graduation party had started, and he was really high. Scott, like most of us, enjoys being the center of attention. He would probably have pooh-poohed the idea of a graduation party, since he thrives on being unconventional, but he seemed to be having a good time.

Last night I worked for two and a half hours filling out a huge grocery order that will be delivered to the boat when we reach Calcite Thursday or Friday. I didn't finish until 10:00 P.M., which is my normal bedtime. By then, I was a little wired and had a hard time falling asleep. It was also uncomfortably warm in my room, which happens any time the boat sits at a dock for a long time. There's no shelter from the sun at any dock I've ever been at. The ship's steel hull acts like a massive heat sink and soaks up the sun's rays all day. To add to our misery, the galley exhaust located over the stove and ovens died just after breakfast on Saturday

Oglebay Norton's *Earl W. Oglebay* cruises past downtown Cleveland on one of its frequent trips up the Cuyahoga River. The river-class freighter, 630 feet in length, was specifically designed to negotiate the narrow and winding Cuyahoga, hauling stone, ore, and coal to a steel mill located up the river. (Author's collection)

and it wasn't repaired until this afternoon. That corner, where I spend much of my time, was like a sauna. I must have consumed five gallons of water today, and my uniform was soaked with perspiration all day. Sleeping will be much better tonight, as it has cooled off considerably since we got out onto Lake Erie. There's a nice breeze to blow away the humidity of the flats. It's an unmistakable fact that the ol' *Calcite II* is a hot boat. I'm going to have some trying days when the hot weather settles in later this summer. I don't tolerate heat well.

I planned on washing a load of underwear in the laundry facilities located one deck down in the engine room, but the washer is currently off limits due to a water shortage. Ironic, isn't it? We're out in the middle of one of the largest lakes in the world and we're short on water. We normally replenish our supply of freshwater in remote and deep regions of Lakes Huron, Michigan, and Superior, where water quality is highest. There's no place on Lake Erie for us to take on water because it is shallow and comparatively polluted, so there's a possibility we'll have to stretch what's left in our potable water tanks until we reach Lake Huron sometime late Tuesday. If we're lucky, we may top off our tanks in Ashtabula, where we can take water from a municipal water line. Not being able to do laundry is a frequent inconvenience for those aboard boats that spend any amount of time on Lake Erie. If you're lucky, you planned ahead and did your laundry before the boat reached the St. Clair River or, like me, your supply of underwear is large enough to get you through a few washerless days.

Tuesday, June 11
Lake St. Clair, Upbound

Busy yesterday. We finished unloading the cargo of coke at Conneaut, Ohio, about 8:00 in the morning, then made the one-hour trip over to nearby Ashtabula to load coal for delivery to Green Bay, Wisconsin. American Steamship's *Charles M. Wilson* arrived just before we did, so we didn't even start to load until about 11:00 P.M. It was a nice delay for those of us in the galley, and I walked uptown after supper. Nothing major, just stopped at the bar where most of the crew had congregated, bought a round and had a Diet Pepsi before I walked up the hill to a little strip mall to buy cigarettes, deodorant, and film. I stopped at a pay phone on the way back to the boat and called my mother. It was a pleasant evening and I enjoyed getting away from the boat for a couple of hours. It's only the second time I've been off the boat in almost three weeks. That's normal for me. I'm not much of an up-the-streeter.

When I returned to the boat, I sat out on a hatch with the watchman and another crewmember who delighted in telling me outrageous stories about cooks they'd sailed with over the years, several of whom are infamous in the fleet. One cook, who used to be on this boat, served tuna salad sandwiches every noon for more than a month, then egg salad for over twenty days. At night he put the leftovers in the night lunch. When one crewmember finally complained that he was tired of the same sandwiches lunch after lunch,

41

the cook commented that the rest of the crew must think they're just fine, because the leftovers were always gone from the night lunch when he checked in the morning. What the crewmember didn't tell the cook was that he and his shipmates dumped the tuna or egg salad over the side every night. Unfortunately, it generated the opposite outcome they were hoping for.

The same cook earned a reputation for being extraordinarily frugal. His second cook related that he found almost all the lunch meat and cheese gone from the night lunch each morning. Every day, the second cook increased the amount of cold cuts and sliced cheese he put into the night lunch, but each morning the supply was nearly wiped out. The second cook couldn't believe how much the crew was eating until he found a huge stash of cold cuts and cheeses hidden in a corner of one of the ship's walk-in coolers. The frugal cook, it seems, took most of the meat and cheese out of the night lunch each evening in an effort to keep food costs down.

Another cook was famous for boiling every cut of meat, whether it was ring bologna or prime rib. One day he put some ring bologna in a pot to boil for supper and then went off for his afternoon nap. When he returned several hours later, all the water had boiled off, leaving the ring bologna to scorch on the bottom of the pot. Unfazed, the cook simply changed the menu that evening from boiled ring bologna to fried ring bologna.

Many of the old-time cooks were obsessed with making sure everything was finished when the meal hour started. The best way to do that, they concluded, was to start cooking food several hours earlier than necessary. Fried hamburgers were often cooked as much as an hour before mealtime and then put in a pan of au jus in an attempt to keep them from drying out before the crew came in to eat.

Other cooks apparently suffered a phobia about running out of a food item listed on the menu, so they frequently prepared twice as much as necessary just to be safe. As a result, many tons of leftover boiled potatoes were buried at sea over the years. Leftovers of more expensive menu items, like meat, reappeared on the menu day after day, until the last scrap was finally consumed. What began as roast beef later appeared as hot roast beef sandwiches before it transformed into barbecued beef on a bun. If some roast beef still remained, it went into the night lunch until it turned green.

One of the great myths about the Great Lakes shipping industry is that the food on the boats is virtually gourmet quality. Not so. Nearly half the cooks on the lakes would not qualify as fry cooks at McDonald's. They usually produce prodigious quantities of food, which impresses the hell out of visitors to the boat, but it's not always well prepared and there's little variety. Back in 1980 I was second cook to one old-timer on the *J. L. Mauthe* who featured roast beef on the menu seven times in one week. Before the end of the week, crew consumption dropped way off, which the cook attributed to the men being tired of eating. What he didn't know was that consumption of peanut butter and jelly sandwiches and cereals reached record highs!

Most cooks on the lakes won their jobs largely through perseverance. They began as porters in the galley; when they earned enough seniority, they became second cooks. When someone became the senior second cook in the fleet, he was sent off to the union's steward school in Toledo. The next season, he started working as a relief cook. If he didn't poison anyone, he eventually worked his way into a permanent position.

Most cooks on the boats don't enjoy cooking. They view their positions as just good-paying jobs. If they could only cook twenty entrees when they started out, they probably still only cook twenty entrees. They have little or no interest in expanding their repertoires and act as though they're doing their crews a favor, no matter what sad-looking, foul-tasting dishes they produce. When interviewed by a newspaper reporter making a trip on his boat, one cook commented, "I tell the crew, if they don't like what I've prepared, they can go next door." The brash message was clear to the crew, one they're not likely to forget.

I generally receive pretty high marks from the crews I cook for. I'm no master chef, but I cook a wide variety of dishes and always do my best to see that they are well prepared and attractively presented. The guys on the boat have little to look forward to each day, except for their meals. If the food's good, it seems to have a positive effect on the attitudes of those aboard. One cook once remarked that he felt the steward served as the ship's social director, because the only real social activity aboard a ship was eating. He may be right.

After supper tonight I walked on deck for the first time this season. I started walking laps around the deck, but there wasn't any breeze on the port side and the bugs were as thick as they are in a northern Michigan cedar swamp in July. I modified my plan and walked back and forth along the starboard side for the equivalent of just over a mile. That's plenty for the first time out.

I know walking is good for my heart, but walking on this deck may do serious damage to a walker's back and legs. There's so much camber to the deck to aid in water run off that it's like walking with one foot on the curb and the other in the gutter. It's a chiropractic nightmare. By the time the season's over, my heart will be as strong as a mule's, but my legs and feet will be all crippled up. Life isn't always easy or simple on a boat.

Wednesday, June 12

Poe Reef Channel, Lake Huron, Upbound

We're adrift right now due to a broken fuel line in the engine room. The boat's entire stern, including the galley and my room, are filled with the heavy, oily smell of diesel fuel. The engineers are working frantically to repair the broken line so we can get power up again, but in the meantime we're just drifting along. There isn't much wind, fortunately, so we're not actually moving very much.

Broken fuel lines are a common problem on diesel engines, due to their vibration. Back in the 1980s one of the engine rooms on the 1,000-foot *James R. Barker* was totally destroyed by fire as the result of a broken fuel line. There's a lot of hot equipment in the engine room that may easily ignite fuel spilling from a broken line. Today we were lucky. Quite a bit of fuel must have spilled, given the density of the fumes here at the stern, but no fire. Ironically, just two hours before the fuel line broke, we held one of our weekly fire and boat drills. Good timing.

While we drifted along, I walked some laps on deck again. It's cooler and much more pleasant today and there weren't many bugs to contend with. It was a pretty evening to walk. We're passing through the channel between Cheboygan, Michigan, on the mainland, and Bois Blanc Island. I've driven from Rogers City to Cheboygan many times in my life and I can identify many of the landmarks along the shore. It makes you feel close to home, yet far away. Earlier today we passed Rogers City, but we were ensconced in heavy fog and couldn't see a thing. Maybe it's better that way. It's been almost three weeks since the boat loaded at Rogers City, and the crewmembers are starting to get a little surly. Other small boats in the fleet continue to run in and out of Rogers City regularly, but we keep getting sent elsewhere for some reason. We're not even sure where we're going after we unload this coal at Green Bay.

We were scheduled to load stone at Stoneport, between Rogers City and Alpena, for delivery to Benton Harbor. That would have put us about twenty-four miles from home, and it would have provided a chance for everyone to see their families, but the trip got cancelled. Apparently, it's impossible to get into the river at Benton Harbor right now because the water is two feet over flood stage. A ship from Oglebay Norton with a load of stone has been anchored there for four days, waiting to get in. Demurrage like that gets costly, and the shipping company is reportedly trying to find someplace else to offload the cargo so its boat can operate again.

I'm starting to get a little worried about how to get my mail. I know a couple of my bills are due late next week. If we don't reach Rogers City or Stoneport, I'll have to have my mother bundle it up and mail it to me somewhere. I suppose she could send it to our fleet's warehouse at Sault Ste. Marie, where we order our groceries. They'll bring it along when they deliver the groceries—if they send us someplace where we can get groceries, that is.

Mail is another headache for bachelor sailors, especially those of us who sail relief. I could have my mail forwarded to the boat through either the marine post office at Detroit or the one at the Soo, except that we never go to the Soo and have been through Detroit on only an irregular basis. About the time I'd have my mail sent to Detroit, we'd spend

The Detroit River mailboat, *J. W. Westcott, II,* swings away from the hull of the *Calcite II* after delivering the mail. Mail service has been provided to crewmembers aboard ships transitting the Detroit River for more than a century. Mail service is also available at the Soo Locks. (Author's collection)

a month running on Lake Michigan. Or I'd have my mail coming to the *Calcite II,* and I'd get transferred to another boat. Then I'd have the headache of trying to get the post office to change my forwarding address. I've been through all that before and it's frustrating. The married guys don't have those problems, and nearly all the crewmembers on this boat are married. They don't know what fun they're missing. Ah, the carefree life of a bachelor.

The second assistant engineer is diabetic and he's constantly bugging me to order sugar-free ice cream, sugar-free jams and jellies, sugar-free ice-cream bars, sugar-free pudding, sugar-free jello, and anything else on the market that comes *sans* sugar. While he's a bit of a pest, I'm willing to order sugar-free products for him, knowing how hard it must be to be diabetic and have a sweet tooth. Now I'm getting reports that the engineer doesn't rigorously avoid things with sugar in them. In the last few days he's been seen eating a thick peanut butter and jelly sandwich, a turnover full of sugary fruit and topped with frosting, and sugar-free ice cream slathered with regular sugar-laden ice cream toppings. Why do I feel slightly used?

We're running again. We just passed under the Mackinac Bridge and are heading toward the setting sun. Word is we lost only forty to fifty gallons of fuel when the piping broke. The oiler on the 4-to-8 watch noticed it when he saw smoke rising from where the fuel was spraying onto the hot exhaust manifold. Good thing he paid attention to what was going on in the engine room or we might have had our second fire and boat drill of the afternoon.

Thursday, June 13

Green Bay, Wisconsin

It's early evening and we just left the Fox River at Green Bay and are headed east again. We unloaded coal at the Ford Howard Paper Company, which is about as far up the river at Green Bay as a freighter can go. It was a scorcher. The temperature in Green Bay got up to 87 degrees, and the temperature in the galley hit 100 degrees for the first time. I was wringing wet by the time we got done serving supper, and went to my room to collapse in front of the fan and sleep for an hour. Many of us later went up on deck for the trip through the city of Green Bay to get back out to the lake.

We had a surprise waiting for us when we got to the dock in Green Bay—two guys from some medical lab came on to do drug tests on the entire crew, part of the company's random drug testing program that is now required by the U.S. Department of Transportation and the Coast Guard. Several guys had difficulty generating the required two-ounce urine sample, which was cause for considerable hilarity among the crew. Even though I had downed several gallons of water in the hours before the test, I barely came up with the required sample. It's not easy to pee when you've got some guy looking over your shoulder.

Surprise of surprises—we finally got some orders this afternoon, and, amazingly, we're on our way to Calcite. Even more amazing, we should get in there about four o'clock

Left to right: Iggy Donajkowski, Tom Flanner, Frank Bruski, Shawn Langlois, John Schefdore, and Mike Fischer lounge on the deck as the *Calcite II* works its way up the Fox River at Green Bay, Wisconsin. Clearly visible in the photo are the hatch clamps that hold the telescoping leafs of the hatch covers in place when the ship is out on the lakes. (Author's collection)

tomorrow afternoon, which is an incredible time for those of us who work in the galley. Once we finish stowing the groceries we have coming and serving supper, we can all go home for a few hours. Eureka! My bills will be paid on time.

What is unbelievable is that the four trips the company has us scheduled for have us loading at Calcite, Stoneport, Cedarville, and then Calcite again. Stoneport's only a half-hour from Rogers City, and even Cedarville is only two hours away. It looks as though we all may be getting home on a fairly regular basis for the next couple weeks if our orders hold.

We passed the old *E. M. Ford* on our way up the river today. She's the oldest ship in the Great Lakes fleet, built in 1898, the year of the Spanish-American War![7] She still

---

[7]Launched as the 428-foot *Presque Isle*, the ship was a conventional ore carrier until she was converted to haul cement after Huron Cement of

The *E. M. Ford* is the grande dame of the Great Lakes shipping industry. Shown here at her berth in Green Bay, Wisconsin, where she was being used to store cement, the *Ford* was built in 1898 and is generally considered the oldest operating vessel on the lakes. Although she has spent most of her time laid up in recent years, it is anticipated that her owners will bring her out during the 1998 season to mark the 100th anniversary of her launching. The beautiful old ship is owned by Inland Lakes Management, which hauls cement from LaFarge Corporation's cement plant in Alpena, Michigan. (Author's collection)

looks good, although it's unlikely she will ever operate again. She's owned by Inland Lakes Management, successor to the Huron Cement fleet, which hauls cement for LaFarge Corporation, one of the world's major cement manufacturers. They're in the process of building a high tech tug-barge, which will probably make boats like the *Ford* obsolete. The tug-barge will have a greater carrying capacity than small boats like the *Ford*, and it will operate with far fewer crewmembers. I took a few pictures when we went past the old girl, just in case her next trip is to the boneyards.

We also saw the *Metis*, a little self-propelled cement barge, tied up near the mouth of the Fox. It looked pretty shabby and doesn't appear to be operating anymore. It still shows Toronto as its hailing port, and I believe that she was

---

Alpena, Michigan, purchased her in 1956. At that time, the ship was also given her present name.

owned by Canada Steamship Lines at one time. I have no idea what she's doing in Green Bay.[8]

I'm enjoying traveling to so many out-of-the-way ports. One of our next trips will be up the Saginaw River, another first for me. When I sailed for Interlake, none of their boats ever hauled into Saginaw or Bay City, the two ports on the busy industrial waterway. We'll be taking stone in, while other boats carry coal and petroleum products to the myriad of docks along the river. I'm looking forward to it.

My sister and her husband keep their boat on Saginaw Bay, and if we happen to get in there on a weekend, I may get to see them. In addition, Ralph Roberts, who has been helping me with photos for my shipwreck book, lives in Saginaw and may visit the *Calcite II* if we're at a decent dock.

Saturday, June 15
St. Clair River, Downbound

After an evening in Rogers City, we're downbound with another load of limestone on our way to Cleveland. It was a beautiful evening while we loaded at Calcite. I was so tired after working all day and then stowing a huge load of groceries, that I didn't do much to take advantage of the weather. In fact, I left the boat about 6:00, returned by 8:30, and was in bed by 9:30.

I did go to my mother's, picked up my mail, mailed a check to AT&T, picked up a couple of t-shirts and two

---

[8]The *Metis* was built in 1956 for Canada Steamship. Originally only 258 feet long, she was a typical "canaller," built to operate on the Welland Canal between Lakes Ontario and Erie. After the locks on the Welland were enlarged in 1959 as part of the St. Lawrence Seaway construction, the *Metis* was lengthened to 331 feet. In 1966 the little freighter was converted to haul cement. In 1991 it was converted to an unpowered barge. *Metis* is currently owned by Essroc Canada, a cement company. There was no tug with the *Metis* when we spotted her at Green Bay, so she was probably being used for cement storage, augmenting what could be stored in the shoreside siloes.

pairs of shorts, washed several uniforms, bought some hand lotion, and washed my car, which was limestone grey after sitting at Calcite for three weeks. Too bad I couldn't have relaxed. I also drove by Sally Schalk's, but her car wasn't there, so I suspect she was working the afternoon shift at Alpena General Hospital. Chances of my ever being into Calcite at a time when she's not working are pretty slim. Sally's an old friend from my high school days, and just about the only single woman I know in Rogers City in my age bracket. I enjoy talking with her.

The captain has caused a lot of dissension on the boat. He treats the mates like they're incompetent much of the time. They're all nervous when he's in the pilothouse, because they know he's going to correct them on just about everything they do, even though most have been working on the boats for years.

It's often said that on a boat the captain is God. There was a time when that was true, but it's not any longer. Neither the company office nor our unions will tolerate a captain who harasses crewmembers. If our young captain doesn't change his ways soon, somebody's going to "drop and dime on him"—call the company or the union and complain.

I know what it's like to work under an abusive captain. My first year with Interlake, I was on the *Elton Hoyt 2d* during the fall with a loud, threatening drunk who delighted in terrifying or discharging crewmembers. There should have been a revolving door in the fo'c'sle to handle the constant turnover of deckhands. I seem to remember that the captain went through more than thirty that season. Whoever drew the character Bluto in the Popeye comic strip must have known the captain of the *Hoyt*, because the overstuffed, bearded brute was the spitting image of the tyrant I served under that long and miserable fall. He was a scary character to have to work for, especially if he didn't like you and there were few on the boat he liked. He definitely didn't like me, even though I busted my butt to try and please him. In retrospect, I don't think he liked himself very much, despite his false bravado.

The chief engineer, first mate, and I were standing out on deck just outside the galley this evening when a small runabout with two girls in it came by. We were talking—

51

about our rambunctious captain, as a matter of fact—and didn't pay much attention to the girls. One of them started waving to attract our attention. Several of us offhandedly waved back and continued our discussion. Once the girl knew we were looking, though, she pulled the bra part of her two-piece bathing suit up and bared her chest. That got our attention! Not to be outdone, her friend then turned her back to us, bent over, and pulled the bottom of her bathing suit down around her ankles. I've seen many young women in passing boats bare their chests before, but that's the very first time I've ever been mooned since I've been sailing. An interesting end to an interesting day on the Great Lakes.

Sunday, June 16
Father's Day
Lake Erie, Westbound

We unloaded at Ontario Stone in Cleveland from 11:00 A.M. until about 4:00 P.M. and are now heading back north to some as-yet-undetermined destination. We're either going to Calcite, Stoneport, or Port Inland. We won't know our destination until the captain talks to the office tomorrow morning. If we do go to Calcite or Stoneport, we won't get in until 11:00 or 12:00 P.M., a lousy time for those of us who would like to go home.

While we were in Cleveland, hundreds of boaters were out enjoying an eighty-five-degree summer day on the Cuyahoga River. All the restaurants and taverns in the flats were busy, but I didn't have much of a chance to stand out on deck and observe the passing scene. Tonight was pizza night on the *Calcite II,* and I was held hostage in the galley making seventeen pizzas. I didn't finish pulling the last one from the oven until we cleared the breakwaters at the entrance to the Cleveland harbor. With that completed, I slipped into a t-shirt and shorts, finished a little paperwork, and am now awaiting the start of *60 Minutes.*

52

Tuesday, June 18
Lake Huron, Downbound

Yesterday afternoon at about 3:00 we finally found out that we were going to Rogers City again. We docked there at 10:00 P.M., which is not a good time for most of the crew, but there was a large contingent waiting at the ladder as soon as the cables were put out. I was one of them. I ran to my mother's to pick up one of my coffee mugs. There aren't any mugs on this boat and I'm tired of drinking out of styrofoam cups. I also visited a local super-market that's open twenty-four hours a day and picked up a couple gallons of vanilla ice cream. It got left out of our last order from the Soo, making it tough to serve pie à la mode, or root beer floats. I was back at the boat by 11:00, but I was slightly wired and had trouble falling asleep. Nonetheless, I was better rested this morning than most of the crew, though I did sneak in a thirty-minute nap this afternoon.

The weather took a rather strange turn last night while we were loading at Calcite. By this morning it was only 42 degrees, and everyone aboard was wishing they hadn't taken their winter gear home. On top of the cold spell, it's also been raining for the past twenty-four hours, making it doubly miserable for the guys who have to work outside. On the other hand, those of us who toil in the galley and engine room are enjoying the respite from the recent bout of hot weather. I usually turn off burners and ovens as soon as we're done using them in an effort to keep the galley from getting too hot. Today, however, I turned everything on just to keep warm. As long as I'm on a boat without air-conditioning, I'm not about to complain about cool weather in the summertime.

We're on our way to Detroit, and then we'll turn around and go back to either Stoneport or Calcite for another load. It's nice to get home, but these short trips are death on the crew. When they're not working and should be sleeping, they're at home with their families. As a result, after two trips into Calcite in just four days, everyone looks a little ragged. A few of the guys joked this morning that they were hoping for a long trip so they could get rested up.

53

Valerie Peacock and her husband Tim "Hollywood" Peacock, handyman on the *Calcite II*, relax on a bench on the ship's stack deck for an evening cruise up the Detroit and St. Clair Rivers. Crewmembers aboard ships in the USS Great Lakes Fleet are permitted to have their spouses aboard for at least one trip each season. (Author's collection)

We have two guests aboard for this trip: April Bellmore, the wife of the chief engineer, and Val Peacock, the wife of the handyman. Both are beautiful ladies, and Jimmy Atkins, my porter, is clearly infatuated with April. During meal hours, Jimmy waits on the unlicensed crewmembers who eat in the messroom. This morning, I told him that it was company policy that guests eat in the officer's dining room. "Every meal?" he asked plaintively. "You mean they can't eat in here at all?" For a minute I thought he was going to cry. Relax, Jimmy, I was just kidding. It's nice to have guests; they break the monotony for everyone.

We also found out that we'll be getting a new captain when we get back up above. Our captain will be going on vacation, and his relief will be Ed Brege, the brother of our first assistant engineer. I've never sailed with Ed before, but he seems to be extremely popular with the crew.

The guys in the deck department are so happy they're

virtually dancing a jig, especially the mates. The situation in the pilothouse continued to worsen almost daily. The captain keeps correcting the mates on the courses they're steering and the reference marks they use to begin turns in the rivers. If they're steering 180 degrees, the captain will say something like, "Where'd you get 180 degrees? The course should be 179. How've you been doing this job all these years when you still don't know the right courses to steer." The next time through that stretch of river, the mate will call for 179 degrees, only to have the captain correct the course—to 180 degrees! That exact scenario occurred the other evening, and Larry Post, the wheelsman on watch, burst out laughing, though the captain never caught on as to why. If this guy carried ball bearings in his pocket and conducted searches for missing strawberries, none of us would be the slightest bit surprised. As one crewman noted the other day, "the captain's elevator doesn't go all the way to the top floor." A new captain aboard our ship will be a great relief for virtually everyone. Ed Brege is reportedly a prodigious eater, so I'm sure he and I will get along fine.

I think the second cook made it through the entire day without screwing anything up—for the first time in the almost three weeks he's had the job. He can do some things that truly amaze me! He's worked in galleys for seven years, but must have had his eyes and ears closed most of the time. He really hasn't learned much. He simply doesn't have any interest in his job; it's just a paycheck to him. The sad thing is that he knows I haven't been pleased with his performance. I think he's tried to do a better job, but he doesn't have any of the skills necessary to be a cook or baker. He'll probably be happy to return to his porter's job when Gene Schaedig returns from vacation in another ten or eleven days. I left a message on the telephone answering machine at Gene's house the other day, telling him to be back here not later than June 1! I'm sure he got a chuckle out of that, and I'll enjoy filling him in on all his relief's shenanigans when he arrives. I don't think Gene will be the slightest bit surprised; he's worked with this guy quite often. Every time he told us about all of the sensational things he was going to bake when he got to be second cook, Gene just rolled his eyes. Now I know why.

Ol' Lake Huron is fog-covered again tonight. Combined with the cold on-again, off-again showers, it makes for a gloomy day. No matter, most of the crewmembers who aren't on watch are sacked out to make up for the sleep they lost last night. The weather's conducive to that. It's the sort of day that inspires napping.

Wednesday, June 19

Lake St. Clair, Upbound

It was 42 degrees yesterday, and 82 today. What a dramatic change in weather in less than twenty-four hours. We spent the entire day unloading stone in the Rouge River at Detroit, and just left the dock and headed back north at suppertime. It's cooled off now that we're out on the open water, but it must have been at least 100 degrees in the galley when I was cooking hamburgers for supper. I was perspiring freely!

We almost lost our four deckhands this morning. As the captain backed the boat up the Rouge on the way to another unimproved dock, the deckhands launched the workboat so they could go ashore ahead of us to handle the mooring cables. They had just passed the stern of the boat when the outboard motor quit. As the deckhand operating the motor frantically tried to restart it, we rapidly bore down on them. Those in the boat saw the ship's massive bronze propeller beating its way through the water toward them, and two grabbed the oars and tried to row the workboat out of the way. Just about the time the captain stopped the engine, one of the deckhands noticed that the fuel line to the outboard had dropped off. He quickly reconnected it and they were on their way and out of harm's way. While the captain stopped the engine, we had a fair amount of way on and wouldn't have been able to stop in the short distance between us and the workboat. With four men in the little workboat, it didn't have much freeboard left, and it's likely it would have been swamped if we had hit it. If there hadn't been a mate on the fantail to radio the captain to stop the engine, the propeller would easily have made mincemeat out of the workboat and its occupants.

I happened to be looking right at Frank Bruski, one of the deckhands, when he turned and noticed the propeller coming toward them. Frank's eyes were as big as portholes! He instantly started rowing . . . with vigor.

It looks like we're on our way to Cedarville, and will arrive tomorrow evening. If the weather's nice, I just might go for a walk. With the tourist season underway now, there should be some activity around the little resort community.

April and Val, the vacationers, are sitting on the swing and bench up on the boat deck for the evening cruise up the St. Clair River. It's a pleasant, warm evening, but overcast and humid. I sat out on a hatch for awhile, but the horseflies got the best of me. They're the scourge of sailors on the Great Lakes, descending in hordes when the winds are calm and tearing off chunks of flesh with impunity. The worst are usually encountered off Harbor Beach at the tip of Michigan's thumb on Lake Huron. They swarm onto the boat and if there's no wind, they'll ride all the way up the lake, making life miserable for those aboard.

Interlake's *Lee A. Tregurtha* passed us in the Rouge while we unloaded, and I saw several former shipmates. Skip Wood, the chief, hung out the gangway in the engine room and the mate out on deck was Scott Savoy. I've sailed many times with both of them, and always enjoyed their company.

Scotty was a Ford Motor Company mate who went with Interlake when they bought the Ford fleet in 1988. A middle-aged bachelor in those days, he was known for being extremely frugal. I remember one year he showed up with a pair of old-fashioned black leather dress shoes that he inherited from an uncle who had died. The shoes were several sizes too large for Scott, but he felt they still had some good years left in them. He was one of the few sailors I've known who carried a sewing kit with him so he could mend his clothes. Good thing, some of his shirts and pants were largely made up of thread added when Scott repaired them. Scotty didn't throw anything away before it was *truly* worn out. He's a good soul, though, with a wry sense of humor. He got married several years ago to an old high school friend, proof positive that there's hope for all of us.

Deckhands carefully climb down into the *Calcite II*'s tiny aluminum workboat as the ship approaches its unloading dock on the river at Saginaw, Michigan. The workboat is used at unimproved docks, where it is impossible to put deckhands ashore with the ship's landing boom. (Author's collection)

I sailed with Skip on both the *Kaye E. Barker* and the *James R. Barker,* where he was first assistant engineer and relief chief for three or four seasons when I served as porter, second cook, and steward. Skip's a good-hearted guy who enjoys bull sessions and is always assured of getting his two cents' worth into any conversation. On the *James R. Barker* Marty Tice and I used to try and find some topic of conversation that Skip wouldn't know anything about, to limit his ability to horn in on our discussions. We never did, despite the fact that when we'd see Skip coming we'd start talking about such diverse topics as brain surgery, cryptography, and the Russo-Japanese War of 1905. We finally faced up to the fact that if there's a conversation going on aboard ship, Skip's going to be part of it.

While we were on the *James R. Barker,* Skip spent most of his time as the first assistant engineer under Chief Engineer Jerry Hassett. In fact, it was Skip who found Jerry after he had been stabbed fourteen times by the second assistant engineer. The chief and Skip had teamed up and given the second assistant a bad end-of-season evaluation. The second assistant got drunk that evening and, according to the chief, went up to the chief's room about midnight where the chief was asleep, and started stabbing him with a screwdriver and a small pocketknife. The chief woke up and started struggling, and the second assistant fled. The chief was on blood thinners at the time, and even though none of the wounds was severe, he was bleeding like a stuck pig. He staggered to the door of his room and called for Skip, who was in the room across the hall. Skip called the pilothouse, then he and another fellow patched the chief up as best they could, using up most of the bandaging material in our ship's first-aid kits. A couple of hours later, a Coast Guard helicopter took the chief off in a basket and transported him to a hospital ashore. That was in early December, and he came back to work for the last trip of the season. The following spring he came to fitout, but was still bothered by his wounds and uncomfortable living in the room where he had been stabbed. As I recall, he sailed only a matter of weeks before he decided to retire.

Although the second assistant was charged with attempted murder, he was eventually found innocent. There just wasn't any forensic evidence tying him to the crime, and there was apparently a lot of testimony about how the chief and Skip had harassed him. He got off, but lost his engineer's license. He is reportedly now teaching school in Florida.

The second assistant said he blacked out after getting drunk that evening and didn't remember anything that happened afterward. He was found asleep in his bed several hours after the chief was attacked, so they tied his door shut so he couldn't get out. A guard was posted outside the room until two state troopers came aboard the next morning when we went to anchor off Ludington, Michigan. The troopers interviewed just about everyone on the boat, after handcuffing the second assistant to a railing outside the captain's stateroom. I sent some lunch up to the errant engineer, something he was particularly fond of as I recall. I knew him when he was a student at the Great Lakes Maritime Academy, and we had spent a fair amount of time talking on the boat. He was a few years older than I was, and had given up teaching to go to the academy back in the late 1970s when there was a real shortage of officers on the lakes. By the time his class graduated, however, the shipping industry had slipped into the infamous recession of the 1980s and you couldn't buy a job on the boats. He stuck around, though, and eventually went sailing in 1988 or 1989 when things finally picked up. His wife, Laurie, a nurse, also went to the academy at the same time, but they divorced somewhere along the line. She graduated with a license as a deck officer, but I don't think she ever sailed.

The infamous stabbing affair actually started in the spring or early summer of 1991 when the second assistant came over to the *Barker* as a relief engineer. At the time, Hassett said the office had told him that the engineer had trouble on his previous boat, and if Jerry wasn't satisfied with his performance they'd get rid of him. Hassett bitched and complained a lot about the office sending him another incompetent engineer. A couple weeks later, Hassett told us that once again the office didn't know what they were talking about. The engineer, he said, was doing just fine and he had no complaints with him.

Sometime in November, the relief engineer became a day-worker, helping Skip, who was then first assistant. As I saw it, Skip spent most of his time in the messroom drinking coffee and eating doughnuts, while the second assistant was given every lousy job that came along. That was a bitterly cold fall, and we had endless troubles with the hydraulic mooring winches. I remember the engineer spent hours and hours in the biting cold working on those winches. In fact, he hadn't planned on having to work outside, and didn't have a warm jacket along, so I sold him an old Eddie Bauer down jacket I had with me. I think the second assistant tried to do the best job he could, but he wasn't very experienced on the types of equipment we had on the *Barker*, and Skip didn't give him much help.

When it came time to do the second assistant's evaluation, the chief, possibly with a little prodding from Skip, did an about-face regarding the engineer's abilities. In his evaluation the chief said he really needed to go back as a third assistant on a steamer and learn the job all over again. That night the chief got stabbed. Some crewmembers morbidly joked that the second assistant even screwed that up. Several engineers who didn't like Hassett vowed to take up a collection to buy the second assistant a bigger knife.

I'll never forget the night of the stabbing. I was second cook and shared a room with the porter. We were awakened around 1:00 A.M. by the first mate, who told us the basic details of what had happened and asked us to stay in our room and lock the door or go to the messroom where some of the crew was congregating. He no sooner left the room than the lights went out. They'd lost a generator down in the engine room, but we theorized that the second assistant was down in the engine room sabotaging the equipment. When the power came back on a few minutes later, our blasted toilet started running and wouldn't quit. The only way to shut it off was to use a screwdriver to close the valve, and we didn't have one in the room. I decided to go next door into the galley to get a screwdriver, fully aware that the second assistant might be rampaging around the ship armed with a knife. I slipped some clothes on, stealthily crept into the galley, and went to the locker where we kept our small supply of basic tools. As I opened the locker, movement in the window attracted my attention. When I looked, the window was filled with a large head with a bushy beard

61

and tousled hair, looking much like the second assistant. I nearly suffered heart failure until I realized it was one of the deckhands who was nervously making his way to the messroom.

Few of us got any sleep the rest of that night. We searched for the second assistant for an hour or so, and someone found footprints in the snow on one of the upper decks. Our first thought was that the despondent engineer had jumped overboard after stabbing the chief. It was snowing heavily at the time, so there was no sense in turning the boat around to try to look for a man overboard. A little later someone got the bright idea to look in the second assistant's room; there he was, sound asleep and snoring loudly. He was probably the only one on the boat that slept well that December night on the *James R. Barker.*

Thursday, June 20
Port Dolomite
Cedarville, Michigan

We arrived at Cedarville about 4:00 P.M., after playing "run silent, run deep" all day. The office said that Oglebay Norton's *Courtney Burton* was supposed to arrive at Cedarville at about the same time we were, so we didn't make any radio calls that would give away our position. The captain hoped we could outrun the *Burton* to Cedarville. If we didn't, we would have to anchor until she was done loading. Well, when the mate finally called the dock this afternoon to let them know what time to expect us, he asked the dock foreman the status of the *Burton*. "Oh, she loaded here yesterday," was the surprising reply. Our antics were unnecessary, not that they would have made any difference.

It's still cool up here at the top of Lake Huron. I never checked the temperature, but I don't think it got much above 60 degrees all day, much to the delight of those of us in the galley. It was a vast improvement over the heat and humidity we had yesterday. Unfortunately, when we finish loading tonight, we'll be heading south. We're taking on a split load—half will go to Cleveland and the other half will end up in Fairport, Ohio. It's likely to be hot down there.

I wanted to make a few more comments about Chief Engineer Jerry Hassett. When I first met him on the *James R. Barker*, Jerry was pushing sixty. He was on the short side, with a pot belly and a swarthy complexion, and I thought he looked Mexican, but I wasn't forward enough to ask him if he was. Later, I heard him talking about his home in Brownsville, Texas, just across the river from Mexico, and in my mind that confirmed the fact that he was of Hispanic origins. I discovered soon afterward that nothing could have been further from the truth. Jerry was born and raised in Sault Ste. Marie, Michigan, on the banks of the St. Marys River. His entire life was intertwined with the Great Lakes shipping industry. Over the years, he worked on tugs, tankers, and bulk freighters of all sizes and vintages, moving "up the hawsepipe," until he was chief engineer on the *Barker*, one of the largest and most modern ships on the lakes. The chief was proud of the rich heritage of our industry, and the role it played in the development of our country. He entertained me for many fascinating hours with stories about his years at sea.

Jerry spent a lot of time in the galley. In fact, some argued that he was in the galley more than he was in the engine room. His post was on the back side of the long work island that ran down the center of the galley, where he leaned against the shiny stainless steel freezers that lined the back wall of the galley. I grumped many times about having to clean the chief's fingerprints off the freezer doors every blasted day.

From his strategic position against the freezers, the chief spent hours entertaining George Rydberg and me with stories, or pontificating on politics, government, today's youths, deck officers, and the like. He could be quite opinionated and boisterous. George occasionally got upset and walked out of the galley.

The chief wasn't always easy to get along with. Once when I was working as a porter, I started crossing off the days on the calendar that hung on the bulletin board in the officer's dining room. It was simply a way to keep track of what day it was. Anyway, after a week or two, the chief asked if I was crossing off the days. "The days go by slow enough out here, I don't need to be reminded of that by seeing those x's on the calendar each day," he said. "I'd appreciate it if you would stop." And I did. But I mentioned the chief's complaint to several engineers, including Skip Wood and Marty Tice. They immediately took up the challenge and started crossing off the days themselves. The chief asked me several times after that if I was still crossing off the days; he quizzed George Rydberg and others on the boat, including the culprits who were actually doing it. I was innocent and none of the others would confess, so he eventually dropped the whole issue, though it was obvious to everyone that he was upset that someone had gone against his wishes. After all, he was *the chief*. I'm sure he still thinks I did it.

On the night he got stabbed, the chief lost a lot of blood and we weren't sure if he was going to make it or not. When the Coast Guard helicopter arrived, they wrapped the chief in blankets and strapped him into a litter. As four or five stout crewmen carried the litter down the passageway leading to the main deck, over which the Coast Guard helicopter hovered, they passed George Rydberg's room. George stood in his doorway, and as the litter was carried past him, the ashen-faced chief looked up and said quietly, "I guess I won't be in to stir the soup tomorrow." With that, both George and I concluded that the chief was going to be all right.

Friday, June 21

St. Clair River, Downbound

The first full day of summer. It's hot and humid with little breeze, and the mosquitoes are so thick you'd think we were sailing through a cedar swamp.

We lost a deckhand last night. He apparently pulled a bunch of muscles in his back lifting a heavy tag line for the self-unloading boom. Back injuries are frequent in the deck gang. The deckhand, Mike Fischer, was picked up at Cedarville by someone from our warehouse at the Soo. Before he got off, though, he had to provide a urine sample for drug testing. We had a monthly vessel safety meeting this afternoon, and several guys complained because Mike had to ride to the Soo in a van. They felt he should have gone by ambulance, given the fact that he could barely straighten up, he was in a lot of pain, and nobody knew exactly what was wrong with him. At least the company arranged to have someone pick him up. I've known of many other sailors who got off boats sick or injured all by themselves, often in ports they weren't familiar with. And the shipping companies wonder why they get sued so often.

Rod Bellmore, one of the deckhands, bought a used twelve-foot aluminum fishing boat that needs some repairs, and he's working on it out on deck. Charlie Brege, one of our oilers, is helping him. Three or four other guys are standing around giving free advice. The work on the fishing boat is what's referred to as a "government job," with materials and equipment provided by the company. Such jobs are a longstanding tradition on these boats, one of the unofficial fringe benefits of sailing on the "Rogers City boats." Most other shipping companies don't tolerate such projects.

This company and its captains, chief engineers, and stewards have always been extremely lax about such things. It's well known, for example, that many galley personnel take a lot of supplies home with them. A couple stewards are infamous for taking on large loads of stores when their boats are on the way to their lay-up docks. When the crews leave the boats, the stores mysteriously disappear. Other stewards order a couple large prime rib roasts every time they get groceries, yet they never serve prime rib to their crews. Stewards have also been known to take kickbacks from the chandlers who supply the boats. The chandlers will charge the company for five hundred dollars' worth of meat, and pass the cash along to the steward. For the chandlers, it's sort of painless graft, since the shipping companies are picking up the tab. One old steward told me that he knew a cook who bought a new car in Toledo and then passed the payment book along to the grocery man to handle. Some second cooks and porters in this fleet have been known to take a load of groceries off their boats every time they get to Rogers City. They want to be *real* careful if they ever work with me. Tradition or not, I'll raise holy hell if I catch anyone stealing groceries from my galley.

It's several hours later now. I just spent some time out on deck talking with the second assistant engineer.

There's little vessel traffic in the river this evening, and even fewer recreational boaters. It's a grey evening and it looks as though thunderstorms may erupt at any time. Severe thunderstorms are forecast for the Detroit area, which we are fast approaching, so they've got the watchman battening down everything out on deck. It's cooling off considerably, and it looks as though it might be good sleeping weather later on.

Friday, June 21
Cleveland, Ohio

We had a bit of excitement this morning. It was blowing quite hard out of the west when we tried to enter the harbor at Fairport, Ohio. The captain attempted to stay over on the west side of the channel so the wind wouldn't set the boat down against the east pier, but he strayed into shoal water and we ran aground. Fortunately, we fetched up on sand and no damage was done to the hull. The wind did carry the stern around to the east, though, and we sat parallel to the shore and almost blocked the entrance between the two piers. The captain tried to get the boat off, but she was stuck fast, so he called for a tug to come from Cleveland to help us. The seas continued to build as we waited for the tug. When the waves eventually lifted us free of the sand, the captain quickly throttled up and headed out into deep water. Instead of making a second attempt to get into Fairport, the captain decided to take the prudent course and go to Cleveland to unload half our cargo. That's what we're doing right now. In another hour or so, we'll sail for Fairport and with a much shallower draft, we shouldn't have any trouble getting in. Hopefully.

It's a bit embarrassing to run aground, especially for the captain. It's basically impossible to hide a 600-foot ship that's sitting sideways in the middle of the entrance channel. All the people in passing boats are excessively friendly at such times, waving and smiling knowingly. Captains of grounded ships aren't likely to wave back. They take refuge in the darkest corner of the pilothouse and try to ignore the

Coast Guard personnel in a small boat inspect the hull of the *Calcite II*, aground across the entrance channel at Fairport, Ohio. The boat ran aground due to shoaling on the west side of the narrow channel. Another boat from the USS Great Lakes Fleet ran aground in the same spot only a week earlier, but no one had warned the *Calcite*'s captain of the problem. As seas increased throughout the day, the captain was able to work the *C-2* free of the shoal. Part of the ship's cargo was unloaded in Cleveland before it made a second, successful attempt to enter the harbor at Fairport. (Author's collection)

fact that their little mistake is plainly obvious to everyone going by. Groundings are not good for the ego.

Many of the crewmembers were actually glad that the captain put the boat aground. They felt he'd gotten his just desserts. A lot of wry comments were made about the Coast Guard forcing him to produce a urine specimen for a drug test. One of the guys wanted to call the pilothouse and remind the captain not to go to the bathroom until after he gave the Coasties a urine sample.

The first mate and I talked at breakfast about how none of the mates would go out of their way to keep the captain from making a mistake, due to his constant superior attitude. With such an atmosphere on the boat, the mate concluded it was only a matter of time before the captain got into trouble. I suggested that the next time we were in Rogers City the mate should return to the boat with a suit and a white shirt and tie on a hanger. If the captain asked what it was for, he could reply, "In case I have to testify at a Coast Guard inquiry." After we went aground this morning, the mate passed me out on deck, winked, and said, "And I don't have a white shirt."

Reports from the pilothouse say that the captain was nice to everyone for several hours after the grounding. By the time we got to Cleveland, however, he returned to his old habit of screaming at people. If he ever has an accident that is genuinely his fault, he's not likely to find too many members of this crew who will stick up for him. That's not a comfortable position to be in. In this business, like most others, you reap what you sow.

It's now several hours later and we're still at the dock in Cleveland. Just when we were almost ready to leave, the self-unloading system broke down. The chief and first assistant have been working on it for an hour and a half, but to no avail thus far.

Crewmembers watch as the *Calcite II* unloads stone—into itself—while tied up in the Cuyahoga River at Cleveland. The ship was carrying a split cargo, with half going to Cleveland and the other half destined for Fairport, Ohio. Once the Cleveland portion of the cargo had been unloaded, part of the remaining cargo had to be transferred from one hold to another to trim the ship before it could leave for Fairport. (Author's collection)

Sunday, June 23

St. Clair River, Upbound

This has been some trip. This afternoon we hit a small boat on the Detroit River, just above Boblo Island. The runabout had been towing a guy who was parasailing. When he came down, the chute or risers got tangled in the boat's propeller and the boat's driver and the parasailor were on the stern trying to get the chute untangled when we arrived on the scene. Their first awareness of the *Calcite II* was when the captain blew a one-blast signal for a port-to-port passage, followed immediately be a series of short blasts—the danger signal. A second danger signal followed, and then a prolonged blast of the whistle that ended when we collided with the boat.

The captain and the watchman were both yelling and motioning for the two guys to get out of the way as we bore down on them. The fellow who had been parasailing finally realized the seriousness of the situation. He dove overboard and began to swim perpendicular to our path. He had a life jacket on. The driver didn't have a life jacket on, and he appeared to entertain notions of remaining aboard his boat to ride out the collision. As the bow of the *Calcite II* loomed over him, however, he, too, abandoned ship.

Our ship smashed into the fiberglass-hulled boat. It careened off and slid down the side as we passed. Both of the guys who had been aboard were outboard of their boat, treading water as we plowed by. When I first got a look at them, they were about half way down the ship's side; my immediate concern was that they would be sucked into our propeller. I started to run for a life ring to throw to the fellow who wasn't wearing a life jacket, but we passed them too fast. Fortunately, they and their boat floated safely past the stern, where they were quickly assisted by other boaters in the area and a Canadian Coast Guard patrol boat.

When the incident occurred, we were in a narrow channel with little maneuvering room. The captain moved as far to the left side of the channel as he could, but there was no way we could avoid hitting the pleasure boat or stop in time. We weren't at fault, but the captain apparently must file a report with the Canadian Coast Guard when we stop to fuel at Sarnia, Ontario, just across the river from Port Huron.

Undoubtedly, the worst part of the whole incident for the captain was to call the fleet manager in Duluth—the same guy he called yesterday after we went aground. We've speculated all afternoon on the gist of that conversation: "Hello, Fred? This is the *Calcite II* calling . . . again." I've seen captains tremble when they made those calls to the office to pass along bad news.

Both of the men in the boat seem to have survived the experience without any injuries. As we steamed off, I saw them climbing aboard their boat. I have no idea how serious the damage might have been to the boat. It seemed to be floating okay, and if it only struck a glancing blow against our hull it may have nothing more serious than a marred paint job. My suspicion is that the driver won't play around out in the middle of the shipping channel in the future. Small boats and big boats don't mix well, and if there's a collision, the small boat and its occupants are at a decided disadvantage.

I told one of the mates that I was going to wear my survival suit and carry a fire extinguisher with me once we enter Lake Huron. After a grounding and collision in the past two days, it seems likely the boat will either sink or catch fire somewhere between Port Huron and Calcite.

Tuesday, June 25
Lake St. Clair, Downbound

We were at Calcite from noon until a little after 10:00 last night, so everyone had a chance to get home. I went to my mother's right after lunch to pick up my mail and hear the latest news, and then ran a few errands before I returned to the boat. I gave the porter and second cook the balance of the day off, so I had plenty to do before dinner. I think I only served six people during the dinner hour, so there were lots of leftovers for the rest of the crew when they came back to the boat. Only a few scraps were left this morning. Not much food gets wasted on this boat.

New captain—not Ed Brege, but Al Gapczynski. The

mates and wheelsmen were more relaxed today than they've been since I came on board. Apparently, Captain Al is fairly laid-back and willing to let his crew do their jobs. It was funny to have dinner with the guys from the 4-to-8 watch, as I do almost every evening, and not hear any horror stories from the pilothouse. It will be a nice break; too bad it's only for a week.

Fewer pleasure boats plied the rivers today than the last time we went through here, which was on a weekend. We didn't hit anyone this time.

Wednesday, June 26
Lake Erie, Westbound

We unloaded at two different docks in Cleveland today; now, we're now on our way to Cedarville to pick up another load of stone for Cleveland again. Oglebay Norton's *Fred R. White, Jr.* and American Steamship's *American Republic* both passed us while we docked in the Cuyahoga. John Meharg, the chief on the "*Fast Freddy*" leaned out the engine room gangway when they went past. He's from Rogers City, the brother-in-law of Jimmy Atkins, our porter, and one of my brother's best friends. The captain on the *Republic*, Ed Derry, is also from Rogers City. Oglebay Norton's *Earl W. Oglebay* was right behind us coming out of the river at Cleveland, though I never saw her until we got out into the lake. My brother, another Rogers City sailor, is the third mate on the *Oglebay*, and there are six or seven other Rogers City men in the crew. While American Steamship is headquartered in Buffalo and Oglebay Norton is a Cleveland-based company, many of the personnel on their boats are from little Rogers City on Lake Huron's northern shore. On a per capita basis, Rogers City undoubtedly produces more sailors than any other community around the Great Lakes. They sail for every company on the lakes. It's unusual to find a ship that doesn't have at least one Rogers City sailor aboard. It's a long tradition those of us from Rogers City are very proud of.

I bought a bunch of lottery tickets from the Ohio lottery today. I don't normally waste money gambling, so they're

71

The *American Republic* passes outbound through downtown Cleveland after delivering more than 20,000 tons of iron ore pellets to a steel mill on the upper Cuyahoga River. On its previous trip into Cleveland, the ship carried a much lighter, but more noteworthy cargo—the Olympic torch. The *American Republic* was selected to transport the torch from Detroit to Cleveland during the Olympic symbol's highly publicized tour of the United States prior to the start of the 1996 summer games in Atlanta. For the voyage, the initials of the *Republic*'s owning companies—American Steamship Company and its parent, transportation giant GATX—were painted on the hull. (Author's collection)

the first lottery tickets I've bought in years. The Ohio lottery jackpot is at $35 million, though, and I just couldn't resist a chance at it. Who knows? My luck has been pretty good lately. Many of the guys on the boat bought tickets. In fact, seventeen of us threw five dollars each into a pool to buy tickets. If any of the eighty-five sets of numbers win, the seventeen of us will split the winnings. That would mean about 1.75 million dollars a year for the next twenty years, or just over one hundred thousand dollars each. Many of the conversations on the boat today were about what we would do if we won the lottery. It was an almost unanimous decision that if we won we'd get off at the mailboat in Detroit later tonight and head to lottery headquarters in Columbus, Ohio, to pick up our winnings. The captain, one of those in our pool, said he'd call the office in Duluth and tell them where we were leaving their boat, so they could send a new crew. A wonderful fantasy. Unfortunately, I suspect that at dawn tomorrow all seventeen of us will be doing what we were doing at dawn this morning, with only fleeting thoughts of what might have been.

Few of the guys said they would continue sailing if they won the lottery. That's really no surprise. If we had money, most of us would find things we'd rather do with our time. I'm sure the same is true of workers in auto plants, supermarkets, and Wall Street offices. This is the best job I've ever had, but there are *many* ways I would rather spend my time. I won't bore you with the details, unless my numbers hit, of course.

Everybody seems happy with our new captain. He complimented my cooking, and I really didn't do anything special today—just bean soup, pizza burgers, tuna melts, stacked turkey sandwiches, and taco pie for lunch, and fried pork chops, sweet-and-sour pork chops, Cajun blackened pork chops, and turkey tetrazzini on spaghetti for supper, along with boiled new potatoes, green beans with bacon, and applesauce. Most stewards would have prepared only one type of pork chops, but it isn't much additional work to offer a variety. The Cajun chops went over the best tonight, while the fried and sweet-and-sour were only slightly less popular. The tetrazzini also went over well; a lot of guys ordered it with a chop of some sort on the side. The crews on every boat I've been on seem to like the variety I offer at each meal. Several entrees makes it interesting for them to come back to eat, and they're almost certain to find something they consider edible.

Thursday, June 27
Lake Huron, Upbound

We're still heading for Cedarville on what must be a magnificent summer day on the beach. It's nice out here, too, but a bit hazy, which limits what we can see.

The guys that stayed up after 10:00 last night got a rare treat. When the boat was near Boblo Island in the lower Detroit River, what was billed as North America's largest display of fireworks was set off from a string of barges moored in mid-river. The fireworks were part of the week-long International Freedom Festival, which involves both Detroit and Windsor, Ontario, its twin city across the river. The fireworks apparently continued for a full hour. I love fireworks and would have enjoyed seeing the display, but after working twelve hours in the steamy hot galley, I couldn't keep my eyes open after about 9:15 P.M.

It's now about 2:30 P.M., and I just finished putting most of tonight's supper in the oven. We're going to have spaghetti, chicken in white wine sauce, and lamb chops sauteed in garlic butter; both the spaghetti sauce and chicken are in the oven heating. You probably don't cook your spaghetti sauce in the oven, but then you aren't preparing two gallons of the stuff, either. If I tried to cook it on top of the stove, I would either have to stand there and constantly stir it, or risk scorching it. Instead, I cover the pot tightly and pop it into a 350-degree oven. It will be nicely done in about an hour or so, without any risk of burning. It's an old trick used by professional cooks around the world.

We didn't clear the Blue Water Bridge at Port Huron to head out onto the open stretches of Lake Huron until about 6:30 this morning, so things have been rather quiet on the boat. Both the captain and chief engineer slept through lunch, after working all night. When the ship is in the confined waters of the Detroit, St. Clair, and St. Marys Rivers, the captain is almost constantly in the pilothouse, backstopping the mate who is actually "in the front window" doing the piloting. Because the boat operates in narrow, winding channels and encounters other shipping traffic, a slight error in navigation could result in a collision or grounding. Years ago, the shipping companies and the Steamboat Inspection Service, one of the predecessors to today's Coast Guard, determined that the number of accidents occurring in the rivers could be cut substantially if there were two experienced pilots on watch, instead of just one. The captain usually sits off to the side of the pilothouse in a chair reserved just for him. On this boat, a recliner perched atop a wooden platform so the captain can see out the pilothouse windows serves as the captain's chair. Looks too comfortable to me. I'd have trouble staying awake in that chair.

The river watches represent the majority of the time captains work aboard ships on the lakes. They also take

Captain Mike Gapczynski stands "in the front window" of the *Calcite II* as it approaches the harbor in Buffalo, New York. Although ships on the Great Lakes are normally navigated by one of the three mates who stand watches, the captain takes over when the ship is maneuvering in harbors or narrow river channels. (Author's collection)

over handling the ship when docking or locking through at the Soo. The long river watches take their toll. Sleep deprivation is a common problem for captains of ships frequently traversing the rivers.

Ships are "piloted" in the rivers rather than "navigated." There simply is no navigational system accurate enough when a ship is in channels that are only three hundred to one thousand feet wide, not even the new global positioning system (GPS) that was widely used during the war in the Mideast. Instead of navigating, the mates handling the ship use navigational aids, like buoys, leading lights, range lights, and other less formal reference points along the shoreline to maintain their courses and gauge the moment to commence turns, and the like. By less formal, I mean such things as clumps of trees, distinctive buildings, and tall chimneys. Over the years, deck officers navigating ships have developed a system of pilotage for the Great Lakes, just like the riverboat captains did along the Mississippi. While trying to keep their ships in deep water, they soon figured out that if they steered on a big red barn at the end of a certain stretch of river, they would be on a safe course. When they were abreast a distinctive clump of birch trees near the bend in the river, they knew it was time to start their turn onto the next course. Eventually, the "courses and distances" for the river systems of the Great Lakes were written down in an effort to create a uniform set of instructions from ship to ship, and to make it easier for new mates to study for Coast Guard pilotage exams.

Out on the lakes, the ship is navigated by the three mates who stand watches of four hours on and eight hours off. Navigation today doesn't involve shooting the sun with a sextant, like you see in the old movies. Navigators primarily rely on LORAN, a radio-based system. The LORAN receiver aboard the ship reads radio signals being broadcast by a number of special transmitters located around the lakes. Based on the angle from the ship to a station and the time it takes to receive the signal, the computer in the LORAN receiver computes the ship's position with a fairly high degree of accuracy—within a hundred feet or less. That's a plenty accurate fix out on the lakes, but it wouldn't help in the rivers. The LORAN outputs are also confirmed by navigational officers who use their radars to fix the ship's position. On the lakes, vessels are almost always close enough to land to have it show up on their radars. By finding a known location along the shore or an offshore lighthouse or buoy, the mate plots the angle and distance on a chart to show the location of the ship and confirm the LORAN data.

Until radio direction-finders came out after World War I, and radar after World War II, captains and mates navigated their ships on the lakes by "dead reckoning." Outfitted with a magnetic compass that provided their heading and a taffrail log that told them how far they had traveled, navigators could plot their ship's location, or approximate location. Magnetic compasses, affected by the iron masses in the earth's crust that are common in the Great Lakes area, were often off by a few degrees. Wind and waves frequently pushed ships off course sideways. If the compass was off a little, or if the ship had been pushed off course by wind or waves, a navigator could only make an educated guess at the ship's location at any given time. If the navigator was wrong—and errors were common—the ship could easily run aground. Until ships were equipped with more sophisticated navigational systems, groundings were almost a daily occurrence on the lakes, and many sailors died as a result.

Some ships on the lakes today are even equipped with computerized navigational systems that will show the location of the ship on a chart of the lakes stored in the computer. Called an electronic chart, it's similar to the navigational systems that are purchased as options in some luxury cars today.

The mates on ships on the Great Lakes are also involved in other shipboard duties. They oversee loading and unloading operations and maintenance of the ship's deck areas. One mate is usually in charge of preparing the payroll documents, such as time sheets. Exactly which mate does

First mate Don Dehring stands watch on the bow of the *Calcite II* as it approaches the harbor at Buffalo, New York, in the midst of an evening sailboat race. (Author's collection)

which job varies somewhat from company to company, but the first mate is almost always in charge of loading the ship. He develops the loading plan prior to arriving at the loading dock, indicating how many tons are to be loaded in each hatch of the ship. Whatever mate is on watch will usually handle loading until it gets down to the last couple thousand tons, which are used to trim the ship. The first mate usually oversees that critical operation, assisted by the mate on watch. The goal is to store as much cargo in the holds as possible, within the draft limits imposed by the lakes, rivers, and harbors the ship will have to transit, and to make sure that the vessel isn't listing, hogging, or sagging. If the boat has a list on, it's tipped to one side or the other because too much cargo was loaded on that side. If the ship is hogged, its center is loaded too deep. Conversely, sagging means there isn't enough cargo amidships, so the middle section rides higher in the water than the bow and stern. The first mate's job is to guarantee that the boat leaves the dock "on an even keel," while carrying as much cargo as possible.

There are many horror stories around the lakes about mates who loaded their ships too deep, and couldn't pass through the locks at the Soo or up some river they had to negotiate. When I was on the 1,000-foot *James R. Barker*, the somewhat lax first mate hadn't read a *Notices to Mariners*, put out by the Coast Guard, which informed ships that the maximum draft at the Soo had been reduced because of low water levels. He would have loaded to the old draft limit if the captain hadn't been listening to the first mate on the radio. When he heard the mate mention the old draft figure, the captain quickly cut in and brought him up-to-date. Other mates weren't so fortunate. Their boats reached the Soo and couldn't get through until after they had lightered off some of their cargo, an expensive and time-consuming proposition. Many mates lost their jobs as a result of such mistakes.

Other mates have made navigational errors so outra-geous that one wonders whether they knew what planet, much less what lake, they were on. A few years ago, the mate navigating the 1,000-foot *Indiana Harbor* drove his ship onto the Lansing Shoal in northern Lake Michigan. The ship actually struck the tall lighthouse that clearly marks the shoal. Another mate put the *Kinsman Enterprise* on the rocky shores of Isle Royale on Lake Superior, many miles south of the passage he was aiming for. I don't think either sails on the lakes any longer; the rest of us still puzzle over why the accidents occurred. They almost qualify for *Ripley's Believe It or Not.*

Out on the lakes, the mate's job can be extremely boring. The autopilot, or "Iron Mike," keeps the ship on course, so there isn't much to do except keep an eye peeled for other traffic. That's even handled by today's collision avoidance radars that sound an alarm whenever another ship approaches. As a result, the four-hour watches in the pilothouse pass slowly.

It's often said that for captains and mates the long hours of boredom are occasionally punctuated by moments of stark terror. The captains and mates must always be ready to respond to the hundreds of things that might go wrong and put the ship in jeopardy—loss of steering, an engine shutdown, another vessel straying into its path, pleasure boaters cutting in front of the ship, and so on. There's a fine line between making a safe passage and being involved in an accident. The case of the *Sidney E. Smith, Jr.* offers a prime example.

In 1972 the *Smith* was upbound on the St. Clair River, in the middle of the big sweeping turn that takes you under the Blue Water Bridge and out onto the waters of Lake Huron. The captain had gone to his room a little earlier to use the bathroom, and he had fallen asleep in his easy chair, tired from long hours in the rivers over the prior couple of days. While the captain dozed, the mate decided that the *Smith* was a bit too close to the Canadian shoreline, so he told the wheelsman to take a little bit of the right rudder off. Unfortunately, when the wheelsman complied with the order, the bow of the ship got caught in the strong current below the bridge. Despite the mate and wheelsman's frantic efforts, the ship took a diagonal course across the river. The officers put progressively more right rudder on, but the ship wouldn't answer the helm. It was in the clutches of the current and headed straight for the American shore. To compound matters, the steamer *Parker Evans* was making a downbound passage under the bridge at the same time. When the *Smith* sliced across the river the Canadian freighter rammed the hapless ship. The tremendous impact

79

of the collision jarred the captain awake and he raced up to the pilothouse. It was immediately obvious to the captain and mate that their ship was mortally wounded, and they sounded the "abandon ship" signal on the steam whistle. All the crew got off safely, but the *Smith* quickly sank to the bottom and rolled over on its side, partially blocking the shipping channel. The hull was later cut up and removed. Today, only one-way vessel traffic is allowed in the stretch of river under the bridge, though few of today's sailors know why. Such a tiny error . . . and such dire consequences.

Friday, June 28
Lake Huron, Downbound

After arriving off Cedarville shortly after 10:00 last night, we had to anchor for more than four hours to wait for another ship to finish loading. Once we got under the loading rig, though, the dock crew didn't waste any time. We started loading about 3:30 A.M. and were finished and on our way by 9:45 this morning.

It's supposedly in the eighties on the beach today, but quite cool out here on the lake. The weather forecasters are calling for temperatures in the nineties in the Cleveland area tomorrow, which is cause for some consternation, since that's our destination. The only thing that may save us from roasting is that we won't be arriving at Cleveland until about 6:00 P.M., and should be out and on our way again by about 11:00 P.M. If we can catch a little breeze out on the lake, we may be all right.

Someone's been raiding my supply of potato chips. Each night, he slips into the storeroom and takes about a half bag of chips, a different kind each night. One night it was barbecue, the next cheddar and sour cream, and last night he took the Ruffles. He leaves the rest of the bag, neatly rolling the top closed. I thought I could head off the culprit last night by locking the storeroom, but he got in anyway. The porter and I are curious to know who's pilfering the chips. It's not a big deal, but my policy is that nobody takes anything out of our storerooms, walk-in coolers, or freezers without my permission. If I didn't have that rule, food items I

80

was planning to use for meals would vanish to leave me in a lurch. This is similar to the case of the missing strawberries in *The Caine Mutiny,* so I don't want to make a big deal out of it. I locked the storeroom again this evening. Expect a full report tomorrow.

One disadvantage of being out on a ship is that if you get hungry for something, you don't necessarily have access to it. At home, if you get a craving for pizza, you can call and have one delivered. Hungry for a burger? Run to McDonald's or Burger King. Need a candy bar or a bottle of pop? You can always find a convenience store open that has what you want. Out here you often must do without unless you've anticipated your craving and laid in a supply of whatever you're likely to develop an appetite for. There are times when I'd pay almost anything for a cold can of Diet Pepsi, a slice of pizza, or a doughnut. Oh well, they're all things I can live without.

Butch Kierzek, the 4-to-8 watchman and an old school chum of mine, probably has the biggest stash of munchies on the boat. Butch has what seems like an insatiable appetite, and he has a little apartment-size refrigerator in his room that's always well-stocked. He doesn't just lay in a supply of chips and pop, though. Butch keeps a real larder in his room that contains enough food to feed the crew for a couple of days. The last time we were in Rogers City, he came back to the boat with about a week's supply of pickled ham—a new one on me—and a big tub of potato salad. He dines on those things when he gets up at 3:00 A.M. to go to work, supplemented by whatever he finds in the galley.

It seems as though the crewmembers on the 4-to-8 watch are required to have gargantuan appetites, at least in the deck department. Mate Don Dehring and Wheelsman Larry Post can almost keep up with Butch's prodigious level of consumption. When Butch was temporarily on another watch, he was replaced by Rod Bellmore, an epicure of world-class proportions. The guys on the 4-to-8 don't eat dinner until they get off watch at about 7:45 P.M., so they're always dining on leftovers. Lately, many of the popular entrees were wiped out by the time the 4-to-8 watch came in, so they've started calling back just before I start serving dinner to check the menu and have me set aside plates for them. That way they don't miss out on anything.

81

Watchman Jerome "Butch" Kierzek operates a winch on the *Calcite II* during docking operations on the Saginaw River, while Wheelsman Larry Post looks on. The *C-2*'s skeleton-like unloading boom can be seen over the heads of the two crewmen. (Author's collection)

There's a wheelsman and watchman like Larry and Butch on each of the three watches. They work under the mate's supervision, since they're unlicensed crewmembers. Wheelsmen or watchmen must be able-bodied seamen. That means they've sailed for at least three years as ordinary seamen and passed a Coast Guard exam on seamanship and safety in order to get the "A.B." endorsement on their merchant seaman's documents.

Wheelsmen work in the pilothouse, where they steer the ship. They stand on a raised platform in the center of the pilothouse, so they can see over the head of the mate or captain who's standing in the front window. The easiest part of the wheelsman's job is wheeling out on the open lakes. There the ship is almost always put on autopilot. There are a few ships, however, that don't have autopilots, including the S. T. Crapo and the Kinsman Enterprise. On those, the wheelsmen steers the ship for the entire four hours they're on watch, including the long and boring courses across the lakes. On ships with autopilots, the wheelsman usually kicks back when out on the lakes, chats with the mate, or reads a book. The most demanding aspect of a wheelsman's job is on the rivers. There's little room for error on river courses, and the wheelsman must steer a sure course on both the straightaways and the turns, not allowing the ship to stray beyond the heading called out by the mate or captain. On the lakes, the wheelsman steers by the gyrocompass. On the rivers, he uses a gyrocompass, navigational aids—range lights and leading lights in particular—and landmarks along the shore. On ships where the pilothouse is at the bow in a traditional configuration, the wheelsman lines up the steering pole that juts from the bow of the ship with whatever it is he's steering on, such as a building or a set of ranges. On ships with the pilothouse at the stern—most of those vessels built since the 1970s—the wheelsman usually uses the vessel's forward mast as a steering guide.

Technically, the wheelsman is only responsible to do what the mate or captain tells him to do, but a good wheelsman makes the mate's job easy, particularly if the mate is inexperienced. On the other hand, some wheelsmen do only what they're told, even to the point where they would allow the mate to wreck the ship. I've often wondered what went on in the wheelsman's mind on the Indiana Harbor when he was told to steer on Lansing Shoal Light, and he continued until the ship had literally collided with the lighthouse. The Coast Guard took action against the mate, but many around the lakes feel they should have gone after the wheelsman as well.

The other watchstander in the deck department is the watchman. Historically, the primary role of the watchman

The deck crew on the *Calcite II* open hatches before arrival at an unloading dock. Watchman Mark "Ollie" Oliver pays out cable from a deck winch, while deckhand Casey Kandow (right) drags the bridle end of the cable. Kandow, a high school basketball star in Rogers City with an athletic scholarship to Michigan State University, worked on the boats during the summer to make money for school. Many college students were once employed on the boats in the summer, but with the downsizing of the Great Lakes fleet, that practice is fairly unusual today. (Author's collection)

has been as a lookout posted in the bow of the ship to watch and listen for other shipping traffic, lighthouses, buoys, and such. Since commercial lake ships were equipped with radar immediately following World War II, that role has steadily declined in importance. About the only time that vessels actually post a watchman in the bow as a lookout is in the rivers, and then primarily to watch for pleasure boaters. The captain and mate in the pilothouse usually know there's a commercial ship coming long before the watchman ever hears or sees it.

Since they no longer spend most of their time stationed up in the bow, the watchmen are assigned many other chores. They mop the passageways in the cabins, burn garbage, get lines and cables ready for making docks, run winches at the docks, sump water out of the tunnel after loading or unloading, fetch meals for the captain when the ship is in a river and the old man must remain in the pilothouse, hose down the cargo hold when unloading, and other odd jobs. Through the 1960s, there was also a deckhand on each watch, known as the "deck watch." When the deck watch positions were eventually eliminated during contract negotiations between the companies and the unions representing unlicensed seamen, the watchmen inherited most of the jobs previously performed by the deck watches.

Saturday, June 29
Off Cleveland

Whoops! We just lost our engine due to another broken fuel line. We're about nine miles out of Cleveland, and we'll just drift along until the engine room crew repair the line.

We passed the *James R. Barker,* my long-time "home," this morning in the St. Clair River. Several guys were out on deck, but I didn't recognize anyone. Captain Brian Laffey was in the pilothouse window, looking at us through binoculars. When he saw me, he dropped the binoculars and started flapping his arms in typical Captain Brian fashion. I flapped back, glad to see an old friend. After waving, Brian appeared to be dashing to the telephone next to the front window—I suspect he called down to the galley to tell George Rydberg to go out on the stern. It was about 9:30 A.M., though, and I'm sure Big George was taking his morning break in his room, where there's no phone. Oh well, word will quickly get around that I'm on the *Calcite II.* The next time we meet in the river I'm sure there'll be a few old shipmates out to exchange waves. My years on the "*Big Barker*" with Captain Laffey, Big George, Chief Hassett, Tiny, Bob Boyle, Moose, Edgar, Crocodile, Bananas, Tom Darnell, Skip, and the others were the best I've had on the lake . . . until now.

Great supper tonight. Saturday is traditionally steak night in this fleet, as in most others. I had New York strip steaks, which I cooked on the charcoal grill on the fantail. Along with the steaks, I also offered steak and onion kabobs with peanut sauce, barbecued chicken breasts, and grilled

marinated chicken breasts with my "secret" marinade—
Italian salad dressing. The kabobs were by far the most
popular entree, followed by the barbecued breasts, followed
by the marinated breasts. We only had four orders for steak
during the meal hour, out of about twenty crewmembers
who ate or had plates put aside for them. That's typical of my
experience on other ships. The vast majority of sailors today
will pass up steaks to try something they haven't had before,
or something most other stewards don't prepare. Two people
asked me for the recipe for the peanut sauce this evening,
so they must have liked it.

There was an interesting conversation in the messroom
this afternoon about some sailors in this fleet who are
survivalists and members of the now-infamous Michigan
Militia. One guy apparently has a trapdoor in the floor of
each room in his house, and he's planning to build a tunnel
to a bunker he's erecting some distance away. He's got
quite an arsenal of weapons and ammunition, including an
AK-47. When questioned, he apparently admitted that he
doesn't know how to use the weapons, but pointed out that
he did have instruction manuals for all his guns. These guys
seem to be afraid of government agencies like the FBI and
the Bureau of Alcohol, Tobacco, and Firearms. They think
they might someday be the target of a raid like the ones that
took place at the Branch Davidian compound in Waco and at
Ruby Ridge. Why they feel someone might want to raid their
homes is unclear. The logic of most of these militia-types is
also unclear. They call themselves patriots, but they don't
seem to support the American system of government. They
arm themselves and train for what they say is an inevitable
confrontation with the government, yet a platoon from the
82nd Airborne would have the soldier wannabes flying the
white flag in a matter of minutes.

Sunday, June 30
Lake Huron, Upbound

A memorable twenty-four hours. We docked at the
mouth of the Cuyahoga River at Cleveland about 7:30 last
night, right across from Shooters, one of the most popu-

lar nightspots in the flats. We no sooner tied up than my brother's boat headed up the river, completing yet another in a series of shuttle runs from the pellet terminal at Lorain to the LTV Steel complex on the Cuyahoga. Gary was on the bridge wing when his boat went by, but with the loud music coming from Shooters and the other clubs in the flats, we couldn't exchange more than a hello.

Our stern was only about a hundred feet from Shooters, and many of us stood out on the fantail late into the evening, watching the myriad of pleasure boats cruising the river and the foot traffic on the boardwalks and listening to the bands. Guys being guys, we were particularly interested in any attractive women who happened by and there were lots of them.

I went to bed about 11:30 P.M., but my room was like an oven and the band at Shooters sounded as though it was right outside my door. I'm not sure when I finally fell asleep, but it was much later than my usual 10:00 P.M.

This morning I was surprised, even shocked, to learn that we'd had a fire aboard the ship around 12:30 A.M. Some boxes of equipment in a storage cage over the engine

A law enforcement boat patrols near the entrance to the Cuyahoga River at Cleveland to keep pleasure boats out of the path of the inbound *Calcite II*. The riverbanks near the mouth of the serpentine Cuyahoga, an area known as "the flats," are lined with trendy bars and restaurants that attract thousands of pleasure boaters during the summer months. (Author's collection)

room started on fire. Later, several crewmembers said they'd smelled smoke coming from a doorway leading to the storage room for several hours before the fire was discovered, but thought the guys in the engine room were burning something. Quite a few crewmembers were near the stern; they quickly broke out fire hoses and extinguishers and put out the fire. It wasn't pure efficiency, though. A mate and a watchman ran out one of the canvas fire hoses. The mate took one end and headed around the after part of the cabin, while the watchman took the other end and went around the front of the cabin, pulling in opposite directions like a scene straight from a Three Stooges movie.

A number of us were upset that those of us with rooms in the vicinity of the fire weren't awakened immediately after the fire was discovered. Some felt that the general alarm should have been sounded. They're probably right. While the fire proved relatively minor and was quickly extinguished, those involved really didn't know the situation at the outset. Fire-fighting procedures call for you to rouse the crew whenever a fire is discovered, even before you try to put it out. What seems to be a small fire can get out of hand very quickly, and our little fire certainly had that potential. Burning debris could have fallen into the engine room and ignited the bilge or a variety of other combustibles, including a massive fuel tank that's located only a few feet from the source of the fire.

When the cabin on the *Cartiercliffe Hall* was gutted by fire in 1979, it started out as a relatively minor room fire, apparently started by a crewmember's cigarette. Several crewmen tried to fight the fire, but it spread too rapidly and they had to run for their lives. By the time they called the pilothouse to report the fire, a number of crewmembers were already trapped in their rooms. Before the mate in the pilothouse could sound the general alarm he and the wheelsman were driven out onto the bridge wing by thick smoke. The engineer and oiler on watch were in the engine room and unaware that the ship was on fire until the engineer called the pilothouse and got no answer. When he sent the oiler to see what was going on, the entire main deck of the ship was engulfed in flames. The oiler was badly burned by opening a doorway leading from the engine room to a passageway inside the cabin. I think a total of six crewmembers died

Deckhand Tom Flanner sprays a stream of water over the side during a fire drill on the *Calcite II*, while Iggy Donajkowski (left) and Gene Schaedig look on. The weekly drills, required by the Coast Guard, provide little in the way of practical experience in how to fight a shipboard fire. (Author's collection)

A bright orange U.S. Coast Guard helicopter hovers over the deck of Canada Steamship Line's *Manitoulin,* waiting to take aboard a man who fell into the lake from a sailboat the previous evening. The man was rescued from the lake by the crew of the *Manitoulin* and was evacuated to a shoreside hospital by the Coast Guard helicopter. (Author's collection)

in the blaze. All would probably have been saved if the fire alarm had been sounded immediately. Unfortunately, the lessons of the past are soon forgotten in this industry.

About 6:00 this morning, after I learned about the fire, Watchman Butch Kierzek called from the pilothouse and told me to look out the galley door. Just a couple hundred yards away was Canada Steamship's *Manitoulin* with an orange U.S. Coast Guard helicopter hovering over its deck. I later learned that those aboard the *Manitoulin* were in the process of recovering the body of a person who had fallen off a sailboat last night, and the Coast Guard was standing by to airlift the body to shore. A sad end to what undoubtedly started out as a wonderful summer weekend for some pleasure boaters.[9]

---

[9]I later learned that the individual pulled from the water was alive, which goes to show you that much of what you hear aboard ship is inaccurate. In the case of the *Manitoulin* situation, someone probably guessed that they had recovered a body and someone else repeated the speculatory comment as fact. Such things happen all the time on the boats.

It was 92 degrees outside today, and about 102 around the ranges in the galley. I worked all afternoon preparing dinner, sweating profusely the entire time. I think I drank enough water to float this boat, and I'm still thirsty, even after a long, cool shower and a switch into shorts and a t-shirt. Now that we're out on Lake Huron, the temperature is dropping steadily. It's supposed to get down into the mid-50s tonight, which should make for great sleeping.

Thursday, July 4
Cleveland, Ohio

Some Fourth of July. I planned a gala picnic for the crew, expecting we would be in the Detroit or St. Clair River at suppertime, on our way north. Because of the thirty- to thirty-five-mile-an-hour winds out of the north, we took a big delay after loading salt at the Akzo Noble salt mine here. We sat idle at the Akzo Noble plant from about 8:00 last night until 1:30 this afternoon before shifting down the river to unload the salt at a storage dock. It's 6:00 P.M. now, and it'll be at least another hour before we're finished unloading and can get on our way.

Once we took the delay, I began hoping we would still be here this evening. Cleveland's scheduled a massive fireworks display, said to be the largest in the city's history, for 9:45 P.M. tonight. The dock we're at is just behind Edgewater Park, where the fireworks will be held, and we'd have had ringside seats for the show. I haven't seen a fireworks display in quite a few years and was looking forward to it.

We loaded stone at Cedarville a couple of days ago and delivered it to Ontario Stone, just across the river from where we're now unloading. Then we shifted up the river to Akzo to load road salt. Because of the wind, the stuff blew all over the boat, and the deck looked as though we'd had an inch of fresh snow. Salt's a nasty cargo. The taste of the stuff has been in my mouth for more than a day now, and everything in my room is coated with a gritty layer, including my computer keyboard. It's corrosive, too, and takes a toll on a ship's cargo hold. Usually, when ships are put into the salt trade, it means they don't have many years left. The salt eats away at the steel until the ship isn't seaworthy anymore and is sent off to the shipbreakers. I'll be quite surprised if the old *Calcite II* is still running five years from now.

Gene Schaedig came back from vacation at Cedarville, so things are returning to normal in the galley. I don't have to keep one eye on the second cook anymore to make sure he isn't ruining something, or doing something that could poison the crew. Geno's not going to win any Betty Crocker baking contests, but he gets the desserts and salads out without any hassles.

Some lucky stiff won 45 million dollars in the Ohio lottery last night. We formed another pool that included twenty-four of the twenty-six crewmembers aboard, and bought 120 tickets, but the winning one eluded us. Too bad. We would have written a page in Great Lakes maritime history if we had won and simply walked off to leave the boat tied up at the dock with the two nonparticipating crewmembers acting as shipkeepers until the company put together a relief crew. I suspect we would have gotten some good press coverage, too. Darn!

I talked to my mother and my daughter Meredith yesterday evening, but Scott was at work, so I missed him. Everyone's doing well—they're all busy with work and summer activities. I feel like I'm on a different planet than they are. It may be quite a while before I see Scott or Meredith, depending on whether the permanent cook assigned to this boat returns or continues to relieve on boats that go to Two Harbors and Duluth.

My first full fifteen-day pay check arrived at my mother's the other day. It was for just over $1,700. I'm not even sure exactly what my pay rate is. It should be about $150 a day, plus overtime—Saturdays and Sundays are always overtime. Today is a holiday so we get double-time. The pay's not bad for a cook! Last year at this time, I was manager of a deli and general store at The Homestead, a resort near Glen Arbor in northwestern Michigan. I made about half what I am now, with *no* fringe benefits. I got to go home every night, but after twelve to sixteen hours at the store, usually seven days a week, and a half-hour drive each way, it didn't leave much time to do more than sleep and try to wash a load of laundry each week. Scott was living with me then, and I

Second cook Gene "Geno" Schaedig glazes freshly made doughnuts in the pantry of the *Calcite II*. The second cook is primarily
responsible for preparing desserts and salads. (Author's collection)

barely ever saw him. The work at the store was much more
demanding and much more stressful than running a galley
on a ship, mainly due to constant staff shortages. I actually
have more free time here.

This is the best job I've ever had and the most money
I've ever made. Before I came to work in the galley, I was
an avid amateur cook for twenty years. During that time,
I thought often of opening a small restaurant or a combi-

nation restaurant and bakery, but I'm leery of going into business. Failures are too common, and just because I'm a good cook doesn't mean I would be a good business owner or be able to run a successful restaurant. This job pays me well and satisfies my desire to be a professional cook without the risk of going bankrupt.

I've had many other jobs I enjoyed, but they always had major drawbacks. When I was a member of the Michigan House of Representatives, I was frustrated by the legislature's inability to get much done, the failure of legislators to make rational decisions, and the constant haranguing of the often uninformed or misinformed electorate. There were many positive aspects to teaching college, but the pay stunk. The pay wasn't much better when I was a college administrator—each day I spent in Lansing was agony since I really wanted to be back up in my beautiful north country. Being an administrator at the Great Lakes Maritime Academy in Traverse City got me back to north, close to my kids, and involved with the boats. It could have been the job to end all jobs, but the constant friction between the faculty and the director made it a miserable place to work. Cutbacks in enrollment because of the 1980s shipping recession resulted in my job being eliminated, but I didn't shed any tears. The marine consulting business was plain fun, and I spent a lot of time aboard ships, but as the industry struggled to stay afloat, there wasn't much money available for consultants. The consulting work got me through a tough period in my life, though, and probably planted the idea in my mind that I would someday enjoy sailing full time. Selling advertising and writing occasionally for *Seaway Review*, a trade publication for the maritime industry on the Great Lakes and St. Lawrence Seaway, was great in many ways, but there wasn't any money and no fringe benefits in it. When I was the advertising director at *Traverse the Magazine*, the constantly changing staff, low circulation, and lack of resources turned it into a high-stress job. I was back in northern Michigan, but I couldn't enjoy it because I was always trying to figure out how to make our sales quotas. After that, sailing became a leisurely walk in the park.

I started sailing full time in the summer of 1989, and my first job was as a second cook on the 1,000-foot *Columbia Star*. There were a lot of things I didn't know when I started, like how to run the big Hobart mixer in the galley, but I struggled through and managed to turn out a lot of good desserts and salads for the crew. What's more, I found that I didn't mind the long stretches aboard the ship. In fact, I was ecstatic much of the time. Still am!

Friday, July 5
Lake Huron, Upbound

We finished unloading and left Cleveland just before 8:00 last night, so we missed the big fireworks. Those who were up around 10:00 P.M., however, said that they could see fourteen fireworks displays at one time as we headed west across Lake Erie, but all from quite a distance. Maybe next year I'll get to see my fireworks.

Everyone was apprehensive when we arrived at the Shell fuel dock just south of Sarnia, Ontario, this morning. Canadian officials recently boarded two U.S. ships at the fuel dock to search for "contraband." On one boat, the *Philip R. Clarke* from our fleet, they reportedly caught the third assistant engineer with five ounces of cocaine and promptly arrested him. We're convinced they must have been tipped off by someone after the boat left Lorain, Ohio. They also boarded a second ship, one from the Interlake fleet, and supposedly confiscated a lot of beer and booze that was being carried for use by passengers. The alcohol had reportedly not been declared on the customs documents filed by the ship before entering Canadian waters. We were expecting them to come aboard our boat—the captain put out the word to get rid of any alcohol before we reached the fuel dock. I had a half bottle of burgundy and a half bottle of chablis that I use for cooking, and I didn't want to throw it away, so I put the burgundy in an empty orange juice jug and dumped the chablis into an empty mayonnaise jar. I tucked them away behind things in the cooler. I suppose I would have been a bit nervous if Canadian officials had come aboard.

We were scheduled to load early tomorrow morning at Stoneport, but another ship is going to beat us to the dock there by about forty-five minutes and the office doesn't want us to take an eight- to ten-hour delay, so we're going someplace else, but we don't know where. It could be Calcite or Cedarville, but the office hasn't made a decision yet. What the heck, we're still seven hours from Calcite and ten hours from Cedarville, so what's the hurry? It's indeed a life of uncertainty we lead on these boats.

Tim Peacock, our handyman, received a lot of razzing about a haircut he got while we were loading in Cleveland the other day. He went to a unisex hair salon in downtown Cleveland to get a badly needed haircut. It looked real nice when the gal got done cutting it, but Tim almost had heart failure when he found out that it cost $22.50. Heck, most of us get our hair cut in barber shops back home for about $8. Tim pointed out that the stylist washed his hair twice. My barber doesn't wash mine once. Not wanting to appear cheap, Tim also gave the stylist a $5 tip, so the total clip job cost him $27.50. After we heard the story, a lot of us asked Tim if we could touch his hair. At breakfast this morning, I told him that if he called the office and explained that he had a $27.50 haircut, they might give him a temporary exemption from the rule that requires crewmembers to wear hardhats when they're working. Tim is taking it all very well, but he's not likely to visit that hair salon again.

Like many crewmembers, I'm long overdue for a haircut, just like Tim was until the other day. I last got a trim back in late May, just a couple of days before I returned to the *Calcite II.* I'm looking pretty shaggy now, and with the hot weather I feel uncomfortable, but I just haven't had a chance to get it cut. The last time we were in Rogers City during the day it was a Monday and the barber shops were all closed. Getting a haircut is becoming a higher priority each day.

My buddy Don Dehring will be leaving when we get to a dock someplace. Jerry Macks, the regular first mate, will be returning from vacation, and Don will be gone for thirty days. He's a family man and looking forward to spending some quality time with his wife and children. Rod Bellmore, our "bull deckhand," will also be going on vacation. The suitcase brigade marches on. Normally, I'd be getting antsy to leave myself, but for some reason I'm content to stay on the boat this year. With my kids all wrapped up in their own lives now, I'm not sure what I'd do with thirty days off. In the past my vacations always centered around doing things with Scott and Meredith. I really don't want to take a vacation this year, but if I have to, I hope it's not until October. I guess I need to get a life as the kids say; I've been living like a virtual hermit for quite a while now. I think I'm ready to get involved in a relationship; now all I have to do is meet a nice lady. There aren't many out here on the lakes!

We had an eclectic dinner this evening: baked ham; Cajun red beans, rice, and sausage; stir-fried beef and vegetables; and baked rainbow trout with crabmeat stuffing. Tomorrow night it's prime rib, a favorite with this crew.

Saturday, July 6

Lake Huron, Downbound

At 7:30 P.M. last night, the office finally decided that we would load at Calcite. We got in there shortly after 2:00 A.M., but the *George A. Sloan* was loading, so we tied up along the north wall. When the *Sloan* left at around 5:30 A.M., we backed into the slip and began loading. Jerry Macks was waiting when we got in, and it was his loud talking out on deck that woke me up at 5:30 P.M. I should have been upset, but it was actually good to hear his voice again.

I ran to my mother's house between breakfast and lunch to pick up my mail, and even managed to get a haircut. I couldn't believe my barber was working over the Fourth of July weekend.

When we started to load, they initially posted a 1:30 P.M. departure time, but the loading went fast and they eventually changed it to 12:30 P.M. Macks, just back from a thirty-day vacation, ran home to Alpena when he got off watch at 8:00 A.M. Later in the morning, he and his wife Bev came to Rogers City to run some errands and have lunch before he returned to the boat. At about 12:30 P.M., Jerry decided he'd better call the tape to see when we'd be loaded, hoping it wouldn't be until around 2:00 P.M. When he listened to the tape, there wasn't anything on it about the *Calcite II*. He even called the tape back to make sure he hadn't missed some information. He immediately knew something was up, and he and Bev hurried to Calcite. When he got to the gate, the guard recognized him and waved him through. By then we had been sitting idle at the dock for about fifteen or twenty minutes waiting for Jerry. The captain was close to throwing off the lines and heading down the lake without him. Jerry's car rolled up, slid to a stop in a big cloud of dust, and our tardy first mate leaped out and ran for the ladder. He was relieved we hadn't left without him, because the company would have made him catch the *C-II* at the mailboat in Detroit at his own expense. Jerry cries if he has to spend any money needlessly.

We also got a wiper today, the captain's younger brother Mark, and a new deckhand by the name of Mark Aikens. He's a big, strapping fellow who's sailed on SIU—Seafarers International Union—boats for the last seven or eight years, mainly the old Huron Cement fleet. He hasn't worked steadily, though, and is tired of sitting in the SIU hall at Algonac, Michigan, waiting for a ship assignment. In our unions—the American Maritime Officers (AMO) for the licensed people and Steelworkers for the unlicensed—you receive your shipping assignments by telephone. In the SIU you still must be present in the shipping hall when a job is posted. Unless you live in the Algonac area, that means staying in some fleabag motel down there while you wait for a job. That's expensive, boring, and frustrating, or so I'm told by the SIU guys I sailed with on the *Kinsman Enterprise* last fall.

The SIU lost a lot of jobs on the lakes in recent years, so it's been tough on union members who don't have enough time in to qualify for a steady job with one of the few fleets that still hold contracts with their union. More and more SIU sailors are looking for jobs with our unlicensed locals.

The Steelworkers had hiring halls back during the boom days of the industry, but today the fleets have taken over the hiring function. All the union does is collect dues and bargain contracts. They're very good at the first, and not so hot at the second. Most sailors they represent haven't had much in the way of pay increases or improved fringe benefits over the past decade. In many fleets unlicensed personnel actually took cuts in pay, vacations, and other benefits when the bottom fell out of the industry during the 1980s. Few, if any, were able to recover those losses since shipping improved. The union seems to lack muscle in contract negotiations. The only union on the lakes that has been able to hold its own in contract negotiations in recent years is the AMO, which represents most of the deck officers, engineers, and stewards working on the lakes.

Monday, July 8
Detroit River, Upbound

Well, we're at anchor again. This time it's due to a malfunction of the main lube oil pump. It failed when we were coming up the river, but the auxiliary pump automatically kicked in and allowed us to continue on to the anchorage just below the Ambassador Bridge. The engineers expect it will take three hours to complete the necessary repairs and get underway again. This ship is jinxed.

We got into Conneaut shortly after midnight and were on our way again about 4:15 A.M., so I slept through our entire unload. We're now on our way to Stoneport to load for Saginaw. If we don't get a change in orders, it will be my first trip ever up the Saginaw River. I hope it's during the day so I can see the sights.

It was a scorcher yesterday, with temperatures around ninety and the humidity about the same. It got up to ninety-four in the galley just before supper, when I had an oven and a couple of burners on. I was pooped by the time we finished serving, and as soon as I got out of the galley I stripped my clothes off and collapsed on my bed for about an hour. It was hot today, too, but the humidity was much lower. It's quite windy right now and severe storm warnings have been posted here in the Detroit area. It's supposed to be much cooler for the next three or four days, with highs in the seventies, which sounds wonderful to me.

Wednesday, June 10
Zilwaukee, Michigan

We got into Stoneport yesterday afternoon at about 3:00 P.M. I took a meal off for the first time this season.

Everything was prepared, and I left Geno and Jimmy to serve the few crewmembers who would be eating aboard ship. As soon as the ladder went down, I headed for the sailor's parking lot where my brother leaves his truck. After walking the length of the lot, I was surprised to find that Gary's truck wasn't there. Fortunately, the chief engineer was just leaving for Rogers City, so I caught a ride with him to Calcite, where I picked up my own car and headed for my mother's house.

Gary is in the midst of being transferred from the *Earl W. Oglebay* to the *Columbia Star,* a thousand-footer flagship of the Oglebay Norton fleet. He had a few days off between boats, so he picked up his truck and headed to Detroit to see his daughter Jenny before catching the *Columbia Star* at the Soo.

I talked to my mother for awhile, and then stopped by the Secretary of State's office to get a new registration for my car. Once that necessary task was completed, I drove down to Alpena to do some shopping at Wal-Mart. It was a beautiful day and a pleasant drive, the longest I've made since coming on the boat back in late May. After shopping, I stopped at Lud's, a local fast-food restaurant, and had one of their giantburgers, a favorite of mine for almost thirty years. It was nice to eat someone else's cooking for a change.

We left Stoneport at around 11:00 last night. I tossed and turned for a couple of hours, the result of drinking a large, caffeine-laden Diet Coke with my giantburger. Around 2:00 in the morning, I woke up shivering. It was c-o-l-d out on northern Lake Huron and I had to break out a wool blanket. This morning I hit my snooze button a couple of times before facing the reality that I wasn't going to get as much sleep as I wanted. I forced myself out of bed, not because I was still tired, but because it was so blasted cold in my room. A hot shower felt good, but almost not worth the agony of having to step out of the shower into the cold environs of my room. I think I dressed in record time.

Thursday, July 11
Port of Calcite
Rogers City, Michigan

We arrived just before supper and the crew left the boat like rats leaving a sinking ship. After serving the three crewmembers who wanted to eat, I went to my mother's for a little while, and then returned to the boat to watch TV and do some work on the computer. We're due out at 11:00 P.M., bound for Detroit.

Oglebay Norton's *Joseph H. Frantz* came in about an hour after we did and is loading in the south slip. She's one of the few boats that I don't have a good picture of, but there's no way to get one here.

Jerry Macks, the first mate, is bothered by the fact that I'm single. I kid him that after he kicks off I'm going to marry his wife, and she and I will spend our days spending his money. I think he's a little bothered by that picture, and he's been trying to come up with someone for me to date. His prime candidate at this point is a supposedly lonely widow who lives out near Posen. He says she's not very good looking, but she's got lots of money. It just happens that the lady went to high school with our chief engineer. The chief confirmed that she's no fashion model, but he says she has a nice personality. I may pursue Jerry's tip, not because she has money, but because she's a nice person. I would like to have someone in my life to do things with, to see when we're in port, to write to when we're not. I should have something better to do when we're in our home port than visit my mother or sit in my room on the boat and write on the computer. It's been a l-o-n-g time since I've had a date, but I'm definitely getting my courage up. If I'd had transportation this evening, I might have driven out to Posen. Maybe I'll do it when we get to Stoneport on Sunday. My car's there now, and Posen's only a short drive. (I feel my courage fading already!)

Yesterday's trip up the Saginaw River was interesting. I expected to see a typical industrial waterway, lined with factories and commercial docks. There was some of that, to be sure, but more shoreline was taken up by marinas for pleasure craft, and there were miles of wooded, undeveloped

101

river frontage. I suspect that the undeveloped property is all within the river's flood plain and therefore not suitable for development. Regardless, it's a pretty river, especially for one that winds its way through an area of urban and suburban sprawl. The river was extremely muddy, though, probably due to the recent heavy rains that pushed the river up and out of its banks on several occasions during late spring and early summer. The water was the color of coffee with a little cream in it.

We see some strangely colored water around the lakes. The heavily polluted Rouge River at Detroit is a slimy black. At Superior, Wisconsin, and Duluth, Minnesota, the St. Louis River is a deep red, similar in color to the iron ore off the Mesabi Range that has made the twin ports so important over the years. Most sailors will tell you the water has been colored by all the ore that has fallen into it, but I found a statement in a book written before any ore was mined around Duluth or Superior that said the water there was red. The author of the book attributed its color to large amounts of tannic acid that found its way into the river from the cedar swamps upstream. At one time, the Cuyahoga River at Cleveland was so polluted it actually caught fire on several occasions. Overall, the water quality of all the rivers around the Great Lakes, and the lakes themselves, seems to be much improved over the past couple decades. There's still too much pollution, though, much of it coming today from recreational boaters. Those of us in the commercial shipping industry add our share, too. One boat I was on last year dumped the galley scraps directly overboard, except when they were in port. In port the soupy, foul-smelling stuff went into a galvanized garbage can on the stern, and then was dumped overboard after we were out in the lakes. Their sewage also went directly overboard, and I'm not sure it was being treated. I was appalled. I've thought of reporting them to the Environmental Protection Agency. I still may, even though several of those involved are friends of mine. There are stiff fines for such pollution, and rightly so.

Friday, July 12
Lake St. Clair, Downbound

Another gorgeous day on the Great Lakes. Lots of pleasure boats are headed in the direction of Port Huron for tomorrow's annual Port Huron-to-Mackinac sailboat race. We'll be at Port Huron on our way back north just about the time the race starts, and that's likely to add another interesting page to our logbook for this season—hundreds of sailboats and a lake freighter don't mix well. Stay tuned.

We had a major change of orders today. Instead of going to Stoneport after we unload in Detroit tonight, we'll travel to Drummond Island to load stone for Saginaw. Drummond Island is another port I've never been to, though I've passed the island hundreds of times. It's located across the St. Marys River from DeTour, right on the main shipping channel. It's a small operation, and they don't load too

The 1,004-foot *Edwin H. Gott* is a virtual twin to the *Edgar B. Speer,* except that the *Gott* was outfitted with a conventional self-unloading boom during the winter of 1995–96. The white boom of tubular steel can be seen on the deck, just forward of the *Gott*'s cabin. The addition of the 295-foot boom, the longest of any ship on the Great Lakes, made the *Gott* more flexible. Prior to installation of the boom, the *Gott,* like fleetmates the *Speer* and *Roger Blough,* could only unload into specially designed hoppers at Conneaut, Ohio, and Gary, Indiana. (Author's collection)

103

many ships in a season, so I'm particularly pleased we're going there.

We passed our fleet's *Edwin H. Gott* earlier this afternoon. She's a thousand-footer with a self-unloading boom that was installed last winter at Bay Ship Building at Sturgeon Bay, Wisconsin. The *Gott, Edgar B. Speer*, and *Roger Blough* were built as self-unloaders, but with shuttle booms instead of the more traditional booms used on other self-unloaders. On the *Gott* and *Speer* the shuttle booms were mounted transversely just ahead of their after cabins. On the *Blough* the boom is built into the hull near the stern. The shuttle booms can be extended about 40 feet out either side of the ship to unload into shoreside hoppers like those used at U.S. Steel's mill at Gary, Indiana, and the P&LE dock in Conneaut, Ohio. Because of their shuttle booms, the three ships were limited as to where they could unload, and less versatile and less competitive than other ships with conventional self-unloading systems. Now the *Gott* sports a regular unloading boom that's 295 feet long—the longest on the lakes. With her new boom, she can unload the ore she carries in piles adjacent to whatever dock she's at, or she can unload into a shoreside hopper. How that will affect the cargoes she carries remains to be seen. We all wonder whether the *Speer* and *Blough* will eventually get deck booms, too.

We passed a Canadian ship named the *Cuyahoga* this afternoon. Her hailing port on her stern was Nanticoke, Ontario, and under her name it said she belongs to Lower Lakes Towing Company, a company I've never heard of. The ship is an old self-unloader with a rounded cruiser stern that suggests she may have been built at a U.S. shipyard on the Great Lakes during World War II.

John Buczkowski, one of our watchmen, later told me that the *Cuyahoga* was formerly Oglebay Norton's *J. Burton Ayers.* A Canadian company apparently bought the *Ayers* and another older ON boat. The *Ayers* is one of sixteen Maritime-class freighters built on the Great Lakes during 1942 and 1943 to support the U.S. war effort. Few survive today. The only one I'm aware of besides the former *Ayers,* is the *George A. Sloan* from our fleet. The *Sloan* was converted to diesel power back in the 1980s, but John tells me that the

An old ship in new colors. After operating for fifty years within various American fleets on the Great Lakes, the 620-foot *J. Burton Ayers* was sold to a small Canadian shipping company in 1995 and renamed *Cuyahoga*. The aging ship was one of sixteen Maritime-class freighters built for service on the lakes during World War II by the U.S. maritime Commission. Three remain in service today. (Author's collection)

Cuyahoga still has its original triple-expansion steam engine, one of the few left in operation anywhere in the world.[10]

Inspired by my friend Ralph Roberts of Saginaw, I've been photographing every boat we pass. Ralph has an in-

---

[10]John Buczkowski was almost right about the *Cuyahoga,* née *Ayers.* She has a Lentz poppet valve, double compound engine, not the more common triple-expansion steam engine. The *Ayers* was one of six Maritime-class boats built at American Ship Building in Lorain for the Maritime Commission during the war. They differed from the ten Maritime-class boats built at the Great Lakes Engineering Works in that they had modified cruiser sterns, transverse framing, and were fitted with Lentz engines. The *Cuyahoga* is the lone survivor of the six wartime ships built at AmShip. Five of the ten Maritime boats built by Great Lakes Engineering Works are still around. Three—the *J. H. Hillman, Jr./Crispin Oglebay/Hamilton Transfer,* the *Mesabi/Lehigh/Joseph X. Robert/Willonnglen,* and the *McIntyre/Frank Purnell/ Steelton/Hull No. 3/Pioneer/C.T.C. No. 1*—are now owned by Canadian firms and used for storing grain and cement cargoes. The other two, Erie Sand Steamship's *Richard Reiss,* originally launched as the *Adirondack,* and USS Great Lakes Fleet's *George A. Sloan,* built as the *Hill Annex,* are in regular service on the lakes. Built as straight-deckers, the three Maritime boats still in operation have all been converted to self-unloaders.

credible collection of historic photos of Great Lakes ships, and visiting with him in recent months reminds me how important it is to document the ongoing history of our industry. The boats we see every day on the lakes may not always be of much interest to us, but in the future boat buffs will place great value on the photos we're taking today that document how things were in the Great Lakes shipping industry during the 1996 season.

Saturday, July 13
St. Clair River, Upbound

I was surprised to wake up this morning and find that we were still at the unloading dock, a redi-mix concrete plant on the old Rouge River south of Detroit. We should have been unloaded and on our way by 3:00 or 4:00 in the morning. The captain, first mate, and a couple other crewmembers had been talking about going to the casino in Windsor, Ontario, while we were unloading, and my first thought was that they hadn't made it back to the boat yet. Once I went into the galley, though, Butch Kierzek, the 4-to-8 watchman, told me that there was trouble with the engine-room generators and very little cargo had been unloaded.

Later on, I learned that when we left Calcite, the engineer and oiler on watch inadvertently left a valve open that connects the diesel fuel and blended fuel tanks. When the engine has been shut off for awhile, the engineers start it on diesel fuel, then shift to blended fuel once the ship is underway. The open valve allowed the two fuels to mix, and it formed a waxy substance that quickly fouled the generators' fuel filters. The generators supply power to the electric motors that drive the unloading equipment. During the night, they shut down the unloading several times so the engineers could change all the filters in the generators. It took them about an hour and a half the first time they did it, but after three or four changes, the time dropped to twenty-five minutes. We quickly ran out of spare filters, though, so the chief and the Duluth office contacted Caterpillar dealers in the Detroit area until they managed to locate a couple more cases.

106

We finally finished unloading about 3:00 P.M., after an unload of about fifteen or sixteen hours. Now we're on our way to Shell's marine fuel dock at Sarnia, Ontario. There, we'll pump off all our contaminated fuel and take on clean bunkers, a process that's expected to take four to five hours. The terminal will then separate the contaminated fuels and pump them back into our tanks the next time we stop for fuel.

The engineer on watch when we left Calcite was my buddy Jon McKinley. Jon's been exceptionally quiet today, and it's obvious he's concerned about repercussions from the screw-up. He told me he figured the office would have to take some action because of all the expenses that resulted from leaving the valve open—the delay in unloading, the additional fuel filters, and the cost of having the Shell people clean up our contaminated fuel. He may be right. I haven't been with this fleet long enough to know how they respond to such situations. In other fleets a guy could be suspended for thirty days without pay, or he could be fired outright. I'd hate to see them let Jon go—he's a bright and conscientious guy.

Last year, one of the heating coils that heats the blended fuel so it can be burned in the engine developed a leak and contaminated the fuel with water. The ship was carrying a full load of fuel at the time, and it all had to be pumped off so the water could be removed. The chief engineer was blamed for the mishap and was forced to retire. He was called to the office in Duluth, taken out to dinner, and told he was going to be let go. The incident is now referred to throughout the fleet as The Last Supper, and there are lots of jokes about people getting invited out to dinner in Duluth. The current chief says that if they call him to Duluth because of the problems we've had in the last twenty-four hours, he's simply going to quit. Hopefully, that won't be necessary.

When I had an eye exam and got new glasses last January, the optometrist discovered that I had the beginnings of a cataract in my left eye—a discoloration of the lens that makes it opaque. At that point, the effects of the cataract weren't noticeable to me. Well, I can really notice it now. I've always looked through the viewfinder of my camera with my left eye, but when I do it now everything's blurred. When it first happened, I thought that either the camera's viewfinder

107

or my glasses were fogged up. When the problem persisted despite repeated cleanings of my glasses and the camera lens and eyepiece, it finally hit me that the cataract must be getting worse. For some reason, the problem is most noticeable when I'm outside in the bright sunlight. Without my glasses on, I'm darned near blind in my left eye. That's a little scary. You may rest assured that I will make another visit to the eye doctor as soon as I get off the boat. Aging is such an interesting, often demeaning, phenomenon.

Butch Kierzek gave me some pictures that he thought I might use in one of my books. One of them was taken on the *Irvin L. Clymer* on Thanksgiving Day 1981. The galley crew was just getting ready to feed the crew when the boat turned to go into the dock at Cedarville in fairly high seas. A prudent captain might have gone to anchor because of the waves, but it's said that the captain's wife was waiting for him at the dock and he didn't want to disappoint her. The ship rolled so badly making the turn that the entire Thanksgiving dinner and all the plates, silverware, pots, and pans in the galley ended up in a heap on the deck. The turkey was in the oven at the time, but as the ship rolled, the door of the oven popped open, and out came the roasting pan and the beautifully browned bird, skittering across the deck as if it was trying to escape. In the photo the galley floor is cluttered with the debris that only a few minutes earlier comprised a carefully prepared Thanksgiving dinner. The cook, Al Chesky, is leaning against the refrigerator with his head buried in his arms, obviously overcome by the devastation of his galley. Gene Schaedig was either the porter or second cook on the *Clymer* at the time, and he told me that the galley crew and some volunteers from the engine room cleaned up the mess with shovels, unceremoniously scooping the remnants of their dinner into trash cans. After cleaning up, someone broke out a bottle of booze and all those involved retired to the officers' dining room for a liquid dinner. Thanksgiving dinner is generally the biggest meal of the year on ships on the Great Lakes, stemming from the days when most boats were laid up before Christmas, but in 1991 there was no Thanksgiving dinner on the *Irvin L. Clymer.*

I thought I was going to have a similar situation when I was cooking on the *Herbert C. Jackson* a few years ago, but it was Christmas dinner, not Thanksgiving. Our second cook got off sick when we unloaded down in South Chicago, and on Christmas Eve I was baking pies in the galley when we started to roll while cutting across Lake Michigan. About 2:30 the following morning, I woke up because the boat was rolling badly and I was sliding back and forth in my bed, hitting first the headboard and then the footboard. I got up and went into the galley to secure a few things and I peered out the windows to see what was going on. The waves were huge, and we were wallowing badly. After awhile, the boat seemed to settle down and I went back to bed. Fifteen minutes later I was sliding to and fro in my bed again. That continued all night. Frustrated that I could not sleep, and realizing that the course we were on was the same one followed by the *Carl D. Bradley* when it sank in a 1958 storm, I finally got out of bed at about 4:00 A.M. and set to work getting Christmas dinner prepared. We regularly rolled so badly that I had to hold on with one hand, trying to dice vegetables and mix dressing with my free hand. Tired from lack of sleep, I also poured generous quantities of steamboat coffee into an already queasy stomach. Just before the guys began coming in for breakfast about 7:00 A.M., I dashed to my room where I spent a few agonizing minutes worshiping the porcelain altar in my bathroom. It was a pattern that was repeated numerous times over the next few hours, and I began to worry that I wouldn't be able to serve Christmas dinner. Fortunately, about an hour before Christmas dinner was scheduled, we cautiously turned into the calm waters of the St. Marys River. Because of the high winds, we anchored just above DeTour, my stomach settled down, and we enjoyed a memorable Christmas dinner. Immediately afterward, I crawled into bed and slept the rest of the day while the crew snacked on leftovers. There have been other times when the boat's motion has made me queasy, but that's the only time I actually became sick.

The only other time I was sick on the boats was when I had the flu while working on the *James R. Barker.* The flu had been making the rounds of the boat and I finally came down with it one morning while preparing lunch. I was browning off some short ribs in the oven and the greasy smell made me nauseous. About the time I pulled the ribs out of the oven, I ran for my room. It was the first of many trips over the next hour, but I managed to get everything ready for lunch before realizing there was no way I would serve it. I turned things over to the porter and second cook, and retired to my room. That afternoon and evening, I was alternately ravaged by chills and fever. I was so weak that I wasn't sure I could get out of bed. After supper, the chief engineer stuck his head into my room to see how I was doing, and I begged him to get me some ice water to drink. After rehydrating, I slept soundly all night and returned to work the following morning, weak, but on the road to recovery. A steamboat is no place to be sick.

Sunday , July 14
Lake Huron, Upbound

A hazy day on Lake Huron, with on-again, off-again rain showers. Because of the limited visibility, I only saw one sailboat today, and that was early this morning. If it was in the Port Huron-to-Mackinac race, I'm afraid it was running dead last.

This is my fiftieth continuous day on the *Calcite II,* and my sixty-first day here this season. I'm beginning to feel that this is *my boat,* but I know I could be bumped off at any time by one of the permanent cooks. What the heck, though, it's been a good ride and I've enjoyed every minute of my stay here. If someone bumps me, they better be ready to turn out a lot of good food for this crew, because they're used to it.

I made pizza tonight, and it went over well, as always. I made seven different kinds tonight: double pepperoni (I usually listed it on the menu as pepperoni pizza, but nobody would order it. Once I started calling it double pepperoni, it became a popular item. It's the same pizza!); pepperoni, ham, and mushrooms (the captain's favorite, and mine, too); Hawaiian, with ham, pineapple, and green peppers (my daughter's favorite); six-cheese (deckhand Frank Bruski's favorite); meat lover's (the favorite of most of the crew, including Porter Jimmy Atkins, who knows he shouldn't be eating that much cholesterol); supreme (Second Assistant Engineer Iggy Donajkowski's favorite); and BBQ chicken (nobody's favorite, but one that everyone wants to try. I got the idea after I saw the owners of the California Pizza

Kitchen on television. The BBQ chicken pizza has been the top-selling pizza in their restaurants since the day they opened). I think I offer enough selections to satisfy even the most discriminating crew. I've also made taco pizza in the past, and I'm going to try a Reuben pizza in the near future.

We were at the Shell dock for about six hours last night, pumping off our contaminated fuel and taking on a clean supply. It was a pleasant evening, and I sat out on deck for an hour or so. Shortly after we got to the dock, the *Columbia Star* passed us on its way down the river. Gary must have been on watch in the pilothouse, because they blew us a salute as they went by. It's quite a thrill to hear a ship blow a deep-throated salute on its whistle when you know it's for you.

Ships in the same fleet will generally salute each other when they pass in the rivers, blowing one long and two short blasts on their whistles. In addition to saluting other ships in the fleet, captains will occasionally salute the homes or businesses of friends along the shore, the mail boat at Detroit (always), the grub boat at the Soo (always), and the flower lady on the St. Clair River (almost always). The flower lady owns a greenhouse in Detroit, and for many years has sent plants or flower arrangements out to the ships on various holidays that occur during the shipping season. We received a plant from her for Father's Day this year. A nice gesture, and one that's always appreciated by the crews.

I'm washing a load of laundry as I make these entries. We have a washer and dryer one deck down in the engine room, almost directly below my room, for use by those of us who live at the stern. There's a second laundry room up forward, for those who live at the bow. All I have to worry about washing is my underwear. We send our galley whites and the ship's bedding to a commercial laundry in Sault Ste. Marie. The laundry is located right next to the Soo Warehouse, where we get our groceries and supplies, so we generally send off dirty linen and get back clean stuff with every grocery order we receive. I bring enough underwear with me so that I only have to wash about once a month. Even then, it's a chore I don't look forward to. I always wait until I'm down to my last pair of socks or skivvies before I make the dreaded trip to the engine room. After being a bachelor for a dozen years or so, I'm tired of *all* domestic chores. If I wasn't getting paid to cook, I wouldn't.

Probably two of the great motivators for me to move up from porter and second cook to steward were not having to wash dishes and not having to make beds. One of the porter's major jobs is to wash all the dishes, pots, pans, and utensils we generate each day during the course of feeding the crew. In this fleet the porter also makes all the officers' beds once a week. In most other fleets the porter and second cook share the bed-making duties. The porter usually does the beds of the deck officers, while the second cook takes care of all the engineers. In my years as a porter and second cook making beds was always the most distasteful part of the job.

Our porter here also makes sure the milk machine is full and keeps a constant supply of Kool-Aid on hand for the crew. Jimmy also peels potatoes, onions, and carrots for me every day, which is pretty standard practice throughout the Great Lakes shipping industry. He and the second cook also sweep and mop the galley, messroom, and dining room twice a day and carry out the garbage after every meal. Whenever they have a little time, there's always cleaning to be done— refrigerators, freezers, walls, tables, storeroom, and so on. A porter on the Great Lakes makes about thirty thousand dollars a year with good fringe benefits, basically for being a dishwasher. If they were doing the same job ashore, they'd be paid minimum wage.

The second cooks in this fleet start their day by preparing breakfast for the crew. Geno comes to work at about 6:00 A.M. and serves breakfast from 7:00 to 8:00 every morning. He also bakes a couple loaves of frozen bread dough, and will often mix up a batch of cookies or some sort of dessert while he's taking care of breakfast. In most fleets the second cooks spend most of their time baking, preparing cookies, cakes, pies, bread, dinner rolls, and desserts from scratch each day. Here, the second cooks use mainly frozen cakes, frozen pies, canned or instant puddings, and frozen bread dough. It's certainly easier than making things from scratch, but it would bore me to death. The products simply are not as good as the ones you make from scratch, so I would feel as though I was shortchanging the crew if I used them. Unfortunately, few of the second cooks in this fleet are interested in cooking. It's just a job to them that provides an annual forty-thousand-dollar paycheck.

The second cook is also responsible for the salad served with the dinner meal every evening, and for preparing the night lunch. The night lunch on this boat is a refrigerator stocked with lunch meats, cheeses, pickled bologna, heat-and-serve pizzas, ice cream and ice cream bars, and condiments. On some boats, like those in the Interlake fleet, the steward takes care of the night lunch. It's kind of a pain in the butt, though, and I'm glad I don't have to worry about it anymore.

When my dad sailed back in the 1930s, he started out in the galley, before going on to get a QMED or oiler's ticket. We have a photo taken on one of the Bradley boats, a predecessor to this fleet, showing the entire galley crew mustered in their cleanest whites on the fantail of whatever boat they were on. There were five people working in the galley at that time: the steward, second cook, night cook, and two porters. Over the years, galley staffs have been downsized, and now there's talk that the shipping companies would like to get rid of yet another person. If we lose another person, I don't see how we can manage to keep the galley clean.

Most of the women who have worked on freighters over the years have been in the galley. At one time it was common to find husband-and-wife teams running the galleys. The husband was usually the steward and his wife served as the second cook. That practice faded out when unions came in and ship assignments were handled on the basis of seniority. When it was no longer a sure thing that a husband and wife would end up on the same boat, the wives generally stayed ashore.

Today, there are quite a few women working in galleys. In this fleet we have one female steward, but I haven't run across any female porters or second cooks thus far. Interlake had a lot of female porters and second cooks, but no female stewards. It's highly unusual to find a woman working in any of the unlicensed positions in the engine or deck departments, although Interlake did have a female deckhand for a couple of seasons. If you find women in the engine room or pilothouse, they're usually graduates of one of the maritime academies that train officers for the shipping industry, like the one in Traverse City, Michigan.

Unfortunately, few of the women make a career of sailing on the lakes. They get married, have children, and give up sailing. As far as I know, the U.S. fleet on the lakes has never had a female rise to become either a chief engineer or captain. There was one female captain on the lakes, but she was with a Canadian fleet.

Monday, July 15
Saginaw Bay

We loaded last night at Drummond Island, and in an hour or two we'll be at the mouth of the Saginaw River, on our way to a stone dock above the I-75 bridge. We won't be at the dock until about 1:30 A.M., so we should be just about finished unloading by the time I get up in the morning.

Though I'm not required to start work until 7:00 A.M., I'm usually in the galley a few minutes before Geno arrives, and I help out by wiping down the tables in the messroom, cleaning the menu board, and making that all-important first pot of coffee. From 6:00 to 7:00 A.M., I drink two cups of coffee, smoke several cigarettes, work on my menus, and chat with Geno. I'm a slow starter in the mornings, and I hate to start working as soon as I get showered and dressed. When I was sailing for Interlake and had to prepare breakfast myself, I went to work at 6:00 A.M. In order to guarantee I'd be wide awake by 6:00, I arose at 4:30 A.M. After showering and dressing, I'd go out into the galley, turn on the stoves, and make a pot of coffee. I'd pour the hot coffee into a thermos and retreat to my room, where I'd generally watch the news on CNBC and work on my menus and other paperwork until it was time to return to the galley and being preparing breakfast.

Here I usually start working about 7:00 A.M. by preparing a pot of soup. Once that's on the stove, I'll make the things I'm going to serve for lunch. When lunch is pretty well squared away, I occasionally begin prepping things for supper. Lunch is served from 11:00 to 12:00, and I usually have all my stuff put away and vacate the galley by 12:15 P.M. About half the time, I'll take a forty-five-minute nap right after lunch, then return and start getting ready for supper. I'm supposed to be off from 12:30 until 3:00, but with dinner served from 4:00 to 5:00 P.M., there's no way I can prepare supper in one hour. I usually work at a fairly leisurely pace during the afternoon, though. The galley's empty and I turn up the radio and putter along, taking frequent breaks. Phil Bandish, the 12-to-4 watchman, and Iggy Donajkowski, the 4-to-8 watch engineer, usually stop in during the afternoon for a short chat. By 3:00 P.M. I get real serious about preparing dinner. I usually work nonstop from then until we start serving dinner at 4:00. I don't like supper at 4:00, and seldom eat then. I'll usually wait until the guys on the 4-to-8 watch come in, between 7:30 and 7:45.[11] I'm generally out of the galley by 5:30 P.M. I go to my room and clean up, maybe lie down and watch television, or write for awhile before I go back out and pull whatever I need for the next day out of the freezers. There are probably at least two evenings a week when I have paperwork to do— grocery or laundry requisitions, time sheets, meal reports, safety training logs, etc.—that might take an hour or so. If I'm putting together a major order from the Soo, it can take two to three hours to complete. After all, I'm ordering about four thousand dollars' worth of groceries.

That's pretty much all I do, day in and day out, seven days a week. I'm mainly a cook, though I supervise the second cook and porter to varying degrees. It's a good job.

The chief engineer talked to the office today, and they told him our little fuel foul-up of the other day cost forty-eight thousand dollars. I think they must have used real sharp pencils to come up with that figure, but it's probably setting the stage for them to take some action against the engineer, or engineers, involved.

Wednesday, July 17
Lake Huron, Downbound

We arrived at Calcite at 10:30 P.M. last night. We had groceries being brought down from the Soo and the

---

[11] The watchstanders actually relieve fifteen to thirty minutes before the scheduled time.

blasted truck didn't arrive until 11:20, so it was almost 12:30 before we got everything put away and I could get some sleep. By then, I was hot and sweaty, and after a lot of vigorous exercise, I wasn't the slightest bit tired. I tossed and turned for probably an hour before I finally drifted off. I wasn't happy when the alarm went off at 5:30 A.M. This boy likes a good night's sleep. I managed to limp through the day without an afternoon nap. If it stays reasonably cool in my room, I should sleep well tonight.

Several interesting things happened yesterday. First, word came from the office that the fuel foul-up "was just an accident and could have happened to anyone," so those involved are apparently and happily off the hook. My buddy Jon McKinley was noticeably relieved and is back to his old self again. Even smiling! Second, as I was getting supper ready at 3:30 P.M., the captain called back and said I was supposed to call Fred Cummings, the fleet manager, on the cellular phone right away. It was a long walk from the galley down to the chief's office in the engine room, where there's a cell phone. I thought perhaps the former porter had complained about the way I treated him, or my food costs were too high, or some such catastrophe. When Cummings got on the line, he *thanked me* for the personnel evaluation I had done on the former porter. (On a scale of 1 to 5, with 1 the lowest, I probably gave the porter an average score of about 1.3.) He said he had checked the porter's personnel file and found there have been many complaints over the years, but the stewards who evaluated him always gave him passing grades. Cummings said he had called the porter at home and told him that if he has one more sanitation complaint against him "he's gone." They still haven't decided if they're going to send him back here or to another ship. If he goes to another ship, he's probably off the hook. If he comes here, he better be able to keep things clean. It was nice Cummings would call me and support the evaluation I wrote. When I filled it out, I was tempted to give him all 3s and not make waves. The guy's a health hazard, though, and in the final analysis I gave him the scores I thought he deserved based on his shaky performance. Now I'm glad I did. It's also good to know that someone in the office actually reads the evaluations we do.

While we waited for groceries to arrive last night, I ran to my mother's in Jimmy Atkins's truck and picked up two boxes of my books I had ordered from Wayne State University Press. Today I signed those for the crewmembers who are aboard. A number of the other guys are on vacation, so I'll wait to inscribe theirs until they get back. I've also got copies that I must put off at Stoneport the next time we get in there for Jim Steen and Charlie Hilla, childhood friends who now work at the quarry.

Muggy and in the high eighties today. It's fairly uncomfortable in the galley, and bound to get worse tomorrow when we're down on Lake Erie. We'll unload at Conneaut in the afternoon, and then go to Ashtabula to load coal. We won't get into Ashtabula until about midnight, and we should be on our way shortly after dawn, so perhaps it won't be too bad. We'll be taking the coal to Green Bay.

We're infested with a plague of Harbor Beach flies. They're the kamikaze variety, attacking without regard for their own safety. When they catch hold of your ankle or the back of your neck, you literally have to beat them to death to get them to let go. They can't be brushed off like regular run-of-the-mill flies and when they bite, it hurts. We'll probably have to continue doing battle with them until we return to the cooler waters of the northern lakes, where flies are a nuisance, not a menace.

After lunch yesterday, I spent about an hour talking with Joe Fairbanks, one of our oilers. Last winter, Joe started building a log home on the outskirts of Rogers City. He's doing it all himself, selecting and felling the trees, peeling them, putting them in place and cutting the corner notches. It's a major project for Joe, and he doesn't plan to have the home finished for several more years.

Joe's a bright and obviously talented guy, but I've never seen anyone look worse first thing in the morning. He's on the 8-to-12 watch, and when he comes in for breakfast around 7:15 A.M. I just nod to him. Anyone who looks that bad shouldn't be expected to talk. Later in the morning, around 10:00 A.M., he usually comes up to the galley to get something cold to drink; by then he's wide awake, smiling, talkative, and almost always humorous. If anything is going to go wrong in the engine room on his watch, I sure hope it's after 10 o'clock. After 10:00, I know he can handle just about anything that goes awry; before 10:00, I'm not so sure.

Thursday, July 18
Conneaut, Ohio

Arrived here right at suppertime, so I walked up the street with Jon McKinley as soon as the galley was squared away. We went up to a little party store that seems to specialize in selling cigarettes to sailors. Cigarettes are extremely cheap here in Ohio, and particularly in Conneaut, though I'm not sure why. I paid $16 for a carton of cigarettes that costs me almost $25 at home. That's a big savings, and sailors who smoke tend to load up on cigs when they're here. On the way back, we stopped at a little bar and had a couple glasses of ginger ale. We sat next to four Canadian sailors off Algoma Central Railroad's *Algolake,* which is loading coal across the slip from us. One of the Canadian sailors was from Midland, Ontario, one was from Cape Breton Island, and the other two were from Newfoundland. Sailors from the Canadian East Coast are apparently dominating the shipping industry, even on boats that operate out of Sault Ste. Marie, Ontario. One of the chaps told me that there were only twenty-one crewmembers on their boat, which is a 730-foot self-unloader. That's five fewer than on the little *Calcite II,* and probably represents a cost-savings of about half a million dollars over a comparable U.S. ship. Based on what they told me, their pay is also 20 to 30 percent less than ours, another significant savings for the ship owners. No wonder it's nearly impossible for us to compete with the Canadians in the cross-lake trades. Interestingly, while things are booming on the U.S. side of the lakes, the Canadians have many of their ships laid up. One of the Canadians said that Algoma has five boats that aren't running. Apparently, the grain trade on the lakes, which has been dominated by the Canadians for many years, is drying up. Most of the grain is now moving through ports in British Columbia, or down the Mississippi. If the Canadian shipping companies lose the grain trade, as the Americans did a number of years ago, it will significantly affect the nature of their industry. They've had the luxury of two-way cargoes for generations, carrying grain from Lake Superior out the St. Lawrence Seaway, and then hauling Labrador ore back into the lakes to steel mills on Lake Ontario and at Sault Ste. Marie. It's a lucrative trade. The Canadian sailors said there are already rumors that one of the big Canadian companies—Upper Lakes Shipping—may not survive.

Another interesting tidbit picked up in the harbor bar: Algoma Central has two captains who are black. One has been a captain since the 1980s, the other got his appointment fairly recently. We don't have any on the U.S. side, and I don't think we've *ever* had one, at least not in the modern era of shipping on the lakes. Hooray for the Canadians.

Deckhand Shawn Langlois signals the deck winch operator to show him how much further the hatch cover has to move before it is fully opened. The *Calcite II* is one of only a handful of ships on the lakes still equipped with telescoping, or leaf-type, hatch covers. Pulled open with a winch, the heavy steel leaves of the hatch covers stack on top of each other at the outside edge of the hatch. Most ships built since 1925 have been equipped with single-piece steel hatch covers that are removed with a motorized hatch crane. (Author's collection)

Jerry Macks told a great story at breakfast this morning. A number of years ago, one of this fleet's small boats loaded sand at Grand Haven in the late fall, and then had to lay in for several days because of weather. Jerry was on the 4-to-8 watch, and for two mornings in a row he saw what he described as the largest buck he'd ever seen. It came out of the woods and walked right down near the boat, totally unafraid. Well, they were still sitting at Grand Haven when November 15 rolled around—the first day of deer-hunting season in Michigan. After listening to Jerry's description of the monster buck, a bunch of crewmembers decided a couple meals of fresh venison would be mighty tasty, to say nothing of the chance to display the buck's huge rack as a shipboard trophy that would bring tears to the eyes of all the sailors who had taken vacations in November to go hunting in Michigan's northwoods. The guys pooled their money and bought a deer-hunting license, then paid eighty dollars for a 12-gauge shotgun at K-Mart or Montgomery Wards. The next morning, they all lined up in the portholes, waiting for the buck to appear. It wasn't daylight yet, but they figured that if they shot from inside the boat nobody would hear the gunshot. Well, like Jerry said, the king of the woods soon appeared. The crewman selected to do the firing took steady aim. To compensate for the fact it was still dark out, Macks switched on one of the boat's powerful searchlights, throwing out a shattering beam of more than one hundred thousand candlepower. Caught in the glare of the searchlight, the proud buck stood transfixed—his retinas undoubtedly burned to a crisp by the piercing light. The shooter took careful aim and touched off the 12-gauge, nearly shattering the eardrums of those watching from the confined quarters aboard the ship. At the roar of the 12-gauge, the buck ducked down, wheeled and ran off, but only far enough so that he was out of range of the shotgun. There he lay down and took a little nap, to the great consternation of those aboard the boat. In the beam of the searchlight and at a distance of only about forty feet, the buck should have been an easy kill for the shipboard sharpshooter, but he missed cleanly.

Today, those who were involved still talk about the big buck that got away, but they're a little vague about the details. After all, they probably were violating about twenty fish and game laws, to say nothing of numerous Coast Guard regulations and company policies. A short time later, the ship reached a Canadian port where they went through a customs inspection. Since it's illegal to have a firearm aboard ship, they hid the 12-gauge down in the unloading tunnel, a wet, dirty place unlikely to be explored by the customs officers. A week or so after the incident, the crewmen who had chipped in to buy the shotgun raffled it off in an effort to recoup their losses and to get the illicit gun off the boat. There were no venison dinners on the boat that fall, no trophy head is mounted on the bulkhead, and I doubt the sharpshooter brags much about what a good shot he is.

We've got two passengers aboard the boat tonight—two welders from a ship repair shop in Cleveland. The sprockets that drive the unloading elevator are in such bad shape they're worried that the buckets will come off and drop down into the sump below it. That would be disastrous, so the office approved some emergency repairs. The welders will work on the system nonstop until it's squared away. We'll be leaving the dock here shortly, but we're making a short jaunt down the beach to nearby Ashtabula to load coal. There are two Canadian boats ahead of us at that dock, so we'll experience a considerable delay. We probably won't be able to start loading there until sometime around 8:00 A.M. tomorrow, and possibly later, which should give the welders enough time to finish their work. If not, they'll stay on until we get to Detroit or Green Bay or wherever.

Friday, July 19

Ashtabula, Ohio

We're not actually at Ashtabula, but at anchor about a mile or so offshore. Just after we left Conneaut at about 10:00 P.M. last night, we encountered a series of violent thunderstorms accompanied by high winds. The weather conditions made it impossible for us to get into the harbor at Ashtabula, so we went to anchor. At about 4:00 A.M., the captain hauled up the anchor and tried to enter the harbor. When he was about two boat lengths off the piers that protect the harbor, he chickened out, perhaps remembering

121

his bad luck when he tried to go into Fairport under similar conditions. He hauled the boat around and dropped the hook again. The winds have been blowing at twenty to thirty miles an hour all day, with waves four to five feet high, so we've been sitting here, wishing we were tied up in the harbor. Our *John G. Munson* got into Ashtabula before the bad weather, and unloaded and left at about 1:30 this afternoon. There's a Canadian ship loading coal at the dock we'll go to, and I suspect she'll be coming out pretty soon. If we sit here too long, some other ship's going to sneak past us and into the harbor, and we'll have to wait for them to load.

Our two welders are still aboard. They finished their repairs on the unloading elevator at about 7:00 this morning after working all night. They've been lounging around the boat since then, bored and wishing there was some way they could get ashore. They're from Cleveland, which kicked off a gigantic three-day bicentennial celebration today, and both planned to participate in the festivities. Their ship repair shop is down on the Cuyahoga River, the center stage for most of the bicentennial activities. The welders and the others workers at the facility were planning a party there this evening to watch the parade of boats—led by Bob Hope—and the fireworks. There are also eleven stages set up along the river where bands will be entertaining the hundreds of thousands of persons expected to attend. Since we can't get into Ashtabula, I suggested to the captain that we enter the old *Calcite II* in the parade of boats. What the heck, we'd probably win the prize for being the longest boat in the parade . . . and the oldest . . . rustiest . . . worst paint job . . . etc.

I'm still in a bit of a quandary about what I'm going to cook for supper tomorrow night. Since it's Saturday, I'll do steak, as tradition dictates, and I'll have some baked cod in cream sauce with it, but I don't know what else to offer. Usually I'd do something with boneless chicken breasts, but in my last grocery order the Soo Warehouse sent me four boxes of *breaded* chicken breasts instead of *boneless* breasts. That's going to really complicate my life for the next couple of weeks, because the guys on this boat really like chicken breast, and I can cook it forty different ways. Boy, when the grocery man makes a mistake in this business, it's not easy to correct. *I know!* I've got some frying chickens in the freezer, so I'll just cut them up and cook them on the grill. Problem solved, at least temporarily. I'm off to defrost the chicken.

There, the chicken's out and so is CSL's *Nanticoke*. She was the boat loading coal; at about 7:30 P.M. she finished and set sail. Coming out, she had to run in the trough of the waves for awhile, and she took a couple heavy seas over her bow in the process. Being loaded, the wind doesn't affect her as much as it would us. Besides that, we've got a real underpowered bowthruster on this boat, which makes it difficult for the old man to control the bow if the wind or seas start to set it down toward one of the piers. For now, we continue to sit here on the hook. Unfortunately, TV reception isn't very good where we are.

The Canadian *H. M. Griffith* is due here at 1:00 A.M. If we don't get into the dock before then, we'll end up waiting for her to load. Everyone in the crew's getting testy because of the boredom, and the engine room reports that we're down to only four hundred gallons of potable water. Hopefully, that'll last until after I get my shower in the morning and make a pot of coffee.

Saturday, July 20

Lake Erie, Westbound

We finally got into the dock at Conneaut at about noon today, after riding at anchor for about thirty-six hours. The wind had gone down considerably, and we went in as soon as the *H. M. Griffith* finished loading and left. Unfortunately, it was a quick load for us, and we were on our way shortly after 6:00 P.M. I would have liked a few hours to wander up the street and stretch my legs, but I'll have to wait for another day.

I spent a couple of hours cleaning my room last night, but you'd never know it now. Everything is covered with a greasy coat of black coal dust. Argh! Guess I should have waited one more day to do the cleaning.

The entire boat's filthy and the deck is littered with spilled coal. The deckhands are suited up in rain gear and rubber boots and already at work hosing it down. Things should be back to normal in a couple of hours. Ships are normally hosed down after loading or unloading. It's part of the routine out on the lakes. One team of deckhands, often assisted by a watchman, will start at the bow, another team will start at the stern, and everything gets washed overboard through the scuppers located at regular intervals along the edge of the deck. If you could examine the bottom of the lake outside any loading or unloading port, you'd find it covered with a layer of iron ore, coal, or stone—whatever has been loaded or unloaded there over the years. The underwater trails of ore outside old ports like Marquette and Duluth must be mind-boggling. Even at Rogers City, the bottom must literally be paved with limestone. Thousands of ships have loaded at Calcite over the past seventy years, and most hosed down as soon as they cleared the breakwaters and headed out onto the lake.

Speaking of the breakwater at Calcite, one of the guys told me the other day that they used to have pigs roaming around on it. The breakwater has always been a nesting area for seagulls, and several years ago there was an outbreak of the disease histoplasmosis in Rogers City, involving mostly people who worked at the quarry. The disease was traced to seagull droppings; most of these birds nested on the breakwater at Calcite. Many people wanted to kill the seagulls, but that would have violated both state and federal wildfowl laws. Instead, several pigs were borrowed from a local farmer and turned loose to forage among the seagull nests on the breakwater. Seagull eggs represent fine dining to a pig, and by allowing the pigs eat the eggs, the population was reduced without actually killing any birds.

Most sailors hate seagulls, by the way. To the birds, freighters are like islands and they often congregate in large numbers on our hatches. Soon, the hatch covers and adjacent deck areas are polka-dotted with the nasty creatures' white droppings. Those who work out on deck also regularly get splattered by the gulls, who like to hover over the deck and travel along with the ship. Getting bombed by a seagull is not a pleasant experience, as any deckhand will tell you. As a result, you won't find many Great Lakes sailors with cute little carvings of seagulls on their mantles at home.

At the Soo Locks, they've gone to extraordinary lengths to keep seagulls away from the locks and the viewing areas

Deckhand Jimmy Atkins hoses down the deck around the *Cal-cite II*'s stern cabin after unloading in Cleveland. The decks are washed down every time the ship loads or unloads. On a "work-boat" like the *C-2*, which makes many short trips hauling coal, stone, or salt, the deck crew has to break out their hoses every day or two. (Author's collection)

where tourists watch the ships go through. They've strung fishing line in zigzag patterns all over the property, installed squiggly wire protectors on top of light poles, and mounted fake owls on many of the buildings. I'm sad to report that those efforts have had little impact on the local seagull population. On more than one occasion when I've gone through the locks, I've chuckled when I saw a seagull sitting on top of one of the dummy owls.

Once, as I grilled hamburgers on the fantail of the *James R. Barker* as we passed through the Soo, I had to duck inside the galley for a minute to do something. When I returned, a seagull stood on top of my tray of raw hamburgers, casually eating his lunch. The seagull beat a hasty retreat just as I grabbed a shovel lying next to the incinerator. I was fully intent on sending the burger bandit to seagull heaven.

Seagulls aren't the only birds attracted to the boats. During the spring and fall migration periods, many birds will land on passing ships to rest briefly, including species not normally found around the lakes—usually birds that live in the far northern reaches of Canada. Many allow you to walk right up to them before they take flight. Either they're indifferent to humans, or they're so tired from their long flights that they don't have the energy to fly off. Sightings of owls and hawks aboard ships are quite common during the migrations, especially on Lake Superior. Whitefish Point and the Keweenaw Peninsula are both on major flyways used by migratory birds, probably because they jut well out into the lake and by crossing there the birds spend the least amount of time over open water. We also seem to attract more than our share of bats on the boats, and many sailors have experienced a moment of sheer terror when they reached into a locker to get a heaving line and rousted a bat. The deck crews are usually quite proficient at dislodging the bats with the high-pressure hoses they use to wash down the decks. We'll tolerate the owls, hawks, and other migratory species, and we welcome the swallows and other birds that dine on the various insects that regularly plague us, but good riddance to both bats and seagulls.

We finally got to fill our potable water tanks at the dock in Conneaut, hooking into a city water line. We had run out of water last night, and the engineers had to take on water where we were anchored. Since we were in fairly shallow water, and the seas had riled things up for a couple days, the water was a putrid brown and nobody wanted to drink it, even though it had been filtered and chlorinated. Jon McKinley had the forethought to fill a gallon jug with good water last night before we ran out, and we brewed our morning coffee with that. I even altered my menu for the day and made cream of tomato soup instead of vegetable beef, so I wouldn't have to use water in it. We'll fill our tanks again when we reach Thunder Bay Island on Lake Huron, an area that produces clean and tasty drinking water.

We'll be in the Detroit and St. Clair Rivers most of the day tomorrow, and we should arrive at Green Bay late Monday. After unloading there, we're supposed to go to Ludington, Michigan, for a load of sand—supposedly the last load of sand that will ever be taken out of that port. The company that has been mining sand from the dunes along Lake Michigan reportedly lost its permit from the Department of Natural Resources. We're supposed to be taking out the last sand they've processed. It's destined for Cleveland, a port we haven't visited in a couple of weeks. Maybe we'll get lucky and get in there at a good time, like right after supper.

Sunday, July 21
Lake Huron, Upbound

We left the St. Clair River and headed out onto Lake Huron about noon. It's been a quiet, rather boring day. Since it was Sunday morning when we went up the Detroit and St. Clair Rivers, there was little pleasure boat traffic, and freighters were scarce, too. There wasn't much activity on the *Calcite II* either. It was "Sunday on the run" for the deckhands. They spent an hour or two doing what's referred to as "sanitary," cleaning the hallways up forward, emptying waste baskets, and generally sprucing up the common areas, before they knocked off for the balance of the day. Sunday on the run is an old tradition, honored by most companies on the lakes, or at least by the officers aboard their ships. If you're not loading or unloading on Sunday, the deckhands will take most of the day off. Those of us in the galley, and the watchstanders in the deck and engine departments, never get a day off. It would be so nice right now. On Wednesday, I'll have been on here for sixty continuous days. That's sixty days of getting up at 5:30 A.M., sixty days of working ten or eleven hours a day, sixty days of preparing two meals a day for the crew. Hey, I'm a bit tired, and a day off would be wonderful. What would

I do? Sleep late and then take a few naps during the day. What else?

The summer Olympics began yesterday, and I watched a few events on television last night. I had planned to do the same this evening, but I can't pick up any station that's carrying the games. We're up off Saginaw Bay, and a long way from any television station. We won't get much in the way of TV until about 10:00 tonight, when we'll pick up the CBS station out of Alpena. Unfortunately, the Olympics are on NBC. Besides, ten o'clock is my bedtime, Olympics or not.

In addition to being reasonably diligent about keeping this log, Ralph Roberts will be pleased to know that I'm taking pictures of darn near every boat we pass in the rivers or see in port. Early this morning, I got what should be an excellent photo of the *Oglebay Norton,* a 1,000-footer that was launched by Bethlehem Steel for their Great Lakes Steamship Division in 1978 as the *Lewis Wilson Foy.* The ship is now owned by Oglebay Norton, the fleet that my brother works for. Another Bethlehem ship, the *Burns Harbor* was the first "footer" I was on. Back in the early 1980s, I made a night passage up the St. Marys River on her. It was a memorable and fascinating experience. I didn't think we'd ever make the tight turn around Neebish Island at Johnson's Point, and when we approached the locks at the Soo, I was all but convinced the *Burns Harbor* was too big to fit into the Poe Lock.

In addition to the trip on the *Burns Harbor,* I've worked on six other thousand-footers, including the *Columbia Star, James R. Barker, Mesabi Miner, Paul R. Tregurtha, George A. Stinson,* and *Edwin H. Gott.* Altogether, there are thirteen footers on the lakes. They actually range in length from 1,000 feet to a few inches over 1,013 feet. The longest is the *Paul R. Tregurtha,* flagship of the Interlake Steamship fleet. She was originally launched in 1981 as the *William J. DeLancey,* and quickly became known to those who sailed aboard her as the Fancy *DeLancey,* because of her plush outfitting. She's got some lavishly decorated passenger quarters, where Interlake entertains and hopefully impresses important customers. Even the crew quarters are among the finest on the lakes. All the rooms are carpeted and equipped with telephones, dropped ceilings, tiled bathrooms and so on. The ship was originally named for the then-president of LTV Steel, the second largest steelmaker in the U.S. It was intended to haul almost solely for LTV, moving iron ore pellets from Lake Superior to LTV's mill at Indiana Harbor, and to the pellet transshipment terminal at Lorain, Ohio, where smaller ships carry the pellets up the Cuyahoga River to another LTV mill. During the bleak years in the mid-1980s, LTV went bankrupt. Although the company owed Interlake millions of dollars, it paid off its debt at pennies on the dollar. At the same time, LTV acted unilaterally to cut the prices they paid to shipping companies like Interlake. With LTV its single largest customer and several ships almost totally involved in hauling pellets for LTV, Interlake and several other shipping companies were forced to accept the reduced shipping rates. They weren't happy about it and Interlake extracted some measure of justice a few years later when they renamed the *DeLancey* to honor Paul Tregurtha, the business partner of Interlake President James R. Barker.

Built in 1981, the *Tregurtha* is also one of the newest U.S. ships on the lakes. No new ships have been added to the U.S. fleet since then, though a number of tug-barges have been launched.

The oldest operating vessel in the U.S. fleet is Medusa Cement's *Medusa Challenger*. The 552-foot cement carrier was launched in 1906.

Cement boats vie with tankers for honors as the shortest ships on the lakes. Cleveland Tankers' *Saturn* is only 384 feet long, while the cement carrier *S. T. Crapo,* operated by Inland Lakes Management, is 403 feet long. Among ships in the major ore, coal, and stone trades, the smallest is our fleet's *Myron C. Taylor,* only 604 feet long, one foot shorter than the *Calcite II.*

Monday, July 22

Green Bay, Lake Michigan

We moved through Rock Island Passage and entered Green Bay about 5:00 P.M. We've lost some time because of weather, so we won't arrive in Green Bay until about 1:30

129

in the morning. We should finish unloading about the time I get up tomorrow.

This could be a day in late October, instead of the third week of July. The temperature got down into the fifties last night, and I'm not sure it got out of the sixties all day. It's not just cool, though. We've had blustery winds out of the southwest and there's a six- to eight-foot sea running, which has created a bumpy ride. The captain called back this afternoon to let us know that we would be in the trough of the seas for awhile when we turned into Rock Island Passage. We secured everything in the galley, but Washington Island provided a little lee for us and the seas abated a bit before we made the haul, so we didn't roll at all. Securing for weather is common in the fall and early winter, but it's a little unusual in July.

When we passed under the Mackinac Bridge and entered Lake Michigan at about 8:00 this morning, we encountered quite a few of the sailboats in the Chicago-to-Mackinac Island race. The winds were calmer then, and the first twenty boats or so that we came upon had set their colorful spinnakers as they raced toward the finish line at Mackinac Island. Altogether, we saw about forty or fifty sailboats and quite a number of powerboats that seemed to tag alongside them. The winds increased about 9:00 A.M. and the sailing crews pulled down their spinnakers before the wind could carry them off. The race participants ran along under their less colorful mains and jibs. Weather conditions for the Chicago-to-Mac race were exactly the opposite of last week's Port Huron-to-Mackinac. Sailors in the Port Huron race had no wind, while those in the Chicago race probably had more than they wanted. There were four- to six-foot seas by about noon today; it must have been an uncomfortable ride for the sailboats still working their way toward Mackinac. With the wind on their sterns, they undoubtedly hobby-horsed pretty good, with the bow diving down between waves, and then lifting high as the next wave passed under them. I made a night passage from St. Ignace to Rogers City on a sailboat about twenty years ago under conditions similar to those the sailors encountered today. I lost my lunch after an hour or two of intense hobby-horsing, and was sick until things calmed down around dawn. It was a long, miserable night. I'm sure a few green sailors suffered aboard the boats we saw today. I certainly empathize with their plight.

When I discussed the thousand-footers yesterday, I didn't mean to imply that big is necessarily best nor inherently beautiful. Most aficionados of Great Lakes ships feel that the thousand-footers are decidedly ugly. Mike Gerasimos, a former skipper with the Ford Motor Company fleet, referred to them as "six decks of ugly." The footers are boxy, and their cabins are out of proportion to their massive hulls. When the various companies contracted to have them built, they chose not to waste any money to make the ships look nice. These huge vessels are strictly utilitarian: big, efficient, cost-effective . . . and ugly.

In the past some companies were concerned about the appearance of their ships. In the 1940s and 1950s, for example, Inland Steel spent extra money to make the *Wilfred Sykes* and *Edward L. Ryerson* look as attractive as possible. Much of the clutter of piping and tanks normally found on the fantails of Great Lakes ships was concealed, their fore and aft masts were raked to give an appearance of speed, they were fitted with sleek smokestacks, and their bows and sterns were tied together by a unique band of grey and white stripes that ran from stem to stern. Many people in the industry undoubtedly scoffed at the extra expense Inland went to in building them, but they are widely accepted as the most attractive steam or diesel ships that ever sailed the lakes. The *Sykes* was converted to a self-unloader a number of years ago, and the unloading boom and elevator destroyed much of her former elegance. Heirs of Edward L. Ryerson, who are still major stockholders in Inland Steel, blocked efforts by the company to convert the *Ryerson* to a self-unloader. Though she may not be as efficient as self-unloaders like the *Sykes,* she is, in appearance, without equal on the lakes today.

Of the big ships on the lakes, I think the 858-foot *Roger Blough* is in a class by itself when it comes to appearance. She was built to the design of the classic Great Lakes straight-decker, with fore and aft cabins, and she has an unobtrusive shuttle-type unloading system, instead of the big skeleton-like boom on deck. For a big boat, the *Blough* is so perfectly proportioned that from a distance she looks like a traditional straight-decker. It's only when you get closer that you realize how massive she is. The *Blough* has a beam of 105 feet, similar to the thousand-footers. She marks the transition from traditionally designed lake freighters to the thousand-footers. Like many transitional species, the *Blough* is an oddity. She can't carry as much cargo as the thousand-footers that followed in her wake, but she's too big to dock in many of the ports served by smaller freighters. During the shipping recession of the 1980s, the *Blough* spent years in lay-up, while ultra-efficient thousand-footers and ultra-versatile smaller ships managed to keep busy. She has become the Edsel of the Great Lakes shipping industry. Nonetheless, as big ships go, the *Blough*'s a beauty in my book. I'm looking forward to the day that I get to board her and relieve Al Chesky, her steward.

Tuesday, July 23
Lake Michigan, Downbound

Well, we're not going down very far, just to Ludington. We'll load sand there, and then head for Cleveland. We finished unloading at Green Bay about 7:00 this morning and left while the city was still quiet. Nobody had a chance to go up the street, even though we were just off the downtown area. We won't be into Ludington until after 11:00 P.M. tonight, so many of the guys will not go up the street there either. We're sort of on the midnight run. We sneak into port after the sun goes down, and slip out again in the early morning hours.

We came out of Green Bay through the infamous Death's Door, a narrow opening through the string of islands that forms the expansive bay's eastern boundary. It is the site of many shipwrecks over the years, dating back to the days of the early French explorers, who named the treacherous passage. There's actually a much quicker way to get from Green Bay to Ludington. By going through the ship canal at Sturgeon Bay, Wisconsin, captains save about four hours' sailing time. When someone asked the captain this morning if he was going to take the canal, he had all sorts of reasons why he didn't want to go that way. My guess is that he may not be too familiar with the canal, though he'd never admit it. I wonder how he'll explain the extra four hours of travel time to the office.

I felt crabby all day today. We loaded coal three days ago and I'm still finding coal dust all over the galley. I put Jimmy Atkins to serious cleaning yesterday, but he overlooked a lot of things, so I gave him more specific instructions today. It's wearing me out, though. I'm tired of having to tell these guys every little thing. My kingdom for a second cook and porter who know how to do their jobs without constant prodding! They're few and far between in this fleet.

By the way, I'm not the only one who's crabby. It's apparently contagious on the *Calcite II*. Nearly every other person I bump into is grumpy and the number of complaints has reached new heights. By their nature, sailors are world-class complainers. We feel that complaining is our *right*—one of the few we have out here. We can't go down to the corner bar for a beer after work, we can't go for a sunset walk on the beach with someone we love, we can't take in a movie in the evening, we can't go out and pull the weeds in our garden, we can't—well, you get the picture. We can't do the things people with normal jobs do, so we complain. We complain about people in the office, politicians, religion, women, the weather, our unions, how much basketball players are paid, the fact that we don't load at Calcite every trip, the lousy boat we're on, and our shipmates. Hell, there are times when I'm convinced that there isn't a guy in the whole crew who really gives a rip about anyone else in the crew. We tolerate each other, that's all. If we weren't stuck on this boat, we'd never associate with any of the other guys. We're like twenty-six people traveling on a Greyhound. As soon as the bus reaches the depot, we all go our own ways and we entertain our friends for months with stories about the oddballs we met on the bus. The present atmosphere on the boat is almost as testy as it gets during the holiday season from Thanksgiving to Christmas, when everyone wants to be home with their families. The guys who haven't gone on vacation this year are near the end of their endurance. The guys who've been on vacation realize how long it's going to be before they get off the boat again. All of us are clearly aware of just how long this season will be. Most of us will be a year older and many events will have transpired in our families and in the world before this season is over. We'll have spent eight or nine months of our lives for a few nice paychecks and comfortable fringe benefits. This isn't really what we want to be doing, not today, not tomorrow. So we complain. It's a right endowed upon merchant seamen throughout the world and I think it's always been that way. It may be one of the lost beatitudes—blessed are the sailors, for they shall be allowed to complain eternally.

I managed to talk to my son Scott on the cellular pay phone today. It was probably a twenty-dollar call, but it was worth it. I don't think I'd talked to him since I returned to the boat in late May. He sounds as though he's doing great. Right now he's taking placement tests at Oakland Community College in Royal Oak, and he's looking forward to classes in the fall. Sunday, Scott and Meredith are going to Chicago for a couple of days. They're going to stay at a hotel on Michigan Avenue—the Magnificent Mile—and immerse themselves in the museums and designer shops. It's the first time they've done anything like this together, so I hope it goes well. For most of the last half dozen years they could barely say a civil word to each other. They're both growing older and beginning to appreciate each other.

I miss them both. We've always had good times together during the summers. It's hard to believe that this year I might not get to see them until the fall. They may both be back at college before I get some time off. Summers in northern Michigan are so incredible, it's too bad that summer is also the busy time for relief sailors like me.

Wednesday, July 24

Manitou Passage, Lake Michigan

It's a gorgeous day, and we're cruising through the Manitou Passage between the Manitou islands and the sand dune-studded shoreline of Michigan's Leelanau County. There's no prettier spot on the lakes, and it's only a few miles from my former home in Traverse City. I spotted a few buildings at The Homestead, the resort I worked at last year. It sprawls along the sandy Lake Michigan shoreline at Sleeping Bear Bay, near Glen Arbor, Michigan. I'm sure the gang at The Homestead is frantically busy right now, coping with a resort full of vacationers and too few staff. I wouldn't trade places with any of them, but it would be nice to say hello.

We got word that Ron Bredow will return when we reach Calcite in another three or four days. Both Geno and Jimmy are scheduled for August vacations, and the rumor is I'll end up with Booger as my porter. Booger came on as a deckhand last time we were at Calcite. He's famous for regularly putting his boots on the wrong feet, and for his nickname, which he reportedly earned through his habit of jamming his finger up his nose to search for foreign objects. Booger's goal in life is to be a steward, but in our few conversations he doesn't strike me as knowing anything about cooking. That's apparently no impediment in this fleet, however. I'm not excited about someone called Booger serving as my porter. The first time he inserts his finger up his nose in my galley, he's history![12]

We finished loading sand at Ludington at 8:30 this morning. On the way out of the harbor, we passed the *Spartan, Arthur M. Atkinson,* and *City of Midland,* three car ferries standing idle. All three look pretty good, although they haven't run for years. Many people still hang onto the hope that some use will be found for the ships, but I'd be mightily surprised if they ever ran again. Maybe they could be converted to floating restaurants or gambling ships.

------

[12]Our fleet may be the only one on the lakes that allows sailors in entry-level positions—deckhands, wipers, and porters—to transfer between departments at will. They don't start earning seniority in a particular department until they move up to the next ratings—watchman, oiler, or second cook. Any entry-level position that opens up is fair game for the sailor with the most seniority with the company. Jimmy Atkins, for example, came aboard the boat as a deckhand, and then moved into the galley when Ron Bredow became the second cook. In all the other companies I've worked for, you only gain seniority in one department. If someone wants to transfer to another department, such as from the deck to the galley, he must start at the bottom of the galley seniority list. The arrangement here gives the office more flexibility to fill positions aboard the boats; guys like Jimmy get more sailing time than if they were restricted to a single department.

Like relics from a bygone era, Lake Michigan car ferries sit idle at their docks at Ludington, Michigan. Built to haul railroad cars, automobiles, and passengers across Lake Michigan, the *Spartan* (left), *Arthur K. Atkinson* (middle), and *City of Midland* (right) no longer operate. Only one car ferry, the *Badger,* is still in operation today, carrying mainly passengers and their automobiles on the cross-lake trip from Ludington, Michigan, to Manitowac, Wisconsin. (Author's collection)

As the boat was checked down to pass over Gray's Reef on northern Lake Michigan, I sauntered outside and was treated to a magnificent sunset. Three levels of clouds layered the western horizon and the red, purple, orange, and pink colors reflected spectacularly off them in the waning light. A Hannah tug and barge passed Gray's Reef Light right at that time. I think I got a great photograph of the tug with the lighthouse and sunset in the background. We'll see if it comes out. Our *George A. Sloan* also slid across the horizon, silhouetted against the sunset, but she was quite a distance from us. I took a couple of pictures anyway, but the *Sloan* will probably be nothing more than an elongated dot in the picture.

One of the priceless benefits of working on the boats is that we see sunset and sunrise each day, or at least each day we're out on the lakes. They're usually stunning; even a hardened sailor pauses for a moment to absorb their beauty.

Thursday, July 25

St. Clair River

It's a reasonably nice night on the river, but the bugs are thick. We had killer flies until we got into the river and then they were replaced by a horde of no-see-ums. The fan in the door to my room was running; by the time I got in there after work, my bed was covered with the little buggers. I remedied the situation by turning off the fan and sucking up the bugs with a vacuum. I'm sitting here in a dark room, because I'm afraid the light might attract more of the little nuisances.

When we passed the Detroit Edison plant between St. Clair and Marine City, the *Columbia Star* was unloading and my brother Gary was on watch. Our chief engineer was out on deck with his binoculars, and he saw Gary walking down the deck about midships. I stood on a hatch and waved, and he waved back. Today, that's the best two brothers could do.

I washed some t-shirts this evening, but I don't like to run them through the dryer and risk shrinking them. So I've got laundry hanging from various cables that run across the ceiling of my room. This place looks like the proverbial Chinese laundry.

Our orders were changed—we're no longer going to Calcite after Cleveland-Ashtabula-Alpena. Instead, we load at Cedarville. There was a great deal of grumbling about that. We'll supposedly go to Calcite after the Cedarville-Cleveland. There'll be lots of crew changes at Cedarville, or on the Alpena leg of this trip. A number of guys will be returning from vacation. Several guys are leaving for various reasons, so they will be replaced by relief crewmen. Our present handyman has to get off because his merchant seaman's card is expiring and he must apply to the Coast Guard for a new one. The bad news is that it's presently taking two to three months for the Coast Guard to process an application, so he could be on the beach for awhile. Guess he should have planned ahead a little and renewed his card before the season started. Even more vacationers will come back once we reach Calcite in about a week. We've got three engineers, a mate, a watchman, a wheelsman, an oiler, the second cook, and two deckhands disembarking over the next week.

That's ten out of twenty-six crewmembers on the ship, so it will be quite a change.

We had a fire-and-boat drill right after lunch today, and it was a joke. This time we actually took the covers off the lifeboats before we cranked them out. Nobody takes the drills seriously. I'm told that on many of the boats in this fleet they don't even hold the required drills. The captain just makes a note in the log book every week stating that a drill was held. After the *Edmund Fitzgerald* went down in 1975, the Coast Guard found that drills were seldom held on the *Fitz*, though log entries were made each week. Behaviors seldom change much in this industry.

Friday, July 26
Lake Erie, Eastbound

We had an exciting morning. Just before 8 o'clock, the third mate called back to tell us a tornado was traveling along the shore abreast of the ship. We all ran out on the fantail and easily spotted the swirling black funnel. It was massive and ominous. It was actually a waterspout, which is a tornado that forms over water. It was about four miles off the Ohio shore, between Geneva and Vermilion, and about five miles from the ship. The amazing thing was how long it lasted, probably thirty minutes or so. While we watched, a disturbance in the water occurred several miles west of the first waterspout. It looked like a swirling mass of white water, rising what appeared to be only ten or fifteen feet above the water. As we continued to watch, though, the swirling column of air sucked the water up to the low-lying black clouds to form a skinny waterspout. It was smaller and lighter than the first waterspout and lasted a shorter time. The waterspouts formed on the back side of a storm front that straddled the shoreline. Shortly after we saw the waterspouts, torrential rains poured down for fifteen or twenty minutes, and the temperature dropped sharply. I saw waterspouts on Lake Ontario, while crossing from Oswego, New York, to the Welland Canal on the workboat *Massey D* in 1974, but it was at night and they didn't show up as clearly. Today I took a number of pictures to document what is a rare phenomenon.

We unloaded our cargo of sand at Cleveland and are now on our way to Ashtabula to load coal for Alpena. It'll be about 11:00 P.M. before we arrive, so we won't have an opportunity to go up the street. That's unfortunate, because I'm out of film; after this morning's events, I'm not excited about putting a hold on the picture-taking business. I seem to be getting good pictures almost every day. The ones I took this morning were probably a once-in-a-lifetime opportunity.

The office called today to say that Ron Bredow doesn't want to be second cook when he returns to work. Booger hasn't even started working in the galley and he's already been promoted from porter to second cook. When I told one of the deckhands who works with Booger, he said, "Well, that'll be the end of salads and desserts for me." That's not a good sign. This is going to be an interesting experience. If the office transferred me to another boat at the end of the month, I wouldn't be heartbroken.

Gene Schaedig, Jerry Maciejewski, Butch Kierzek, and John Sobeck (left to right) watch a waterspout along the Lake Erie shore from the fantail of the *Calcite II*. Waterspouts are tornadoes that form over water, sucking up tons of water from the lake. They seldom last long. (Author's collection)

Crewmembers (left to right) Wayne "Wiener" Selke, Frank Bruski, and Tom Flanner strain to crank out one of the *Calcite II*'s two lifeboats during an "abandon ship" drill, while other crewmembers are satisfied merely to watch. The old lifeboats are difficult to launch, and if it actually became necessary to abandon ship, most crewmembers would probably opt to use one of the vessel's state-of-the-art inflatable life rafts. (Author's collection)

Wayne "Wiener" Selke, a wheelsman I've known for years, gave me a surprise gift today—a complete set of military recipe cards from his days in the navy back in the 1950s. The same recipes were used by all branches of the armed forces. It's a real collector's set, and I can't believe Wiener passed it along to me. He said he had no use for the cards any longer, they were just taking up space on his basement storage shelves. Well, I'm darned glad to have them! Many of the recipes were still being used when I was in the army from 1964 to 1968. I'll have to try a few of the military classics on the guys. I assure you, the food in the service wasn't anywhere near as good as the food here on the boats. (Tonight's dinner on the *Calcite II* featured sweet-and-sour shrimp, linguine with clam sauce, blackened whitefish, and roast pork loin. A few of the guys complained that there were too many good choices. "When in doubt," I tell them, "order the sampler platter.")

Monday, July 29
Lake Huron

It's been a busy couple of days. We got into Alpena yesterday at 4:30 P.M., a nearly perfect time for those of us in the galley. I had supper ready, but let Geno and Jimmy serve it. I caught a ride to Rogers City with Wiener Selke and his wife, visited my mother for awhile, stopped and got some cash from an ATM, and took my brother Gary's pickup to Alpena. There I did some needed shopping at K-Mart, stocking up enough film to last me a month or so. I also dropped off five rolls of film for developing, with the hope that I'll find a way to pick them up the next time we're in Alpena. I stopped at Lud's, ate a giantburger, and was still back at the boat by 7:30 P.M. John Buczkowski, who was going on vacation after standing the 4-to-8 watch, drove Gary's truck back to Rogers City, and will leave it in the sailor's parking lot at Calcite so I'll have transportation the next time we get in there.

We finished unloading coal at the LaFarge Cement plant at about 11:00 P.M. and departed for Cedarville. We arrived there at 7:00 this morning during a heavy downpour, finished loading and headed back out onto Lake Huron at 3:00 P.M. We're on our way to Cleveland again, then Ashtabula to load coal for Alpena again. Our schedule calls for us to go to Stoneport.

I've got a big grocery order in, but I don't know where to have it delivered. I thought we were going back to Cedarville, but that's been scratched. After we unload at Alpena, we're now supposed to go to Stoneport to load stone for Benton Harbor, to South Chicago to load coal for Boyne City and finally, to Calcite. I don't think we can wait that long, though, so I may have our groceries sent to Stoneport.

The weather is wretched, the worst we've had this summer. It's been raining steadily and it's windy and cold. The temperature in Marquette, Michigan, last night was only 34 degrees, and I'll bet it'll be in the 40s on northern Lake Huron tonight. I may have to close the outside door to my room tonight. There's a pretty stiff wind blowing in right now, and it's nippy. By morning it may be sub-nippy. It's good weather for sleeping, but it's hell getting out of bed in the morning.

Tuesday, July 30
Detroit River, Downbound

Another depressing grey day, with rain on and off, more on than off. I had a reasonably good day in the galley, completing all my month-end paperwork and making out new time sheets for the first pay period in August. I also sent a fax to Soo Warehouse, to tell them to bring our groceries to Stoneport. We don't know where we're going after that, and I can't afford to gamble with our groceries. We could get stuck over on Lake Michigan for a week, and we'd be out of almost everything except meat by then. There isn't much paperwork in this job, fortunately. Despite the fact that I have a master's degree in administration and have held a number of administrative positions, I despise paperwork. I guess that's one reason I'm out here. I'm just not the type for offices, desks, and paperwork.

It's interesting that my great love in life is writing. I didn't start writing seriously until I had left the regimen and stress of offices. My first book was written at a table in front of the living room window in a Charlevoix condo. Book number two was written at a cheap particle board computer desk in the corner of the spare bedroom in my apartment in Traverse City. My third book was written in my old bedroom at my mother's house in Rogers City. Book four is, at this point, being written aboard the *Calcite II*, working at my computer balanced on the corner of a two-drawer file cabinet at the foot of my bed. Maybe if I had an office to work in, I'd get writer's block. Little chance of that, though, since there's no possibility that I'll ever work in an office again. This is my retirement job, except for writing.

Scott "Booger" Cooper's second day as second cook didn't go much better than his first. He baked a batch of cookies that had to be fed to the seagulls, and the box cake he made looked like a tank ran over it. Baking isn't easy, especially if you have no idea what it is you're doing. He's going to try raised doughnuts tomorrow. That ought to be interesting. He did ask if I would help him, though, so that's a good sign. The only problem is I don't have time to be his baking teacher. Although he performed better at breakfast this morning, he cooked the hash browns so far ahead of time they were inedible by the time the crew came in to eat. Everything else seemed to come out okay, and the potato salad he made for supper went over well. He's a nice kid, but I'm not sure he'll ever be a good cook—no food sense.

Ron "Shortcut" Bredow didn't learn anything while he was on vacation. He makes the same mistakes now that he made previously. He doesn't know anything about galley sanitation, and he doesn't appear to be able to learn. It scares me to have him working in my galley. I don't want anyone getting sick. What really bothers me is that there are apparently several other porters working on ships in this fleet who are as bad, or worse, than Shortcut. Boy, am I looking forward to working with them. Arrrgh!

Thursday, August 1
Lake Huron, Upbound

I didn't make any entry last night. We got into Ashtabula just as supper was ending, so Booger and I walked up to a little shopping center about a mile or so from the dock to pick up some necessities. It was a gorgeous evening, and we bumped into about half the crew on our walk. Nobody was in a hurry to return to the ship. When I finally went back to the boat, I hung around out on deck and talked with the guys until bedtime. I slept like the proverbial log after my little walk and a lot of fresh air.

Booger has found the solution to this second cook stuff. Today he put out store-bought doughnuts and defrosted a frozen cake and pie. The pie was pecan, which required some warming in the oven, so I guess he *did* do some baking.

Fred Cummings, our fleet manager, called me on the cellular phone today to ask if I'd be willing to go to the *Edwin H. Gott* later this month. They want me to switch with the cook who's over there, because they've got some important

143

guests coming aboard for a trip. I'm not sure who's cooking on the *Gott* right now, but he's apparently not a passenger-quality cook in the eyes of the office, whatever the heck that means. I don't cook any differently for passengers than I do for the crew.

At supper tonight, Jerry Macks, our first mate, was commenting on how much fruit juice the crew drinks. The night lunch is always stocked with four or five of the most popular flavors, including the expensive blends like cran-raspberry. Jerry noted that back when he started sailing thirty-plus years ago you got one small glass of juice with breakfast. On one boat he was on, the steward was a real stickler about the little plastic glasses only being filled so high with juice. The porter who filled the glasses each morning wouldn't always get the same amount in each glass, so after all the juice was poured, he evened them out by sipping from those glasses that were a bit too full. Only a porter on a Great Lakes freighter would employ such a creative solution.

Macks and the guys on his watch also complained that they were hungry for pickles, so I brought out a gallon jar from one of the walk-in coolers. You see, it's tradition in this fleet to have pickles only on Sundays. Stuffed olives are eaten only when turkey is on the menu. Fish and cole slaw are served on Fridays, in case any of the Catholics want to abstain from eating meat. Applesauce is the traditional side dish with pork. I could prepare pork chops in pecan cream sauce, or sweet-and-sour pork, and some of the crew would be upset if I didn't include applesauce. Such traditions drive me *nuts*, so I tend to rant and rave at porters and second cooks when they tell me we can't have pickles because it isn't Sunday.

On many boats on the lakes, you can tell what day of the week it is by what's on the menu, and vice versa. There's a set seven-day menu that never varies: fish on Friday, steak on Saturday, turkey or chicken on Sunday, hamburgers on Monday, and so on. It doesn't take much menu planning, but it does get a little boring. I'll go along with steak or prime rib on Saturdays, and I usually offer some kind of fish on Fridays, but in small quantities because few people eat it. Other than that, my daily menus are a mystery to everyone but me. When the crew heads for the galley, they have no idea what they'll find. Variety *is* the spice of life!

We'll be in Alpena at about 6:00 in the morning, and at Calcite by 5:00 P.M. This weekend is Rogers City's annual Nautical Festival, so most of us want to arrive at a good time and go down to the beer tent at Lakeside Park, where everyone congregates. It's a chance to see a lot of old friends. That's particularly true for me, since I haven't been around Rogers City much during the past twenty years. I've got my fingers crossed we won't have any delays.

Jimmy Atkins, now a watchman, was going around the boat this morning with a gas monitor, checking for methane gas that might be escaping from our coal cargo. Lots of ships carrying coal have suffered explosions when concentrations of methane gas ignited. A few years back, two engineers were killed on the *Middletown* when methane ignited and caused a flash fire. It's not a new problem, though. The *R. J. Hackett,* built in 1869, and the prototype for virtually every single Great Lakes bulk freighters built from then until the 1970s, was destroyed by a fire in 1905 that resulted from a methane explosion. Now the company issues little hand-held monitors, about the size of a box of Fig Newtons, that allow us to detect any concentrations of methane that may prove to be dangerous.

Saturday, August 3
Lake Huron, Downbound

In a stroke of rare luck, we got into Calcite at 6:30 P.M. yesterday. Two boats were ahead of us, so we had a long delay. Unfortunately, I had a large order of groceries coming down from the Soo, and the blasted truck didn't arrive until 8:00 P.M. As a result, I didn't get off the boat until almost 9:30 P.M. I visited my mother for awhile and then went down to the beer tent at Rogers City's Nautical Festival until about 12:30 A.M. –well past my bedtime. I had a great time meeting old friends I hadn't seen in twenty or thirty years and I didn't want to go back to the boat. Some hadn't changed much since our high school days; others were literally unrecognizable to me. Recognizable or not, I enjoyed talking with all of them. Most were at least mildly surprised to learn I was sailing. I'm curious where they expected I would be at this point in my life, but I was afraid to ask since I didn't want to embarrass them . . . or myself.

We've had three engineers come aboard during the last couple days. A new guy came on at Alpena to relieve John Schefdore; John Bellmore and Tom Brege returned last night at Calcite, relieving Iggy Donajkowski and Jon McKinley, who were happy to be going on vacation. There's a lot of tension in the engine room right now, as almost everyone aboard feels there's going to be a clash between the chief engineer and Tom Brege and John Bellmore. Nothing of note happened today, though, so we'll have to wait and see.

Booger made an apple torte today that was quite delicious, but Shortcut Bredow started washing dishes in cold water again. He says the hot water bothers his hands. "Wear rubber gloves," I countered. Our dishes *will* be washed in hot water, sensitive hands or not. It's no fun working with a porter and second cook who don't carry their own weight. Too much of my time is spent giving directions, helping them, and keeping an eye on them. As a result, I'm angry or worried too much of the time. Maybe the move to the *Gott* is coming at a fortuitous time.

Sunday, August 4
Rouge River

We just made the turn from the Detroit River into the Rouge on our way to Levy's stone dock. It's hot and sticky today, but it seems to be cooling off some now that the sun is sinking lower in the western sky.

I made seventeen pizzas for supper tonight, giving the crew a chance to break the pizza consumption record set last year on the *George A. Sloan*—sixteen pizzas eaten between dinner and when I arrived in the galley at 6:00 the following morning. With the overnight unload and some new crewmembers who are heavy hitters at the mess table, we might break the old record. Two of our new deckhands, Earl Marino and Casey Kandow, really put away the food. They look like Mutt and Jeff. Earl's short and stout, while Casey must be six feet, four inches tall. Casey was a basketball star in high school last year, and was recruited to play at Michigan State University, one of my alma maters. He's out here earning money for school, something you don't see too much anymore. When I got out of high school, many young guys who were college bound, or in college, worked on the boats during the summer. It's hard to beat the money you make here and there are few opportunities to spend it.

We should have been unloading here in Detroit by about 9:00 or 10:00 this morning, but we had engine problems and spent much of the night drifting in Lake Huron. The problem was a malfunctioning cam shaft and fuel pump on one cylinder of our Nordberg diesel. The repairs weren't completed until almost noon, so we had a pleasant after-noon cruise down the St. Clair and Detroit Rivers. I didn't have much of a chance to enjoy the Sunday boating traffic on the river, though. I spent most of the afternoon getting the pizzas ready and envying the guys sitting out on deck.

When we were in Rogers City Friday night, I stumbled on a source of boat pictures that I hadn't thought about before. I ran into John Meharg, my brother Gary's best friend and an engineer with Oglebay Norton, at the Nautical Festival beer tent. I mentioned to John what a hassle it was to gather artwork for a book, and he replied that he has a lot of pictures he's taken of boats over the years. Many are from his early days as a sailor, back in the 1970s. He even took some in various engine rooms he worked in. Best of all, John said he has all the negatives for his photos, so it would be easy for me to get prints made. He's going to drop them off at my mother's house. I can't wait to get my hands on them. What a treasure trove! I'm sure there are sailors and former sailors all around the Great Lakes who have wonderful boat pictures that deserve to be preserved in museum or archival collections so that future generations will understand what it was like to sail aboard freighters on the inland seas of North America. Finding those photos and ensuring they are preserved will be a mission of mine. Old Ralph Roberts truly inspired me.

Monday, August 5
Lake Huron, Upbound

Another of the *Calcite II*'s famous fiascos occurred last night. When they started to unload at the stone dock, the first thing off the end of the boom was a bunch of coal. Apparently the system wasn't properly cleaned after we unloaded coal at Alpena the other day. We unloaded onto an existing pile of light-colored, almost white, limestone last night, so the coal was obvious to all observers, including the dock foreman for the company we were delivering to. The guys on deck quickly shut down the unloading system. Deckhands were dispatched to climb the mountainous pile of limestone, pick out the errant pieces of coal, and put them into five-gallon pails. On the ship, other members of the deck gang shoveled as much coal as they could off the conveyor belt, and hosed down those areas that had been missed in the last cleanup. After a several-hour delay, the unload was resumed amid much speculation that the customer would refuse to pay for the contaminated cargo. I didn't envy the captain having to report yet another screw-up and delay to the office.

I was totally frazzled by the time I finished supper to-night. It was hot and humid all day and I spent the entire afternoon working over a hot stove. I couldn't drink enough to keep from dehydrating, and I was running on empty by the time supper was over. I went to my room, which was reasonably cool, stripped to my skivvies, and collapsed on the bed for about an hour before I got up the energy to take a much-needed cool shower.

We'll be at Calcite at 3:00 A.M., about the worst possible time. My mornings are always busy, so there's no way I can sneak away from the boat to even make a quick trip to my mother's. From Calcite we go to Gary and South Chicago, so I'm hoping this hot spell is a short one. We'll spend the better part of a day at the south end of Lake Michigan. If it's hot we're going to be in real trouble. My kingdom for an air-conditioned galley! Better yet, my galley for an air-conditioned kingdom!

Tuesday, August 6
Lake Michigan, Downbound

It's a great day to be out on the lakes. Ashore, it's hot and humid, temperatures climbed to near ninety and the humidity is almost as high. Out here on the northern lakes it's simply perfect, except for a humidity-induced haze that limits visibility. It should be good sleeping tonight here on the boat, but I'll bet those people on the shore who lack air-conditioning will be miserable. We might even luck out when we reach the lower end of the lake, where the heat and humidity are often stifling. We won't be into Gary until tomorrow evening, after the worst of the day's heat has passed. If we're lucky we'll unload and sail over to South Chicago to load coal before the sun comes up. If there are no boats ahead of us at the coal dock, we could be back out on the lake before it gets too hot. If we had to sit a whole day at the coal dock, the boat would be like an oven.

We got into Calcite about 3:00 A.M. today, and were gone by 9:00. Despite the late hour of our arrival, most of those who weren't on watch went home. I stayed aboard and got a good night's sleep. I guess that if I had a wife waiting for me at home, I might look at things differently.

We passed our *George A. Sloan,* Calcite-bound, just after we went under the Mackinac Bridge. A short time later, our *Arthur M. Anderson* and *Cason J. Callaway* both steamed past us like we were standing still. They, too, are headed down the lake, but at a much faster speed than we are. We run along at only about eleven miles an hour, while the triple-A boats, such as the *Anderson* and *Callaway,* probably make fourteen or fifteen miles an hour. Of course, we've got three-thousand aging horsepower, and they've got well over seven thousand. It's like a senior citizen with a bad limp racing a middle-aged marathoner. The triple-A boats were built in the early 1950s, while this old bucket came out in 1929, so we've got twenty-plus additional years under our keel.

The triple-A boats were built to handle the surge in cargo during the Korean War. A total of eight nearly identical ships were built for Pittsburgh Steamship—predecessor to the USS Great Lakes Fleet, for Cleveland-Cliffs, Interlake

Steamship, Ford Motor Company, and Columbia Transportation—now operating as the marine division of Oglebay Norton. Seven of the eight ships are still around, although Interlake's *J. L. Mauthe* is not presently operating. The eighth ship, Ford's *William Clay Ford,* was scrapped a number of years ago, though her pilothouse survives at the Dossin Great Lakes Museum on Belle Isle in Detroit. All of the remaining triple-A boats, except the *Mauthe,* have been lengthened and converted to self-unloaders, which has allowed them to remain viable. The triple-A, or AAA, designation by which all ships in the class are known was actually an accounting code assigned by Pittsburgh Steamship to the three boats they had from the class, the *Anderson, Callaway,* and the *Philip R. Clarke.* In those days, captains and chief engineers were paid at varying rates, depending on the size of their ship and the type of propulsion system used. The bean counters in the fleet's accounting department devised a coding system that covered all the possibilities. It's interesting that the triple-A label eventually came to refer to any ship in the class, regardless of which fleet owned it. The class probably should have rightfully been known as the *Anderson*-class, since the *Arthur M. Anderson* was the first of the boats to be launched. Nonetheless, they're triple-A boats and triple-A boats they shall remain.

The latest scuttlebutt is that Captain Dick Sobeck is coming over here around the middle of the month, making the switch from his current berth on the *Sloan.* Almost everyone aboard sees that as an improvement over the current captain, but many crewmembers noted that Dick can be temperamental. "He's completely fair, though," one of the guys added. "He's just as likely to holler at an engineer, or the cook, as someone from the deck department."

Like many of us, Dick is known to indulge in a little screaming and hollering if things don't go right. That's not unusual out here. Few sailors have any training in today's "human resources management" techniques. I'm not sure they'd work out here anyway. Haphazard employees seem to advance just as far and as rapidly as those who are highly motivated and achievement-oriented. Advancements are always a matter of seniority, and the shipping companies and crews aboard the ships seem unusually tolerant of sailors who do lousy jobs. I'm not sure there are any rewards for those whose performances exceed expectations.

Wednesday, August 7
Lake Michigan, Downbound

Welcome to the *M/V Sauna*. Whew! It's hot and humid, and it gets worse the farther down the lake we go. It's 6:00 P.M. and the temperature in Chicago is still 101 degrees. I surpassed that about 3:30 this afternoon. It was 106 degrees near the stove when I was preparing supper. Fortunately, I got things done quickly and turned the ovens and burners off. Once that was done, the temperature dropped to a mere 96 degrees. With the humidity, though, the 10-degree drop in temperature made little difference. As soon as supper was over, I stripped down and took a long, cool shower. What a treat. I actually feel human again.

Thunderstorms are predicted for this evening, which will supposedly drop the humidity to a more bearable level. We're *very* lucky that we're going into Gary and Chicago at night. If we'd been in there this afternoon, we may have all expired from heat stroke.

We got a fax today from the Lake Carriers' Association, the trade organization that represents almost all of the U.S. shipping companies on the lakes, warning the shipping companies and shipboard personnel about expired merchant marine documents. Our captain decided that he would check the cards of everyone in the crew to make sure they were still valid. He started with First Mate Jerry Macks, who was on watch in the pilothouse at the time. Wouldn't you know it, Jerry's seaman's card has expired. Now he'll probably have to get off until he can get the card renewed, a process that reportedly takes two to three months. Jerry's going to get a lot of flak about this and it could prove an expensive oversight on his part if the Coast Guard makes him stay on the beach until he gets a new card.

The thunderstorms just struck and they're doozies! I fled my cabin because the rain was being driven through my screen door and halfway across the room. With the deluge coming down, there was no way I could go out to close the watertight door. My carpet and the foot end of my bed are soaked, even though the rain only lasted about five minutes. I retreated to the messroom, where one of the guys was having a late supper. He said that Ron "Pootzer" Buczkowski, our third mate, left the messroom just long enough to get about halfway up the deck before the rain started. He must have gotten soaked to the skin. With the amount of water rushing down the deck, he's lucky he didn't get washed overboard.

It's quit raining where we are, but I still hear thunder all around us. We're probably in for more before the sun sets. If it helps get the humidity down, let it come.

I just talked with Frankie Bruski, the 4-to-8 watchman. Frankie was up in the pilothouse when the thunderstorm struck. He said that although it was dead calm before the squall line hit us, the winds increased to fifty miles an hour with some gusts as high as sixty-five miles an hour after the storm began. I believe it. The wind blew in through my door with such force it was almost impossible for me to pull the door open on the other side of the room. For a couple of seconds, I thought I was trapped. I've partly closed the watertight door to my room now, just in case we get a second storm.

Several people were caught out in the rain. The chief's wife and Booger were standing back on the fantail when it started. Although their rooms were only about one hundred feet away, they were both thoroughly drenched by the time they got inside. My carpet's still pretty wet, but my damp bedding is drying quite nicely, thanks to a fan blowing directly on it.

Tomorrow's my birthday. I'll have to try to remember to call my mother and the kids so they can wish me a happy birthday. It will be a year ago tomorrow when I turned fifty that I decided to leave The Homestead and return to the boats.

Last year, I was supposed to have my birthday off (and it would have been the first day I'd had off in about a month) but someone didn't show for the opening shift and I got an emergency telephone call at 7:00 A.M. I went into work and found the store an absolute disaster. By the looks of things, you would have thought the two people who were working had just started that day. That whole situation pushed my stress level past the breaking point. Later, during that awful day, I called the union and registered to go back to work on the boats. Over the next month, I moved out of the place I had been living for the previous eight years, stored most of my possessions in my mother's basement, and shipped out as steward on the *Edwin H. Gott.*

Turning fifty was traumatic for me. I suddenly felt old, and I was totally dissatisfied with the lifestyle I was leading, particularly my job at The Homestead. Hell, my job at the resort *was* my life. All I did last summer was work and sleep, although I occasionally had to deprive myself of needed sleep in order to wash my dirty clothes. Some life! Before I worked at The Homestead, I completed the research for *Graveyard of the Lakes* and wrote the first couple chapters. In the sixteen months that I was at The Homestead, I did not write one additional word. There was never any time for luxuries like writing, reading, or taking a drive to one of my favorite haunts, such as Frankfort or Harbor Springs. The day I turned fifty, I decided to take charge of my life again. In less than thirty days I was back on the boats. Now, just a year later, *Graveyard of the Lakes* is almost finished, this book is a third done, and I hope to begin work on a historical novel when I get off the boats this winter. I'm also financially comfortable again; I suppose that's a big factor in my current satisfaction level. I was just getting by when I was at The Homestead, and there was little prospect of any significant pay increases or having the company provide any fringe benefits, such as insurance. When you hit fifty and you don't have any health insurance, it really wakes you up . . . or shakes you up.

Thursday, August 8

My Birthday

Lake Michigan, Upbound

A birthday on the boats isn't much different than any other day. The chief's wife put up a Happy Birthday sign in the galley, and most of the guys commented on the passing of another year, but that was about it. I managed to get through to my mother and Scott on the cellular phone, but I haven't gotten in touch with Meredith yet. I'll try again later, but she's probably working late this evening at the Traverse City restaurant where she waitresses in the summer. I'll talk to her in the next couple days, since her birthday is on the twelfth. She already has her birthday gift and a card from me, but I know she always waits to hear from me on her special day.

We lucked out on the weather. Both the temperature and humidity are down considerably today, and it's a good thing, too. We were delayed at the KCBX coal terminal in South Chicago and didn't get away from the dock until about noon. By then the boat was starting to heat up. We cooled off as soon as we got out onto the lake, though, and the temperature's supposed to drop even more once we head up toward the top of the lake.

We should pass through the Pine River channel at Char-levoix at around 8:00 tomorrow morning on our way to the power plant at Advance, near Boyne City; it will be about 4:00 P.M. when we leave. Both would be good times for us

Deckhands Frank Bruski and Tom Flanner use a heaving line to pull one of the *Calcite II*'s steel mooring cables ashore at U.S. Steel's Gary Works in Gary, Indiana, while Third Mate Ron Buczkowski pays out cable from one of the boat's steam-powered mooring winches. (Author's collection)

154

to go out on deck and watch the tourists watching us. I'd love to see someone I know from Charlevoix! I haven't seen many of my Charlevoix friends in the past eight years.

After unloading on Lake Charlevoix, we're now scheduled to load limestone at Stoneport. I'm afraid we're going to be in there early Saturday morning, however, so it's doubtful that I'll be able to get home, even though my car is parked on the dock there. No sense fretting, though. We're a long way from Stoneport, and we could easily take some delays yet.

Friday, August 9
Lake Charlevoix

What a glorious summer day! It got up to a high of eighty, but there's no humidity, and it's as pleasant as a day in Hawaii.

We entered the Pine River Channel at Charlevoix at about 12:30 this afternoon; I spent the hour it took us to get through to Lake Charlevoix out on deck in the sunshine. There were several hundred people lining the banks of the channel when we went through, and they were an interested and friendly lot. The *Calcite II* and crew will star in many vacation videos. Anticipating a lot of kids would be present along the channel, Ron Buczkowski and some of the guys from the forward end went up the street yesterday and bought a bunch of candy bars and suckers. As we moved slowly through the channel today, they tossed the treats to kids along the banks. Last time we went through they didn't have any candy, so they tossed ice cream bars from the night lunch! We'll be going back through the channel at about 8:00 tonight, so I hope they've got some candy left. I'm sure there'll be a big crowd on hand, particularly since it's Friday evening and many tourists will be wandering the shop-lined streets of "Charlevoix the Beautiful."

I still haven't seen a single familiar face on our trips through Charlevoix. That's a little disappointing. Many of

Crewmembers on the *Calcite II* watch the tourists watching them as the ship enters the Pine River channel at the popular resort community of Charlevoix, Michigan. During the summer months, thousands of tourists and local residents line the riverbanks to watch ships slowly work their way through the narrow channel that connects lake Michigan to Lake Charlevoix. The *Calcite II* was carrying coal for a power plant on Lake Charlevoix. (Author's collection)

the locals steer clear of downtown Charlevoix during the summer because it's so crowded with tourists.

We got a revised itinerary this afternoon, and everyone's pretty excited. It has us making four trips from Calcite to Detroit, and one from Stoneport to Saginaw. If those orders hold, we'll be in Calcite about every two and a half days over the next two weeks. By then the crew will be a complete wreck from lack of sleep. They'll be thankful if we get a long trip over to Lake Michigan or a stone and coal run to Lake Erie.

It's really cooling off outside, and a stout wind kicked up. If it doesn't die down shortly, I doubt the captain will attempt to run out through the channel. We could stay tied up here at the power plant, or we could sail over to Charlevoix and anchor off the end of the channel, like we did the last time we were here. A delay would be great, because without one

156

we're going to get into Calcite at 6:00 A.M., and I'm not going to have a chance to go up the street. A couple hours delay, though, and I'll be able to run up between lunch and dinner.

Saturday, August 10
Straits of Mackinac

Another fabulous day on the northern lakes. The weather was absolutely perfect and we docked at Calcite from 8:30 A.M. until 3:00 P.M. I went up the street for about an hour in the morning and for another two hours in the afternoon. It was great to get away from the boat for a little while. I didn't do anything significant, but I managed to get three rolls of film developed, wash several weeks' accumulated limestone dust off my brother's pickup that's parked at Calcite, chat briefly with an old friend who works at the Rogers City Post Office, buy some zucchini to make Italian sausage soup, talk to my brother on the phone for awhile, mail some catalogs and magazines to him care of the mail boat, and pick up my mail from my mother. I didn't do anything exciting, mind you, but it goes into my log as a rather exceptional day.

When I walked into my mother's house this afternoon, she was talking to my brother on the phone. It's the first time I've been able to talk with him since he boarded the *Columbia Star*. He sounds as though he's adapted to life on a thousand-footer quite well, but he did complain a little about seldom having time to go up the street. He's sailing with a few old friends of his, and there are a number of guys on the boat who were there when I was second cook on the *C-Star* in July 1989. Phil Ketola, the steward I worked for, is back over there again. Phil's an old steamboat cook, with many years on the lakes, and I learned a great deal in the month I was with him. Gary's been out on the boats since late April and it sounds like he's ready for a vacation.

Unfortunately, it doesn't sound as though there are enough relief mates to go around, so he may have to wait awhile longer. It may work out that he'll spend the rest of the season on the *Star*. I think he'll appreciate working on a thousand-footer when the weather gets bad this fall. They ride much better in heavy seas than the smaller boats, much better.

I've spent a lot of time on thousand-footers, and I only remember one time when one actually rolled much. We started down Lake Michigan one fall on the *James R. Barker* and she began to roll pretty good. After about half an hour, Captain Bob Simmonds hauled her around and headed back to the Straits of Mackinac, where he dropped the hook until things settled down.

There was also a letter waiting at my mother's from Rick Covill, an engineer I sailed with last fall on the *Kinsman Enterprise*. Rick's from New Hampshire and sailed saltwater before taking a shore job at a mill in his hometown. He returned to sailing last year; the first boat he shipped on was the *Enterprise,* which is probably in worse condition than any boat in the U.S. fleet on the lakes. When Rick came aboard in Duluth, it was obvious that he wasn't too impressed with the old girl. I'm sure he wondered what he'd gotten himself into. Shortly after he came aboard we set sail across Lake Superior at the tail end of a strong November storm. Like the *Calcite II,* the rooms in the stern cabin on the *Enterprise* open onto the deck, rather than onto an interior hallway, as is the case in newer ships. It was bitterly cold and spray from the waves battering the hull blew against the cabin. When Rick tried to leave his room, he found the watertight door had frozen shut. He banged on the door and threw his weight against it, but couldn't get out of his room until the oiler came around to call the watch and pried the door open from the outside. What an ignominious beginning to his stint on the *Enterprise!*

Rick's soft-spoken with a wry New England sense of humor that he often employs to liven his comments about the goings-on aboard the ship. He's a delight to sail with and we became good friends in the month we spent together. We wrote each other several times during the winter. I sent him a copy of *Steamboats and Sailors* and a Great Lakes navigational chart so he could show his children the places we went on the lakes. I hadn't heard from him since the three-week hiatus I had in May. At that time, Rick was on the *Kinsman Independent.* When I wrote back, I encouraged him to try to get on with one of the other fleets on the lakes, particularly the Great Lakes Fleet. Rick went on our *Arthur M. Anderson* on June 1, and it looks as though he's going to be there until the end of the season. I wish I'd known that earlier, because a week ago both our boats were at Calcite at the same time. In fact, I walked past the *Anderson* on my way back to the *Calcite II* at about one in the morning, not knowing that Rick was on watch in the engine room. The *Anderson* also passed us in the Straits of Mackinac on our last trip down Lake Michigan. From here on out, I'll keep a watch for the *Anderson*. It'd be great to talk to Rick, even just to wave to him in passing. If he stays with our fleet, though, it's likely we'll eventually sail together again.

Sunday, August 11
Lake Michigan, Downbound

I forgot to mention that our orders got changed just before we got to Calcite yesterday. We're picking up a trip that was scheduled for the *George A. Sloan*, taking a load of stone to Buffington, near Gary, Indiana. We should be there just after midnight. After unloading, we'll slide over to the KCBX coal terminal at South Chicago to load petroleum coke for National Steel at Detroit. It's a good thing I took on some extra milk when we were in Rogers City, or the cow would have run dry long before we returned to Calcite. We already know we're going to have a delay at South Chicago. A boat will be loading at the coal terminal when we get there about 6:00 A.M. tomorrow, so it's going to be about 2:00 P.M. before we slide under the loader. Fortunately, the weather is relatively cool, because a boat really cooks when it's sitting in the Calumet River. I've got my fingers crossed that this cool spell holds for the next twenty-four hours.

Al Gapczynski, who came on at Calcite as captain, says he'll only be here "until we get to the next stone dock." Ed Brege is now scheduled to come over as our permanent captain; he'll board the next time we're at Stoneport, Calcite, or Cedarville, in about five days. Ed is the brother of Tom Brege, our first assistant engineer, and he's popular with those who have sailed with him before. That includes nearly

159

everyone on the boat except me. I don't think I've heard a single bad word about him.

Tom and the chief engineer spoke of his appetite for fresh fruits and vegetables at dinner tonight, and I hope we'll be able to get a load of supplies before Ed comes aboard. If not, he might be a little unhappy. I cooked two quarts of fresh green beans for dinner, booty from the chief's garden. Tom laughed and said that Ed could eat that many himself. He's apparently also addicted to oranges, and the chief said he's seen Ed take a ten-pound bag of oranges to his room every day. With the scanty supply we have on hand, he'd only be able to do that for about two days before we ran out! With luck, we should be able to get groceries at the next stone dock. They'll be coming aboard at the same time as Ed, so he'll probably never know how totally unprepared the steward was for his arrival.

I got my birthday presents when I was at my mother's yesterday. She got me a pink, button-down collar shirt from Lands End, which I picked out of the catalog some time ago. Meredith and Scott got me two coffee mugs when they were in Chicago. I've collected mugs for quite a few years now, but only mugs with a special significance. These will remind me of the first vacation my two adult children took together. One is from Planet Hollywood, and the other is from the Hard Rock Cafe in Chicago, both key stops on Scott and Meredith's vacation itinerary. They're nice additions to my collection.

My mother talked me into taking a Lands End sale catalog back to the boat with me. I almost didn't take it, since there really isn't anything I need right now. Thumbing through it, though, I found a winter parka that will be a perfect replacement for the Lands End parka I've been wearing the past six or seven years. It looks a little shabby these days, probably only suited to be worn on the boat. I got myself a great-looking parka at a great pre-winter price. You can't beat that. I called my order in on the cellular pay phone last night, so my parka will probably be waiting the next time we get to Rogers City.

I've been using the cellular pay phone quite a bit this year, even though it costs about $3.50 a minute. When we're in port, I don't always have time to walk to a telephone ashore, so if I need to call my mother or the kids, I generally use the cell phone, which is located in the emergency generator room next to the galley. Most of the time, I try to keep my calls short; so far the highest billing I've had for a call was just over twelve dollars. That's not bad.

Most U.S. boats on the lakes are equipped with cellular pay phones, installed by a company in Cleveland. The caller activates the phone by sliding a major credit card through a magnetic reader and the cost of the call is charged to the credit card. I figure that since I don't make a lot of calls and because I'm usually disciplined enough to keep my calls short, using the pay phone is cheaper than using my own cellular phone. I bought one four or five years ago, when the kids were in school and it was often difficult to get hold of them. If we were in port during the day, they were in school. By having my own cell phone, I could call them in the early evening, when I was most likely to catch them. I had the phone deactivated the year I didn't sail, and I've been reluctant to get it turned back on. I just don't make that many calls anymore, and when I have to contact someone, I use the pay phone. I'll probably use it tomorrow to call Meredith and wish her happy birthday. My little girl's turning 21.

Monday, August 12
South Chicago, Illinois

Too hot! It got up to 115 degrees in the galley while I cooked dinner tonight. That drains your energy pretty fast. It's cooling off outside, though, so it may be okay by bedtime. The problem is that we've been sitting here at the coal dock since early this morning, waiting for Interlake's *Charles M. Beeghly* to finish loading coal. When she departed about 3:00 P.M., we shifted under the loader and started taking on our cargo of petroleum coke at 4:00. It'll probably be midnight before we're finished loading.

I saw a few people I knew on the *Beeghly*, though I found it difficult to remember their names. As the "*Beagle*" backed out past us, one of the mates walked over to the ship's side and yelled hello, but I didn't recognize him. My eyesight isn't that great, and he wore sunglasses and a hard hat. Scott Briggs, the captain of the *Beeghly*, came out on the bridge wing to chat for a couple of seconds when they were abreast of our fantail where I was standing. Scotty and I sailed together a lot over the years on half a dozen different boats.

The *Beeghly*'s stern was only about twenty feet from our stern, so we got a good look at her. She's one of two Interlake boats that I never sailed on. Mike "Redneck" Westbrook, our second mate, and I talked about how the *Beeghly* originally launched as the *Shenango II* for the now defunct Shenango Furnace Company's fleet. Mike noticed that there was some paint scraped off the side of her rust-red hull and some green paint showed through. The Shenango boats all boasted dark green hulls, so the green paint undoubtedly goes back a few years. The fleet folded in the late 1960s and most of the boats were picked up by other companies.

The Shenango boats were always a little special. They were built with a lot of frills normally left off freighters on the lakes in the name of economy. At least one of their ships—the *Wilpen*—featured a pipe organ in the passen-

Medusa Cement's *Medusa Challenger* was built in 1906, giving her the dubious honor of being the oldest operating vessel on the lakes during the 1996 season. Seen here on the busy Calumet River near Chicago, the *Challenger* hauls cement from the company's plant at Charlevoix, Michigan, to terminals around the lakes. Launched originally as the straight-deck bulk freighter *William P. Snyder* for the Shenango Furnace Company's fleet, the ship was converted to carry cement in 1967. (Author's collection)

ger quarters, and the *William P. Snyder, Jr.* displayed a beautiful fireplace in its passenger quarters. Two of the old Shenango boats still sail: the *Beeghly* and the *William P. Snyder*, which operates today as the *Medusa Challenger*, carrying cement for Medusa Cement of Charlevoix, Michigan. While the *Beeghly* is a fairly new boat, built in 1959, the *Challenger*, née *Snyder, Jr.*, dates back to 1906, making her the oldest U.S. boat operating on the lakes. Her hull is painted grey now, but if you scraped off enough layers of paint, you'd probably find some of the original Shenango green on her.

Coming into the Calumet River this morning, we passed the *Captain Georgi Georgiev*, a Russian freighter, at one of the docks that handles general cargo. Her stack was brightly painted, but the rest of her hull looked pretty shabby, with lots of peeling paint and rust. That's unusual, or at least it used to be unusual. Whenever Soviet ships came into the capitalist lakes, they were always immaculate. The *Georgiev* is the second former Soviet ship I've seen lately that appeared poorly cared for, a commentary no doubt on the present financial condition of the former Soviet republics. Heck, the *Georgiev* looked even worse than the *Calcite II*.

I sailed a few years ago with Paul Cojocaru, an oiler who defected from a Rumanian ship. He had been a chief engineer in the Rumanian merchant marine, one of the largest in the world. While his ship was docked on the East Coast, he walked off and flew to Cleveland, where he stayed with friends. There he applied for political asylum. After the Soviet empire crumbled, Paul said that Soviet bloc freighters were stranded all over the world, left without funds to purchase fuel and supplies or pay their crews. It wasn't even clear who owned the ships, as their titles were often disputed by the various republics.

There's another relic of a bygone era sitting in a slip just astern of us—the *Milwaukee Clipper*. I don't know much about her, other than she was a cruise ship on the lakes and may have run between Milwaukee and Chicago on day trips. That trade ceased to exist after everyone got automobiles. Despite continued attempts to resurrect some sort of service for the *Clipper*, she languishes at her berth on the Calumet River. She looks out of place here. Sporting what appears to be a new blue-and-white paint job, she is a pristine oasis of gentility amid the blue-collar dirt and debris of docks, steel mills, coal terminals, and scrap yards. She, too, will be cloaked in a grimy layer of dirt before long, and look as tired and run down as everything else along this industrial ditch.

I must write up a grocery order to fax into the Soo, but it's just too hot tonight. Maybe first thing in the morning.

Tuesday, August 13
Lake Michigan, Upbound

Well, we're temporarily back up in God's Country, and it's cool again. We left South Chicago about 1:00 A.M., and it was still a little warm and sticky until early afternoon. Now we're up near the Traverse City area, and the weather's perfect. Unfortunately, this is probably only a brief respite. We're on our way to Detroit, so by this time tomorrow, there's a good chance the temperature will start to creep up again.

I started the day by getting my least favorite task out of the way—my grocery order. It took me an hour and a half, and I was exhausted by the time I was finished. It was my longest grocery order ever, running to six and a half pages. I don't think the dollar value of the order will necessarily be that high, though, because I didn't order that much meat. What I did order is lots of fresh fruits and vegetables. This is the time of the year to purchase them, and the crew never seems to get enough.

Wednesday, August 14
Lake Huron, Downbound

We passed Rogers City at about 8:00 A.M. today, and should be at the headwaters of the St. Clair River at 8:00 this evening. We'll be at Detroit at 5:00 or 6:00 tomorrow morning. We're unloading on the back side of Zug Island, in a rather remote area of the National Steel complex. I was in there once on the *Herbert C. Jackson*, and I remember that we tied up to a clump of trees. We sure don't get to many nice docks.

There was another minor fire on the boat today. They were swinging the boom over the side to run off stone that spilled during our last unload and an electrical panel started on fire when a breaker stuck. Someone carelessly stowed a tarp above the electrical panel, and it caught fire from sparks from the malfunctioning breaker. Fortunately, the guys working in the area quickly put the fire out. Interestingly, both of the fires we've had occurred on the 12-to-4 watch. I'm beginning to think everyone on that watch should be sent to firefighting school, just to be safe.

This morning, the ship's four-thousand-gallon sewage tank, located in the bow, began to act up. Guys on their way down to clean the unloading tunnel noticed it was giving off foul fumes, and evil-looking bubbles oozed out of one of the vents. The chief said someone put something like bleach or Sani-flush down their toilet that killed off the bacteria in the tank. The tank will continue to act up until the bacteria reestablish themselves and start working on the sewage. They halted the bubbling by flushing several cups of fuel oil down one of the toilets. I can't say I understand the chemistry of that procedure, but it worked.

When they have problems with the sewage tank, the guys living up forward suffer. The odor permeates every nook and cranny of the forward cabin. To say the odor is unpleasant is a serious understatement. Another advantage of living aft. We also don't have to listen to the deafening racket made by the unloading system when we're discharging cargo. On the other hand, we have the ship's powerful whistle right over our heads, and it can be rather annoying, especially when it's foggy outside and the thing is blasting every two minutes. It ruins a night's sleep. We also get quite a bit of vibration from the ship's propeller, though that's fairly constant. I seem to adjust to it quite easily. What I have trouble with is the steering gear, which is located almost directly below my room. Every time the wheel turns a little, I hear the big metal gears of the steering system going ka-chunk—ka-chunk—ka-chunk, ka-chunk, ka-chunk, ka-chunk. Whether in the rivers or maneuvering near a dock, the constant racket can drive you mad. It reminds me a lot of the noise made by helicopters passing overhead in Vietnam. That was a deep-throated whack, whack, whack

Oiler John Sobeck squirts a little lubricant on the *Calcite II*'s steering gear. The complicated steering motor and gears move the ship's massive rudder. (Author's collection)

sound that gradually faded into the distance. It was never quiet in Vietnam, and it's never quiet on a steamboat. This is not a good line of work for a light sleeper.

Rodney Altman, one of the senior wheelsmen on the boat, complained at supper tonight about the difficulty he has in picking something from the menu. "Too many good choices," he said. Such complaints always put a smile on the steward's face. Tonight's menu included crab and vegetables in Alfredo sauce served on fettucine, fried inch-thick pork chops, pork loin medallions in pecan cream sauce, and sauerbraten. Rodney's comment touched off a brief conversation among Rod and some of the other guys in the room about some of the stewards they've sailed with over the years. According to Rod, one cook he sailed with deep fried everything, including beef liver. Mike Westbrook mentioned a cook he was with boiled everything, including prime rib. It's amazing that crewmembers tolerate such poor cooking. You'd think they'd eventually send the so-called cook packing, or throw him over the side on some dark night out on the lake. I probably would. One of the guys asked if I used a cookbook, or if I had all my recipes memorized. I confessed that I refer to my cookbook for about half the dishes I prepare. I don't have the best memory, and I'm not about to try and memorize a couple hundred recipes. Heck, I still have to look up the four-digit PIN number for my ATM card. Anytime you see a cook coming aboard without a cookbook or two in his baggage, though, you're probably not going to be impressed with his cooking. That's been my experience. I've been with a couple cooks who never used a cookbook, and I still remember all the dishes they prepared. There weren't that many and they were repeated over and over and over again throughout the season.

Saturday, August 17

M/V *Edgar B. Speer*

St. Marys River, Upbound

Much has happened. Thursday afternoon, Fred Cummings, our fleet manager, called the boat to say that he was switching me with the steward on the 1,000-foot *Edgar B. Speer* so that I could cook for some VIP passengers who are coming aboard in a couple weeks. I got off at Calcite yesterday at noon, spent the night at my mother's, and boarded the *Speer* this afternoon via the *Ojibway*—the "grub boat" at the Soo. I'm not sure how long I'll be here.[13]

Yesterday morning, when the *Calcite II* was a couple hours out of Calcite, the captain called me up to his room and quizzed me about our porter. It seems that the porter went forward to straighten up the captain's room, and walked in on him as he was getting out of the shower. The captain was irate and told me he was going to call the office about firing him. About an hour and a half later, just as the boat slowed to go into Calcite, he called back to the galley and told me to fill out a separation form for the porter, discharging him "with cause." In other words, he was fired. I had the task of informing the porter that he was to pack his bags, which didn't break my heart at all.[14]

The porter's dismissal created an interesting situation. Since Bobby Bauer won't board the *C-II* until tomorrow, Booger was appointed acting steward for the trip from Calcite to Detroit and back. When he learned Thursday afternoon that he was going to have to fill in for me, he asked quite seriously, "How stupid can those guys in the office be, leaving *me* in charge?" With the porter's firing, Booger was going to serve as the second cook and porter as well as steward—the entire galley staff. Booger was already shook up at the prospect of having to do the cooking for two days,

---

[13]The *Speer* is actually 1,004 feet in length overall, with a beam of 105 feet. She was built at American Ship Building in Lorain, Ohio, in 1980. The *Speer* is powered by two V-18 diesel engines that produce a combined total of 19,260 horsepower, making her and her sister ship, the *Edwin H. Gott*, the most powerful vessels on the lakes. Most of the other thousand-footers have 14,000–16,000 horsepower. Like all the "footers," the *Speer* is driven by twin screws—twin propellers—that aid in maneuvering the big boat. The ship's namesake was a former president and chairman of the board of U.S. Steel. Speer died the year before the ship bearing his name went into service.

[14]The porter was eventually reinstated. Apparently you can't fire a guy for not being smart enough to stay out of the old man's bathroom while he's taking a shower.

The 1,004-foot *Edgar B. Speer,* moored on one of the approach piers to the Soo Locks, waits for the black railroad bridge ahead of it to be raised. Towering over the railroad bridge is the International Bridge, which links Sault Ste. Marie, Michigan, and Sault Ste. Marie, Ontario. Though there are four locks at the Soo, only the Poe Lock can accommodate thousand-footers like the *Speer.* (Author's collection)

but the thought that he was going to be in the galley alone was almost too much for him. Fortunately, the office found someone from Rogers City to join Booger in the galley. Unfortunately, because he had more seniority than Booger, he took the second cook's job, just when Booger was starting to crank out some great desserts.

My twenty-nine hours ashore was a pleasant interlude, though I had trouble sleeping in my own bed. Jimmy Atkins, who's still on vacation, rode with me to Stoneport so I could pick up my car. I spent the evening washing it and Gary's pickup, both of which were heavily coated with limestone dust. I arrived in the Soo about 11:00 A.M. today, which gave me a chance to do some shopping at the local Wal-Mart and some of the tourist shops down by the locks. I bought some new underwear and picked up a couple t-shirts.

I got aboard the boat just minutes before supper—steak and burgers—that Second Cook Tom Schroeder was beginning to prepare. I did a quick change into galley whites and pitched in. Because we were going through the Soo Locks

169

Porter Jake Gajewski takes a cigarette break on the *Speer's* stern while the ship is being lowered in the Poe Lock at Sault Ste. Marie, Michigan. Over Gajewski's head is a hoist used to lift groceries and supplies from the main deck to the poop deck, where the galley is located. (Author's collection)

and many of the crewmembers were busy, it was a slow supper, which was nice. I managed to handle things without much difficulty.

My porter is Jake Gajewski, from Cheboygan, the brother of an engineer I sailed with last year on the *Gott.* He seems to be a good soul, willing to do anything to help out. Tom's a bright guy, from near Ishpeming in the Upper Peninsula, and appears to be a cut above any of the second cooks I had on the *Calcite II.* Over here on the "red boats," the second cooks still consider themselves bakers.

After U.S. Steel bought Michigan Limestone and the Bradley fleet many years ago, the boats of the old Pittsburgh Steamship Company were referred to as the red boats because they had red hulls, the color of iron ore. The former Bradley vessels had grey hulls, the color of the limestone they hauled, and they began to be referred to as the grey boats. When Transtar bought the fleet from U.S. Steel, however, they painted all the hulls red, much to the chagrin of the Rogers City sailors. They also had diagonal stripes painted on the bows. One of those stripes is grey, continuing to some degree the Bradley fleet heritage. The other diagonal stripe is black, for no good reason, I suppose, other than it looked good with the grey and red.

Sunday, August 18

Entering Two Harbors, Minnesota

I haven't been to Two Harbors, or any place on Lake Superior, since the *Calcite II*'s first trip of the season. It's good to see the rocky Minnesota shoreline again.

Today was a typical first day on a boat. I spent a lot of time trying to find things. I wasn't particularly pleased with what the regular steward left me to work with. We definitely cook differently. For supper tonight, he left out Cornish hens and chicken, which is a slight overkill on the poultry. I oven fried the chicken, and it went well, but Cornish hens aren't that popular on the boats. Too much work for too little reward, I suspect. Fortunately, they went over well with our passengers—the wife and three young children of one of our engineers, John Boutin, our fleet's hull engineer, his wife Sue, and their son. John's as much of a boat buff as I am. While we waited for the *Speer* to arrive at the Soo we discussed various aspects of the history of the industry.

The Boutins are getting off here at Two Harbors, and one of the secretaries from the office and two of her friends will join us to ride as far as the Soo, where the engineer's wife and children will also leave. We'll enjoy a respite from passengers until about August 30, when we have a group coming on that the office wants to impress. These people paid about six thousand dollars at a fund-raising auction in Duluth to purchase a trip on the *Speer*. I'm not sure how many people will be in the group, but six thousand dollars is a lot to pay and the company wants to make sure they leave the ship feeling they got their money's worth. Much of that responsibility will be mine. I've been told I can buy *anything* I want in the way of groceries for their trip.

I discovered that I know three of the crewmembers here on the *Speer.* Tom Prince, the engineer who has his family aboard, was at the Great Lakes Maritime Academy when I worked there—I probably admitted him. Another engineer was a cadet on the *George A. Stinson* when I cooked there and Cam Nelson, an oiler, is the son of Herb Nelson, who was dispatcher for our union for many years. Cam first sailed as a deckhand and member of the roving conveyor crew on the *James R. Barker* when I was second cook there. He was straight out of high school and quit after a short time because he missed his girlfriend and his car. While he was on the *Barker* he was a prodigious eater of chocolate chip cookies, to the point that I baked a double batch virtually every day. I suspect he still likes cookies, among other things, because he's gained about seventy-five pounds in the six or seven years since I last saw him. He's now the spitting image of his dad.

This is a marvelous ship, virtually a twin to the *Gott.* While I'm here I want to explore the ship from one end to the other.

Tuesday, August 20

St. Marys River

The Boutins got off at Two Harbors and Margy Kruger, secretary to the president of USS Great Lakes Fleet, came on for a short trip with two of her friends, Dianne Isaacson and Joan Burke. Margy has been with the fleet for thirty years, beginning as secretary to Bill Ransom, an old friend of mine from Rogers City. She's on her third corporate president now, an indication of her amazing staying power. She's a pretty redhead, both intelligent and perceptive, and has a great sense of humor. Like me, she's been divorced for many years. When the guys from the 4-to-8 watch back on the *Calcite II* put together a list of women I should check out, Margy was on it. Now that I've met her, I think the guys were right on target. I spent a couple of hours talking with her and her friends last evening, and that led to her asking me to call when I get to Duluth—if I get to Duluth. It would

172

be nice to be able to get to know her better, but since she's in Duluth and I'm in Rogers City, that's going to be difficult.

Margy and her friends got off the *Speer* at the supply boat this morning, and were going to board the *John G. Munson* a few hours later to make the trip back to Duluth. My cousin Jack is the chief engineer on the *Munson;* I hope he'll put in a good word for me with Margy.

When I first met Margy, I kidded her about being a plant from the office, sent to see if my cooking was any good. She denied it, of course, but yesterday she got a call from Fred Cummings, the fleet manager. She later admitted to me that the first thing he asked her was if I could cook. She swears that she told him I was an excellent cook. I'm sure the office also questioned Captain Bill Craig about my performance. Since I haven't been on boats that get up to the Duluth

Captain Bill Craig of the *Edgar B. Speer* poses for a picture with Margy Kruger, longtime secretary to the president of the USS Great Lakes Fleet. Kruger and two friends made a trip aboard the *Speer* from Two Harbors, Minnesota, to Sault Ste. Marie, Michigan. Although none of the ships on the lakes carries paying passengers, many have "passenger quarters" that are available to fleet management personnel, important customers, and other VIPs. (Author's collection)

173

area, all they know about me is what they've heard from the captains of the ships I've been on. I know I've received good reviews from captains like Mike and Al Gapczynski, but it's almost as though the office doesn't believe that they accidentally hired a decent cook.

Margy's friend Dianne lives in New Orleans and works for a food service company that supplies restaurants. Her accounts include many of the top restaurants in the Crescent City, and she's offered to show me around when I get down there this winter. Another stroke of good luck.

I made pizza for supper tonight, and I think the crew was impressed. When the guys see the variety of pizzas I prepare, they almost go into shock. As steamboat pizza goes, mine is right up there.

Bill Craig, the captain of the *Speer,* is one of the finest I've sailed with. He's bright, soft-spoken, and every bit a gentleman as is Bob Simmonds, who was captain on the *James R. Barker* for many of the years I spent over there. We've been having a good time planning for the six passengers who will be boarding near the end of the month. Few captains are interested in such arrangements, and if they get involved, they've often got some pretty kitschy ideas, but Captain Craig's are very tasteful. When jobs on freighters were in short supply back in the 1980s, Bill worked for the Coast Guard in Cleveland as a liaison between the Coast Guard and the industry on aids to navigation. He knows my friend Captain Jim Wilson and many of the Coast Guard people I met in Cleveland through Jim. I understand why the people in the office want to send important passengers here. They'll be as impressed with Captain Craig's intellect and gentle personality as I am.[15]

I miss my friends on the *Calcite II,* and I sent them a postcard telling them that when we went through the Soo this morning. I've made friends with a couple of the guys here, a mate and deckhand who've been friendly. Some of the others are a little standoffish, but I hope they'll come around in time. I guess it's always like this when you go to a new boat. Some crewmembers will always stay at arm's

---

[15]I found out later that Captain Craig's nickname in the fleet is Wild Bill because he's known for having a bit of a temper.

length until they figure out whether you're a good cook and a good shipmate.

Wednesday, August 21
Gary, Indiana

Right after lunch today, we had the best fire drill I've ever participated in. There was supposedly a fire in the engine room paint locker. We broke out hoses and a fire team went down to the scene of the "blaze" with air packs on and full firefighting equipment. Everyone took the drill seriously. Afterward, we all got together and critiqued the exercise and discussed several problems that we will remedy next time around. The Coast Guard would have been impressed! It sure beat the "break out a hose and spray water into the lake" drills they have on almost all the other ships on the lakes. The next time we have a fire drill, the captain will have us evacuate someone from down below using a Stokes litter. That will be good training, because moving someone from the engine room or conveyor tunnel in a litter is not easy; it's something that must be done occasionally when someone is injured.

The first draft of the menu for the group of passengers who will be arriving later this month is finished. Captain Craig is reviewing it now. I'll try to finalize it on the way up the lake so I can put in a grocery order for any supplies I need. I think the menu is quite impressive, but I'll go over it a few more times before I'm satisfied. I imagine the captain will fax it into Fred Cummings at the office who, I'm sure, will be pleased with it. It's an eclectic menu, which I'll include here once I've finished it. I also want the second cook to take a look to see if he has more suggestions on desserts and salads.

One thing I miss here on the *Speer* is the freedom to go outside during the day to get some fresh air and see the sights. On the *Calcite II* you stepped out the galley door and you were on the main deck. The galley on the *Speer* is one deck up from the main deck, and if you go out the galley door you're on the fantail where all you see is what you've

175

Deckhand Frank Bruski leads crewmembers aft for one of the weekly fire and boat drills held on the *Calcite II*. The pro forma drills are required by the Coast Guard, but are generally regarded as a nuisance by crewmembers. (Author's collection)

left behind. The only window we have in the galley also faces aft, so we can't see if any ships are coming. I miss that, and haven't taken any pictures since I've been over here. I suppose I'll adjust in time.

Thursday, August 22
Lake Michigan, Upbound

We got out of Gary about 9:00 this morning and are heading up the hot and humid lake under threatening skies. There are severe storm warnings posted for the Grand Rapids, Michigan, area, so we may get rained on tonight.

My tentative menu for the Mark Johnson party that's coming on later this month is almost finished, and the captain has given it his blessing. I'll put off a grocery order when we go through the Soo tomorrow. I've ordered all the special things I need to cook for the group. It's going to be fun!

I forgot to mention that I had an interesting conversation with Captain Craig after breakfast yesterday. We talked about having guests aboard, and the captain expressed his disgust with the decor in the messroom and dining room and the ship in general. If the fleet spent more than $1.98 for decorating services, they paid too much. The decor is probably best described as outdated industrial. The walls are painted a hideous gold color that hasn't been popular since the boat was built in 1980; the messroom walls are "attractively" decorated with objets d'art, such as a station bill, Coast Guard documents, instructions on how to rig a breeches buoy, and a cheap calendar from Bartley's Sales and Service in Superior, Wisconsin, purveyors of sporting goods. The captain is embarrassed by the appearance of the messroom and dining room; if he wasn't just the relief captain, he'd make major changes.

Captain Craig also discussed at some length one of the senior officers in the fleet who is a known thief. He apparently hauls a lot of stuff off the boat all season long, which bothers Captain Craig immensely. I don't think Craig would knowingly take a number-two pencil off the boat. There seem to be quite a few thieves in the fleet. In the short time I've been here, I've heard about captains, chief engineers, assistant engineers, stewards, porters, and deckhands who regularly steal from the boats they're on. Captain Craig assumes the office is aware of what's happening, as they seem to be well-informed about the goings-on aboard the ships by crewmembers who call the office every chance they get, yet they have done nothing to stop the thefts. The whole

177

situation frustrates Captain Craig. I don't think I would steal anything off a ship he was on!

I'd like to write to Margy Kruger, but I'm not sure what to say. Maybe I'll just bide my time and see what develops.

Friday, August 23
Whitefish Bay, Upbound

We just passed the *Columbia Star*, but I didn't see any sign of Gary. He's on the 8-to-12 watch, and it's only about 6:45 P.M., so he's probably taking a nap or watching the news on television before going to work. I even tried to call him on the portable marine radio I've got with me, but there wasn't any answer. With us running down Lake Michigan and the *Star* always going down Lake Huron, I'm not likely to see much of him while I'm over here. I guess maybe I'll have to break down and write him a letter.

Speaking of letters, I wrote a short letter to Margy Kruger last night, and mailed it at the Soo when we went through there earlier this afternoon. I tried to keep it light and funny, but I did mention that the *Speer* never gets to Duluth and suggested that perhaps she'd like to drive up to Two Harbors some evening and have dinner with me. That's risky, I know, but it should clarify the situation. If she doesn't show, it'll be clear that she's not really interested and I'll back off. If she does show, we'll just have to see what happens. It would be nice to spend an evening in the company of an attractive woman with a good sense of humor. It's been about two years since I've done that. Yes, that's right, it's been two years since I've had a date! You see, the old story about a sailor having a girl in every port is just a myth. Sorry to disappoint you.

It's hard to develop or maintain a relationship with a woman while you're out here on the boats. Up until last year, when I was off the boats my life centered around Meredith and Scott. I felt bad that I was gone so much of the time, so when I was on vacation or off in the winters, I was at their beck and call. I spent my time with them rather than at places where I might meet a woman, although I did meet and date the mother of a hockey player whose team played

Scott's. If I did meet someone, it might be three to four months before I saw her again. Add to those difficulties the fact that many women simply aren't interested in getting involved with someone who is gone for more than half the year. The prospects of a sailor having a long-term relationship are pretty slim.

The biggest roadblock to meeting someone is probably my personality. I'm a little timid around women. It takes a real act of courage for me to ask someone out. I'm getting better, probably because I'm getting desperate.

The menu for the party of guests due later this month is finally finished. Here it is:

MENU
M/V Edgar B. Speer
USS Great Lakes Fleet, Inc.

The galley staff has developed the following menu for your trip aboard the *M/V Edgar B. Speer*. It would be helpful to us if you would take a few minutes at your earliest convenience and indicate your choices of luncheon and dinner entrees for each day of your stay. Following a tradition as old as the Great Lakes shipping industry itself, you may select more than one entree. When you've made your menu choices, please give this form to a member of the galley staff. Thank you.

FIRST DAY OF THE VOYAGE

Breakfast
German Apple Pancakes
(The following breakfast items will be available each day.)
Eggs or *Egg Beaters* to Order
Omelet
Egg Beater Omelet
Muffin with Egg, Cheese, and Canadian Bacon or Sausage
French Toast
Buttermilk Pancakes
Bluebcrry Pancakes
Fresh Fruit with Orange Butter
Breakfast Meats of the Day

Lunch
Salad
Cucumbers in Sweet & Sour Cream Sauce

Entrees
Spinach Quiche
Shrimp and Chicken Kabobs on Wild Rice
Steak Kabobs with Onion and Mushrooms on Wild Rice
with Peanut Sauce
Dessert
Raspberry Sorbet

Supper
Salad
Spinach Salad with Garlic Tomato Dressing
Soup
Cheese Soup in Brioche
Entrees
Tarragon Chicken on Fettucine
Barbecued Jumbo Pork Loin Chop à la Great Lakes Fleet
Side Dishes
American Fried Potatoes O'Brian
Steamed Cauliflower
Dessert
Bananas Foster

DAY 2 OF THE VOYAGE

Breakfast
Eggs Benedict

Lunch
Salad
Steamed Shrimp with Basil Vinaigrette Dressing
Entrees
Vegetarian Pizza on a Tortilla
Barbecued Chicken Breast Pizza on a Tortilla
Spinach Pie (*Spanikopita*)
Dessert
Athenian Rice Pudding

Supper
Salad
Fresh Garden Salad with Raspberry Vinaigrette
Soup
Seafood Bisque
Entrees
Orange Roughy Florentine
Pork Loin Medallions in Maple-Vinegar Sauce

Side Dishes
Broiled Stuffed Tomato
Caramel-Pecan Sweet Potatoes
Dessert
Raspberry Walnut Torte

DAY 3 OF THE VOYAGE

Breakfast
Crepes with Fresh Berries

Lunch
Salad
Crab Salad
Entrees
Almond Chicken Salad
Shrimp Creole on Rice
Dessert
Kiwi-Strawberry Tart

Supper
Salad
Antipasto
Soup
Minestrone
Entrees
Spinach Lasagna
Chicken in White Wine Sauce on Rice
Side Dishes
Sauteed Tomato, Zucchini & Onions with Parmesan Cheese
Dessert
Raspberry Fudge Cheesecake

DAY 4 OF THE VOYAGE

Breakfast
Ham and Egg Souffle

Lunch
Salad
Sockeye Salmon Salad
Entrees
Club Sandwich
Club Sub
Chef's Salad

181

Grilled Marinated Chicken Breast on Salad Greens
Dessert
Baklava

Supper
Salad
Greek Salad with Feta and Anchovies
Soup
Mulligatawny
Entrees
Broiled Lake Superior Whitefish with Cucumber Sauce
Broiled Whitefish Parmesan
Cajun Blackened Whitefish
Beef Burgundy on Rice
Side Dishes
Green Beans Almondine
Potatoes au Gratin
Dessert
Pineapple Meringue Torte

DAY 5 OF THE VOYAGE

Breakfast
Breakfast Burrito with Garlic Pepper Sauce

Lunch
Salad
Four Beans in Sweet & Sour Marinade
Entrees
Tomatoes Stuffed with Tuna Salad
Tomatoes Stuffed with Shrimp Salad
Chicken Breast Pastie with Provolone and Vegetables
Steak Pastie with Mushrooms and Onion
Dessert
Crème Brûlée

Supper
Salad
Broiled Tomatoes, Peppers, Onions,
and Provolone with Basil Vinaigrette
Soup
Gazpacho
Entrees
Pasta Primavera
Honey-Mustard Chicken Breasts

Side Dishes
Long Grain and Wild Rice and Steamed Asparagus
Dessert
Peanut Butter Pie with Hot Fudge Sauce

DAY 6 OF THE VOYAGE

Breakfast
Huevos Rancheros

Lunch
Salad
Peach and Pepper Salsa on Tortilla Chips
Entrees
Chicken Breast Fajita
Steak Fajita
Grilled Chicken Breast on Penne Pasta with Tomato Cream Sauce
Dessert
French Apple Bread Pudding with Hard Sauce

Supper
Appetizer
Shrimp Cocktail
Salad
Artichoke Hearts and Sea Scallops with Honey Dijon Vinaigrette
Soup
Cream of Fresh Mushroom Soup
Entrees
Grilled Marinated New York Strip Steak
Chicken Breasts with a Mélange
of Garden Vegetables in Puff Pastry
Side Dishes
Sauteed Mushrooms
Baked Acorn Squash
Baked Potato with Sour Cream
Dessert
Kahlua Cream Puff with Hot Fudge Sauce

The Galley Staff

M/V Edgar B. Speer

Mark Thompson
Steward

Tom Schroeder	Jake Gajewski	Ken Ehlers
Second Cook	Porter	Passenger Porter

I'm pleased with the menu. The guests coming aboard told the office that they preferred to eat light lunches and they weren't big on red meat. Given those limitations, I think I came up with a menu that is quite contemporary with interesting variations. For most meals, the crew will eat the same things as the guests, with a little red meat thrown in to keep them happy. I think I've served almost everything on the menu aboard ship at one time or another, so it's not as though I'm abandoning the cooking I normally do. I've built a lot of fruits and vegetables into the menu, because this time of the year we can get outstanding produce. The captain gave his blessing to the menu, but he didn't really say much about it. His only concern was whether I would be able to pull it off with the staff I have. I don't see any problem, particularly since I'll have an extra porter—a passenger porter—who can help to prep things, peel vegetables and the like. I will have to give Tom some help with the desserts, since all the dessert recipes are mine, ones I know will go over well with the guests.

We'll be in Two Harbors about 5:30 P.M. tomorrow, right at the end of the dinner hour. Those of us in the galley couldn't ask for a better time. I'm definitely going to go up the street. I've never gone up in Two Harbors before, so it should be interesting. It's a small town in a tourist area, so there ought to be some activity on a Saturday evening—and it even looks as though the weather is going to be superb. I'm trying to talk Jake, the porter, into going up with me. I don't think he goes up the street too much, but I'm sure we'll have a good time, even if we do nothing more than wander around Two Harbors.

Tomorrow afternoon will complete my first week on the *Speer*, and I have to admit the time has flown by. That tends to happen whenever you change ships. There are so many things to do and so many new things to get used to when you switch ships that the days fly by. Tomorrow I'll also complete three continuous months on the lakes. That's ninety-two workdays with only last Friday afternoon and Saturday morning off, ninety-one days of getting up at 5:30 A.M. and putting in ten to twelve hours in the galley. I started to burn out over on the *Calcite II*, but I seem to have found my second wind.

The crew seems to be warming up to me. Quite a few of

the guys stuck their heads in the galley to compliment me on dinner this evening. I prepared fish and chips, boiled cod with drawn butter, meatloaf, and Italian stuffed meatloaf. The Italian meatloaf, stuffed with slices of ham, pepperoni, and mozzarella cheese, always goes over well on the boats, though crewmembers are often reluctant to try it. I got lucky tonight. Cam "Camshaft" Nelson, who sailed with me a number of years ago on the *James R. Barker*, was the first person to eat—he chose the stuffed meatloaf and really liked it. I think he told some of the other guys how good it was when they came in to eat, which was all the encouragement they needed. Not a single person had the regular meatloaf, which is unusual. There are usually a couple of guys who refuse to try anything new.

The boiled cod went over much better than I had anticipated, probably because a lot of the guys on here are of Scandinavian heritage. I think the crew is starting to accept the fact that I'm a pretty good cook. A few even strike up a conversation with me if I happen to be taking a break in the messroom.

We got a fax today that we'll be getting a passenger porter by the name of K. Ehlers next trip. Nobody has heard of Mr. or Ms. K. Ehlers, so I've got my fingers crossed that it's somebody with a little bit of experience. This is no time to break in a new person when you have six important passengers aboard. I'm sure the office took that into consideration when they decided to send K. Ehlers over here (yeah, right).

Saturday, August 24

Two Harbors, Minnesota

We tied up here at the DM&IR ore dock at Two Harbors at about 6:30 P.M. on a beautiful summer evening. I took a shower after work and walked up town. It was a wonderful evening to get off the boat and go for a stroll, and my first time up the street in Two Harbors. I've been in here about half a dozen times before, but either the weather was bad or we were in during the day or night, so I never got off the boat. It seems to be a real nice town, not unlike Rogers City. Unfortunately, the only businesses that were open

185

were a few restaurants, the local Dairy Queen, and a couple of gas stations. That's surprising, given that Two Harbors is a tourist community and there were tourists wandering around. Maybe it's because the county fair is going on this week and all the locals are taking it in. Anyway, I walked to a Holiday gas station on the edge of town and picked up the couple things that I needed before leisurely walking back to the boat. I wanted to pick up a coffee mug to add to my collection and commemorate my first visit to Two Harbors, but all I could find was a chintzy-looking Minnesota mug that I didn't like. Maybe next time.

I called my mother from a pay phone while I wandered around town. Not much news from the Rogers City end, except that she forwarded some mail to me that I should

Even the 1,000-foot *Presque Isle* is dwarfed by the massive iron ore loading docks at Two Harbors, Minnesota. Though the *Presque Isle* looks similar to other thousand-footers that operate on the lakes, it is actually an integrated tug-barge. The tug is securely locked into a notch in the stern of the barge. The *Presque Isle* is owned by Litton Corporation, perhaps better known as a manufacturer of microwave ovens. Its "hailing port" is Los Angeles, California, headquarters for Litton. The diverse company at one time also owned a shipyard on the lakes. (Author's collection)

receive when we go through the Soo early Monday. I also tried to call Meredith and Scott, but both were working. Mer leaves for college at Western Michigan University tomorrow to start her senior year. She's waiting tables at Dills in Traverse City tonight for what may be the last time and then leaving early tomorrow. Early, by the way, has a totally different meaning for Meredith than it does for the rest of us. I'll bet she doesn't get on the road south until mid-afternoon. *That* is early for Mer.

Meredith's return to Western woke me up to the fact that summer is nearly over. Next weekend is Labor Day weekend, the end of the tourist season in the north country. Soon the trees around Lake Superior will turn colors and the viewing stands at the Soo Locks will empty out, except for a few senior citizens who travel in the fall to miss the crowds and take advantage of the end-of-season motel rates. I hate to see a summer pass without enjoying at least a little of it, but that won't happen this year. I came out sailing before Memorial Day, and I'll definitely be here until sometime after Labor Day, so I missed the summer of 1996. When you're out sailing, you're in a different dimension than the rest of the people on the planet. Months disappear from your life. All sorts of things happen back on the beach that you only hear about later. After I've been out here for awhile, I lose interest in what's happening in the world, except for important events, such as the bombing at the Olympics and the jet that crashed in the Everglades. Those are about the only things that happened this summer that piqued my interest.

I just wandered into the messroom and ended up having a rather extended conversation with John Dehring, Don's older brother. Don is a mate on the *Calcite II,* and a good friend of mine. John's currently the first assistant engineer over here and one of a growing number of Rogers City sailors who made the decision to sail on the big boats like the *Speer,* even though they never get into Calcite. John and Don's father, Pete Dehring, was a captain with this fleet; he retired off the *John G. Munson* a few years ago. Sailing is obviously a tradition in the Dehring family, and that's not unusual on the lakes. There was a time on the *James R. Barker* when we had a father-son team aboard. The father was a wheelsman and the son was a watchman. Al and Mike

187

Gapczynski, whom I sailed with on the *Calcite II* this year, are both relief captains and the sons of Art Gapczynski, a long-time steward with this fleet. Art's third son, Mark, was also on the *Calcite II* this year as a wiper and relief handyman. Tom Flanner, a young deckhand on the *Calcite II,* whom I often refer to as "the deck stud," is the son of an assistant engineer on our *Arthur M. Anderson.* It's common for one generation to follow another onto the boats, despite the hardships a sailor in the family causes. Sons who spend much of their early years without a father present at home still decide to become sailors. I think it's largely a matter of economics. If you want to live in Rogers City, for example, sailing is one of the few jobs available where you make good money.

Sunday, August 25
Lake Superior, Downbound

It's 8:15 A.M., and I'm killing time while the porter and second cook sweep and mop the galley and messroom. We had a heavier-than-usual breakfast crowd this morning. The deckhands were called out to work at 8 o'clock, so we had about ten people eat, two to three more than usual. Breakfast is my least favorite meal of the day. You don't get many people eating, but the minute you start working on something else and you're a mess up to your elbows, someone shows up and wants a couple of pancakes. I also get bored with the breakfast menu. There are only so many things you can do. I offer eggs, Egg Beaters, omelets, pancakes, French toast, several kinds of breakfast meats, and usually either egg-and-muffin sandwiches or a breakfast burrito. Once in awhile I'll also prepare sausage biscuits and gravy, but that's a heavy item and only a few people choose it. Every other day I make hash browns or fried potatoes, but only one or two crewmembers order them, so it's almost a waste of time.

Jerry Walls is aboard for the trip to Lorain. I'm not exactly sure what his title is, but I know he is responsible for safety in the fleet. He's a tall, slender, very preppy looking fellow who used to sail, though I don't know whether he was deck or engine. His wife went to Lake Superior State shortly after I left and Jerry knows a few of the faculty members with whom I taught.

At Lorain we'll anchor offshore and offload into a couple of our smaller boats that will haul the pellets up the Black River to U.S. Steel's mill. Thousand-footers can't make it up the river there. One of the guys said that the *Philip R. Clarke* and *Myron C. Taylor* will make the shuttle runs. The *Taylor* is a Rogers City boat, so I should know a few of the guys over there. The regular captain on the boat is Paul Dubbs, who lives down the street from my mother. Too bad it's not the *Calcite II* making the shuttle runs. That'd be fun. I'd probably have the whole crew over here on the *Speer* at meal hour.

It's after supper now, and I'm relaxing for awhile before I go back in the galley and pull the stuff out of the freezer that I'll need for meals tomorrow. I've also got to bag up my galley whites to send to the laundry at the Soo. Then my day is done at last.

Jerry Walls cornered me just before lunch and asked if I would write a short piece about galley sanitation for the fleet's October newsletter. Mark Malay, one of the other stewards, put a few ideas together and Jerry wanted me to add my thoughts to Mark's material and write a brief article. I finished it right after lunch and printed it out on my portable ink-jet printer so Jerry could fax it to the company that prints the newsletter. He showed me a photocopy of the September newsletter. It's got two pictures of Margy Kruger in it, modeling clothing with the fleet logo on it, but the photos didn't copy well and her face is just a black blob. From what I could see, it looks as if she's wearing her hair down in the photos; she pulled it back in something resembling a ponytail the whole time she was on the boat. I'll know more when the blasted newsletter comes out in a couple of weeks. She certainly has a lot going for her— brains, looks, and a pleasant personality are always an unbeatable combination. I'm intrigued by her and curious whether she'll respond to my note. It was a funny note, so I bet she will. We'll see.

Jerry Walls also told me that there's a flap brewing in Rogers City. Some company is auctioning marine artifacts, and they advertised the bell off the *Carl D. Bradley.* It's not the bell off the *Bradley* that sank in a November storm in Lake Michigan in 1958, but the original ship of that name. That boat was renamed the *John G. Munson,* and then renamed a third time after the current *Munson* was launched in the 1950s. It ended its career as the *Irvin L. Clymer,* scrapped a few years ago at Duluth. Throughout its years on the lakes, its bell was engraved *Carl D. Bradley.* That bell was stolen at some point as the boat sat idle in the frog pond at Rogers City, prior to being towed up to Duluth. Now, apparently, it has resurfaced. When one of our fleet's captains from Rogers City notified the office, they immediately contacted the sheriff's department and prosecuting attorney in Rogers City, asking for the return of their stolen bell. The bell is supposedly presently owned by a judge in the Rogers City area. I don't know who that could be, but he's likely to come out of this with egg on his face. The office, by the way, said they will donate the bell to a museum if it's returned. I'm going to suggest that the bell be donated to the historical museum in Rogers City, home to generations of sailors who crewed the ship. That's where it belongs and that's where it'll be most appreciated.

I found out yesterday that I'm sailing with my third shipmate who is a defector from the former Soviet bloc. Ziggy, one of our deckhands, walked off a Polish freighter eight years ago when it docked at Duluth, and asked for asylum in the U.S. A Polish mate named Stan on the *Gott* last fall did basically the same thing, though I can't remember which port he defected at. When I sailed with Interlake, we had an oiler named Paul Cojocaru, whom I mentioned before. Paul was a chief engineer in the Rumanian merchant marine before he defected. It's nice that defectors like Ziggy, Stan, and Paul found jobs on the Great Lakes. After all, many early sailors on the lakes came here from Europe to escape tyrannies similar to those that drove Ziggy, Stan, and Paul to take the drastic action of fleeing their homelands.

According to Jerry Walls, K. Ehlers, soon to be our passenger porter, has little or no experience in a galley. That doesn't come as good news to any of us. We'll have to make some adjustments in who does what around here. Jake already volunteered to make up the passenger quarters and keep the passenger lounge and pantry straightened up. That means the passenger porter will have to wash Jake's dishes so he has the time to go upstairs. Tom also said he's willing to play waiter for the passengers, if that will help out. It will. The captain feels that's a sound approach, but the overtime bill for Tom, Jake, and me will be staggering. That's okay as long as we get the job done and duly impress the passengers. We will.

We're in one of the television wastelands right now, between the tip of the Keweenaw Peninsula and Whitefish Bay. The only channel that's coming in is the public television station from Marquette and they're broadcasting a Lawrence Welk rerun. That's too exciting for me, so I guess I'll curl up with a book.

Monday, August 26
Lake Huron, Downbound

This has been an interminably long day. We received supplies when we went through the Soo at about 8:30 this morning, and that disrupted the entire day. Oh well, we'll get back on track tomorrow.

A thick priority mail packet from my brother was waiting for me at the Soo. (The locks are one of the two places we get mail— the other is the mail boat at Detroit.) Among the stuff Gary sent was an item in a trade publication about a recent coal fire aboard the Canadian *H. M. Griffith.* They loaded coal at the Superior Midwest Energy Terminal in Superior, Wisconsin, and headed down the lake. Before they got to Whitefish Point, they discovered smoke coming out of the hatch covers, a sure sign their cargo was on fire. When they got inside Whitefish Bay, they went to anchor and started up their self-unloading system so they could dump the burning coal into the lake. They apparently dumped about three thousand tons overboard. I guess the Michigan Department of Natural Resources is upset that the coal was dumped into their clean waters, and may fine the captain. I'm sure Canada Steamship Lines, which owns the *Griffith,* will be happy to pay any fine. It's better than having their ship go up in flames. Coal fires are notoriously hard to extinguish and they've claimed quite a few ships over the years. If the

Griffith hadn't been a self-unloader, it could have been in real trouble.

In his note Gary also said that the captain on the *Columbia Star* seems to have his sights set on breaking the cargo record for coal shipments from Lake Superior. The record of 70,600 net tons was set in 1986 . . . by the *Columbia Star*. Gary says that they keep carrying 100–200 tons more every trip, inching their way closer to the record. On their last trip they carried 69,525 net tons, departing the dock with a draft of 28 feet, 6 inches. When the record was set in 1986, they supposedly heaped coal 6 feet high over the hatch coamings, and then used deck hoses to rinse it down enough to get the hatch covers on. It's kind of a frivolous enterprise, but it's probably fun for the guys on the *C-Star*.

After we cleared the locks and headed down the St. Marys, we passed the *Columbia Star* heading back up to Superior. Gary was on watch at the time and he blew a whistle salute as they approached, before coming out on the bridge wing to wave as they passed. Our captain called down to the galley to let me know the *Star* was approaching, so I went down to the main deck with the hope I would get a chance to see Gary. I also tried to call him on the radio on channel nineteen, their shipboard working channel, but got no answer. Maybe next time I'll get to talk to him.

We're on our way to Lorain this trip, instead of our normal run to Gary. U.S. Steel and Kobe, a Japanese steelmaker, are partners in a steel mill on the Black River at Lorain, but this ship is too large to maneuver up the river. When we reach Lorain, we'll anchor offshore and transfer our cargo into smaller ships that will carry it up the river. There were supposed to be two boats available to shuttle the cargo, but today the only boat available is the *George A. Sloan*. The *Sloan* is a little puddle-jumper, and she carries only 12,000–13,000 tons in a load. Since we're carrying in excess of 60,000 gross tons (a gross tons, or long ton, is 2,200 pounds), it would take the *Sloan* five or six trips to unload us. That could take awhile. My guess is they'll locate a second ship before we get to Lorain.

I sailed on the *Sloan* briefly last fall and know most of the guys who are over there, so it'll be fun to have them alongside for awhile. It's a Rogers City boat, captained by Dick Sobeck, a shipmate of mine when I first started sailing on the *Calcite II* in 1968. When I was over on the *Sloan* last fall, they set the Great Lakes record for pizza consumption. The twenty-six crewmembers did away with sixteen large pizzas. Maybe I'll have pizza when they're alongside us. If the guys on the *Sloan* get wind of it, I'll bet they'll come scampering up the ladder like Eisenhower's troops assaulting the beaches at Normandy. The only problem is, I'm not sure I can make enough pizzas to feed the two crews.

Amazingly, today was my tenth day on the *Speer.* That doesn't seem possible. The pace here has been pretty frantic, with passengers every trip and much left to do yet before we get *the* passengers when we get back up to Two Harbors.

Tuesday, August 27

St. Clair River, Downbound

It's just after breakfast, and we're almost to Lake St. Clair. That'll put us into Lorain about 7:00 this evening. Jerry Walls and the captain checked the position reports for all our ships this morning; the only boat that can shuttle cargo for us is the *Sloan.* The first mate expects it will take at least seventy-two hours to transfer all the cargo using just the one small boat. That'll put us two and a half days behind schedule, which could mean that the passengers we've been planning for could end up taking a trip on the *Gott* instead. That'd take the cake, given all the work we've put into getting ready for them. It's too damp outside to paint today, so the captain has the deckhands scrubbing down the passenger quarters.

John Dehring told the guys here stories about the steward on the *Sloan.* He's known widely throughout the fleet for his somewhat inflated ego. He's a reasonably good cook, but he talks too much and is famous for sticking his nose where it's not needed or wanted. As a result, he's unpopular with the crews. The steward on the *Sloan* is one of those guys who generally serves specific entrees and vegetables on the same day each week. According to John, you know exactly what you're going to have before you even get to the messroom. One of our deckhands here also worked with the *Sloan*'s steward for awhile and said that they ran out of Kool-Aid

193

once, a real no-no on the small boats where it's hot most of the time. Not wanting to be ragged by the crew, the cook cleverly filled the Kool-Aid jug with banana popsicles that he melted down. The guys on the boat wouldn't have noticed, except several liked banana popsicles and were surprised to find the ship's supply had disappeared overnight. John figures as soon as we tie up next to the *Sloan*, the steward will be over to tell us what we're doing wrong.

It's early afternoon now, and we just finished our monthly safety meeting. Following an old tradition, we each received a dollar for attending the meeting. The topic for this meeting was about proper lifting techniques to prevent back injuries. It was particularly timely on this boat, because our handyman just got off in Two Harbors after he injured his back lifting a pump.

Back injuries are very common on the boats. Earlier this year, a deckhand on the *Calcite II* hurt his back putting the heavy steel cable stays on the self-unloading boom to prevent it from swinging loose if the boat rolled. The end of the cable that attaches to the boom is extremely heavy, and you have to lift it over your head to get it on. Occupational safety people say you should never lift heavy objects over your head, but on the boats it's a daily occurrence for many crewmembers.

Jerry Walls also talked a little about using safe proce-dures when handling mooring cables, since we'll have some strange mooring setups during the shuttle unload at Lorain. He mentioned the mate on the *Gott* who lost all eight fin-gers last year when he picked up a mooring cable that had dropped onto the deck and somehow the cable tightened up and pulled his hands through a fairlead—a sheave through which the cable runs. I went aboard the *Gott* just a trip or two after the accident had happened, and the crew was still very shook up about it.

Serious accidents like that aren't uncommon on the boats, unfortunately. Being a merchant seaman is a haz-ardous job, and always has been.

Falls are also common causes of injuries. Crewmen are up and down steep ladders all over the ship and at docks. In addition, members of the deck crew constantly work around open hatches. I already mentioned the deckhand on the *Kinsman Enterprise* who was killed when he fell into an open hatch while they were closing the hatch covers after unloading at Buffalo. Back in 1990 or 1991, a wheelsman fell into the cargo hold on the *Mesabi Miner* while the boat was tying up at the dock at Lorain. Fortunately for him, the hold was full of iron ore pellets, and he fell only about twenty feet, instead of the fifty he would have fallen if the hold had been empty. Even so, the guy was a physical and emotional wreck afterward. He was taken to the hospital right away, but returned to the ship several hours later to collect his gear. He suffered no permanent damage, thank God, but you could still see the impressions made by the marble-sized iron ore pellets in the side of his face. I'm sure he hurt for several days afterward and never again walked close to an open hatch. The crewman on the *Kinsman Enterprise* who was killed had been drinking prior to the accident; the guy on the *Miner* was talking to the mate on watch and didn't pay attention to where he was walking.

You'll also get some oddball accidents on the boats occasionally. I think it was on Christmas Eve 1989 when Jan Dean, a mate on the *Herbert C. Jackson*, suffered a painful spiral fracture of his leg while we were docking the boat at South Chicago to unload. It was brutally cold and snowing very heavily; Jan was out on deck giving the captain "distances off." He ducked into the forward cabin for a couple minutes to get warm, and then went back out on deck to stand along the railing to give the captain the distances between the ship and the dock. He turned abruptly to move farther aft, but one of his feet had frozen to the deck. As he twisted rapidly, his leg snapped. Apparently, the snow on his boots had melted when he went into the cabin and the water dripping from the boots froze to the deck while he stood there along the rail. It was a strange accident. To get him off the boat and into the waiting ambulance, we put him in the steel basket we used to lift groceries aboard the ship. He got banged around a little in the process of getting in and out of the basket, and you could see the agony on his face.

At fitout on the *Jackson* one spring, an engineer injured his leg when he tried to stop the massive jacking gear with a piece of pipe or a big wrench, I don't remember which. The wrench or pipe stuck in the gear, which made another revolution and whacked the careless engineer in the leg.

195

It hurt so much he was convinced his leg was broken, so I called an ambulance. The engineer was down in the lower level of the engine room, connected only to the main deck by extremely steep and narrow stairs. The EMTs were unsure about how they were going to get the guy out of the engine room. They finally strapped him in a Stokes litter, a basketlike stretcher, and carried him to the engine room gangway. We then used the grocery hoist to lift the basket up the side of the ship to the main deck. The injured guy dangled over the less-than-pristine waters of the Rouge River on the way up the side of the ship; if the litter had broken loose he'd probably have drowned. We carried him across the deck of the *Jackson*, lowered him down onto the deck of the *Lee A. Tregurtha* moored between us and the dock at Ford's Rouge Steel plant in Dearborn, Michigan. Once we got him across the *Tregurtha*, we used that ship's grocery hoist to lower him thirty or forty feet down to the dock. The whole process took several hours and the poor guy was in excruciating pain the entire time.

Quite a few years ago, my brother Gary fell while painting the unloading boom on one of *Columbia*'s ships and slammed his arm against the steel boom so hard he broke his wrist. The ship was on its way up Lake Michigan at the time, so they had a Coast Guard boat come out and take him off. It was a long time before they could get him to a hospital, and he was in agony every minute. He ended up with a bunch of evil-looking pins in his wrist and a long medical leave from the boat. Last fall, the *Middletown* was docking in Cleveland in a driving rainstorm and Gary stepped over one of the mooring cables, slipped and fell. He stuck out his arm to break the fall and broke it. That got him another eight or nine weeks of medical leave, and a growing reputation for being accident prone.

Coast Guard helicopters are also available to evacuate injured or ill crewmembers from ships if there are no other alternatives. The only medical evacuation I witnessed was when Chief Engineer Jerry Hassett was stabbed on the *James R. Barker*. We were on our way down Lake Michigan at the time in a blinding snowstorm and a chopper came out from the air station at Traverse City to take the chief off. They sent down a medical corpsman to stabilize the chief's condition, and then lowered a basket to lift him up to the

196

chopper hovering about a hundred feet above the deck. The chief later said that the trip from the deck up to the chopper was almost worse than his stab wounds.

I've only heard of one instance when a helicopter landed on the deck of a ship to take off a crewman. I can't remember the details anymore, but it involved either the *George A. Sloan* or the *Myron C. Taylor*. A crewman had to be medevaced, but the only Coast Guard chopper nearby wasn't equipped with a basket that could be lowered to the ship. Because of the urgency of the situation, the helicopter pilot decided to land on one of the ship's hatches. I assure you, that was an extremely dangerous venture. Hatch covers aren't that big and if the ship had rolled or a gust of wind come up as the chopper was setting down, it could easily have resulted in disaster for the crewmen aboard the Coast Guard rescue bird. A crewman I know who was on the ship supposedly got a picture of the chopper on the deck and I'm going to make a serious effort to get a copy. As I say, it's the only instance I know where a helicopter actually sat down on the deck of a freighter.

The latest word on the shuttle situation is that the *Calcite II* is on her way down Lake Huron to unload stone in Cleveland, and then she will come over and assist the *Sloan*. That's great news. It'll speed up the unloading process, at least a little, and I'll get to see the gang. If they're around at supper time, I'll definitely do pizza for them. It'll also mark a brief reunion for two brothers from Rogers City. John Dehring is the first assistant engineer on the *Speer*, while his brother Don is third mate on the *Calcite II*. They seldom see each other during the sailing season, but they should have at least a brief opportunity to catch up on family gossip while we're loading the *Calcite II*. Don was also one of my better customers on the *Calcite II*, and it wouldn't surprise me at all if he came over here looking for a free meal.

Well, it's now 8:00 P.M. and we're in the process of anchoring off Lorain, but there's no sign of the *Sloan*. She's apparently had some engine problems and is still at the dock in Cleveland. We haven't had any report on the nature of their difficulties, but we know that they tipped ship this afternoon. You tip ship in order to get the propeller and stern tube out of the water so you can examine them. You accomplish that by putting ballast water in the forward tanks to lower the bow in the water and raise the stern. We're on location and ready to start unloading, but we've got nothing to unload into. This could *really* be a long unload for us. I'm glad I've got lots of groceries on board.

Jerry Walls was looking for ideas for things he could put into the fleet's newsletter, so I suggested that he run a column on some of the crewmembers' hobbies. I mentioned several, including the fancy weaving that Tom Brege does on fishing poles, and the scale model boats that Tom Lanthier, our first mate, builds. He talked to several other crewmembers and decided it was a good idea, so he started collecting material for future issues of the newsletter by taking my picture in the galley with copies of my two books. I've posed with those books so many times that I think I'm going to start charging. They don't want to buy the books, just take pictures of me holding them! Cheapskates.

It's now 8:30 P.M. and we just got word that the *Sloan* has some sort of problem with the coupling that connects her engine and propeller shaft. It's serious and they'll have to call in a technician from the company that built the coupling. The latest word is that the *earliest* the *Sloan* can be over here to start taking on pellets is 3:00 P.M. tomorrow! I think the whole crew is in shock. Jerry Walls is quiet. He's seeing this whole charade from our standpoint rather than from the perspective of the office. Things that seem to make sense in the office in Duluth look pretty ridiculous to us out here on the ships. This is apparently one of those cases.

Wednesday, August 28

Conneaut, Ohio

Yup, Conneaut. About 9:00 last night, the traffic people from the office called and said they were going to scuttle their plans to shuttle our ore up the river at Lorain. Instead, we were ordered to head for Conneaut, the only dock on Lake Erie that we can unload at because of our shuttle boom. In order for us to unload, the dock must be equipped with a hopper within reach of our boom, and at the right height. There are only two of those, the dock here at Conneaut, and the one in Gary, Indiana. We arrived early this morning and started unloading around 8:00 A.M. The *Roger Blough* is supposed to be down here about 2:00 P.M., so they're going to be delayed until we finish our unload, which won't be until around 6:00 tonight. What a fiasco.

It's early evening now and we're headed back north. We cleared the dock at Conneaut at about 6:30 P.M., passing the *Blough* on our way out.

I was greatly relieved when they finished unloading and turned the conveyor system off. It's noisy in the stern cabin area and the constant roar of the system grates on your nerves after awhile. On this boat the housing for the loop belt elevator that carries ore from beneath the cargo hold up to a hopper that feeds the shuttle boom is actually tucked into the front of the cabin. As a result, it's loud when the machinery is running. The *Columbia Star* was built the same way and the room shared by the second cook and porter was directly adjacent to the loop belt casing. There were many nights when we unloaded that it was virtually impossible to sleep. On the Interlake thousand-footers like the *James R. Barker,* the loop belt casing is in front of the cabin, outside, so it's much quieter during unloads. The best arrangement from my viewpoint, is on the older self-unloaders, like the good old *Calcite II.* Since they have their self-unloading booms at the bow, there's no noise at all in the stern cabin during an unload. It's in the stern cabin, of course, that the galley is located as well as the steward's room.

The captain and I chatted in the messroom after dinner about how handy ATMs are. Our conversation was sparked by the fact that the first mate had posted a draw list for the unlicensed crewmembers. It's a long tradition that sailors can get a draw against their pay aboard ship. Most fleets let you get one twice a month, and you basically draw up to the total net earnings you have coming. A lot of guys will take a draw so that they have some spending money when they're in port. About the only time I ever took a draw was when I knew I was getting off the boat and might need some traveling money to get home. Now with ATMs, that's really not necessary anymore. It's easier to use an ATM than try and get a company draw check cashed in most places.

When I mentioned ATMs Captain Craig started to laugh. He said that when ATMs were still new, Jake, the guy who's now the captain on the *Blough*, told him how handy ATMs were. Speaking with a heavy Finnish accent, Jake told Bill, "I yust go to da machine wit my Sears card, and it give me money." "Your Sears card?" Bill asked. "You mean your Sears card works in ATM machines?" "Ya," said Captain Jake enthusiastically, "I put in my Sears card and I get da money." Bill thought that sounded a little strange, but he figured it must be true. Later, Bill approached an ATM machine with his own card to get some cash. While the machine was processing his withdrawal, Bill looked up and immediately started to laugh. There, over the machine, were the logos of all the various ATM systems, and prominent among them was Cirrus. "Ya," Bill thought to himself, "Jake uses a 'Sears' card in the ATM!"

Thursday, August 29
Detroit River, Upbound

It's just after breakfast and I've been run out of the galley so the porter and second cook can mop without me being in their way. Everybody seems a bit surly this morning, but I'm not sure why. Maybe it's the weather. There are patches of heavy fog in the river and the captain's got the engines checked down so much we're just inching along. I thought for a while during breakfast that I was having a nervous breakdown. Every time I looked out the stern window, I saw the Renaissance Center in downtown Detroit. That's pretty strange. I did a double take, not realizing that we're barely making any headway. When I glanced out a third time and we were still within sight of the RenCen, I got a little scared. I actually spent a few minutes trying to figure out what the heck was going on. It wasn't until the mate and wheelsman from the 4-to-8 watch came in for breakfast and I overheard them talking about being checked way down that I caught on to what was happening. My mind is still intact.

There was a big turnout for lunch, and I had Philly steak-and-cheddar subs. Making up twelve or fifteen of those, with a couple of ham and cheese and pastrami and cheese subs thrown in for good measure will keep you hopping, especially when you get half a dozen guys lined up at the window waiting to be served. The crew is served cafeteria style on this boat and on most other ships built since the early 1970s. On older boats, the porter waits on the unlicensed crewmembers eating in the messroom, and the second cook waits on the officers in the dining room. That's a pain and three hours of wasted time each day for the porter and second cook. That's one reason I liked the thousand-footers when I worked as a second cook. It gave me a lot more time to make desserts and salads.

We're now in a race with the *Middletown* to see who gets to Silver Bay, Minnesota, first. The *M-Town* is just ahead of us going up the St. Clair River, but she's supposed to stop at the Shell fuel dock at Sarnia to take on bunkers. We were planning to fuel there, too, but now we're just going to press on, hoping to get far enough ahead of the *Middletown* that she can't catch us. If she does, we may have a delay getting into the dock at Silver Bay. We're supposed to load two holds at Silver Bay, and then go on to Two Harbors to finish off the balance of the load. Normally, in a split load like that, they'd load first at Two Harbors, but some other boat is supposed to be in there and they didn't want us to take a delay, hence the decision to send us first to Silver Bay. If the *Middletown* passes us on Lake Huron or Lake Superior it will be a moot point—we'll end up with a delay at either dock.

I didn't get much of a break this afternoon. After lunch, I went out on deck for about half an hour. The weather was magnificent and there was a good deal of ship traffic on the St. Clair River. We were almost to the Detroit Edison plant between Marine City and St. Clair, and I thought maybe Gary's boat would be in there unloading. No dice, though. They may just be on their way down Lake Huron now, so we'll probably pass them sometime tonight. I did see Oglebay Norton's *Armco* and two salties—foreign ships that came into the lakes through the St. Lawrence Seaway— in the thirty minutes or so that I was out on deck. I got pictures of all three, and noticed one advantage of being on a thousand-footer: you're much higher up off the water, actually above the decks of most ships that pass. Because of that, you get a different perspective when you take photos. On the *Calcite II*, I usually looked up at every ship that passed, so all I got in the photo were the hull and cabins.

From the deck of the *Speer*, though, I looked down on the three passing ships and the photos I took will show their decks quite clearly. The photos I took from the *Calcite II* may be more dramatic, but the shots I took today give you a better overall view of the ships. Both types of shots have their place.

After my brief stint on deck, I headed back into the blasted galley to prepare pizza for supper. I had to make the dough and cut up all the meats and vegetables, and that's a major process. I took one fifteen-minute break around 2:00, but other than that I worked straight through until the dinner hour was over at 5:15. Today, I made fifteen pizzas, three of which were small ones. All the others were large or super size. That's out of the way for another week or ten days and I'm glad of it. My back is sore from leaning over the counter all afternoon. Now I need to wash a load of laundry. Isn't that just great? It would be so nice just to kick back and read or watch a little television and let my aging body recover from a hard day at the office. No such luck.

Saturday, August 31

North Shore, Lake Superior

Well, our long-expected passengers are finally aboard. Mark Johnson, Deb King, Elliott Bayley, Anne Lewis, Sarah Nelson, and Joe Ehlers came aboard at about 3:00 this afternoon at Two Harbors. They're a relatively young group—mostly forty-something—and I think they're going to be fun to have aboard. I went up and talked to them for awhile in the passenger quarters after they came on and we fed them supper at about 6:00 this evening. Supper was interrupted several times because we were backing out of the harbor at Two Harbors, and they didn't want to miss anything. I don't blame them. You can eat anytime, but getting a trip on a lake freighter is almost always a once-in-a-lifetime experience. Supper went fine, by the way. Tom, Jake, and our new passenger porter, Ken Ehlers, did yeoman service, and everything went smoothly. It's all downhill from here.

Captain Craig's wife Phylliss is also aboard. She got on

yesterday when we went through the Soo, and will be playing hostess while we have the passengers aboard. Captain
Craig and Phylliss presently live in Grand Rapids, Michigan, but Phylliss is originally from the Soo. She worked for
a number of years as secretary to the president of what
was then Lake Superior State College—my alma mater. She
knows many of the professors I had while at LSSC, and it's
been fun to chat with her. Phylliss is an enthusiastic lady
and should fit right in with our passengers.

We're now on our way to Silver Bay, Minnesota, just a
short distance down the shore from Two Harbors. We loaded
two holds of ore at Two Harbors, and we'll finish up the load
at Silver Bay. That's going to take awhile, probably sixteen
to twenty-four hours. That means we'll have the passengers
aboard for seven days instead of six. We should be back to
Silver Bay on September 7, and Erik Melander will relieve
me. Erik's the guy who got drunk and was relieved during
fitout on the *Calcite II*, which led to my getting called to
work much earlier than I'd expected. He'll be here on the
Speer until Bobby Bauer returns from his vacation around
the first of November. As for me, I'm going on the *John G.
Munson* around the tenth. I'll deadhead on the *Speer* back
to the Soo, and then spend a couple days at home before I
catch the *Munson*. It'll be the first time I sailed on her, and
I'm looking forward to it.

The *Munson* was built in the early 1950s and she's the
queen of the old grey fleet, the biggest of the stone boats
from Rogers City. My cousin Jack Thompson is the chief
engineer there and it's going to be a thrill for me to finally
sail with him. Jack's older than I am and I idolized him
when we were kids. I haven't seen him much in recent years,
except for a couple of times we passed the *Munson* while it
was unloading in the Rouge River and Jack was leaning out
the engine room gangway. Those were brief conversations,
though, and I'm looking forward to having a good long chat
with him. His mother, Dorothy, has always been one of my
favorite aunts and I see her regularly around Rogers City.
She always keeps me posted on what Jack's up to, and I'm
sure she'll be pleased to hear that we're shipmates.

My stint on the *Munson* will be a short one—just a week
or ten days. Where I go after that I don't know. There aren't
many guys going on vacation in October, so I may have some

The *Speer*'s passengers display "monkey's fists" made for them as mementos of their trip by Gerald "Gomer" Swanson, one of the ship's watchmen. From left to right are Phylliss Craig, wife of the *Speer*'s captain; Joe Ehlers; Sarah Nelson; Anne Lewis; Captain Craig; Deb King; and Mark Johnson. Missing from the photo is the photographer, Elliott Bayley. Heavy monkey's fists were traditionally tied into the ends of the heaving lines to make them easier to throw to personnel on the dock. (Author's collection)

time off. If that's the case, I'll try to sail the winter run into January or February. I don't expect to get called back to work too early in the spring and I don't want to have five months off. If I can keep it down to about three months I'll be happy.

Jake and I are going up the street for a little while when we get into Silver Bay. We both need cigarettes and a few toiletries and we're hoping some store that handles such things will still be open. This is a busy tourist weekend up here, so maybe we'll be in luck.

Monday, September 1

Silver Bay, Minnesota

It is the end of a fourteen-hour day and I don't mind saying that my tail is dragging. With passengers aboard, it's like cooking six meals a day and that's a challenge. The passengers eat fifteen minutes after each of the crew's meal hours end. You just have time to get the dishes washed, wipe things up a little, and then start preparing another meal. Like most passengers, these six ate steamboat portions today. My guess is that they'll start slacking off tomorrow; asking for smaller portions and even skipping an occasional meal. That's the usual pattern. New sailors are like that, too. They come aboard and gorge themselves for the first week or so before they revert to saner eating habits.

One of the reasons it seemed like such a long day was that Jake and I went up the street for a little while last night. Like me, he seldom strays from the boat, but he was almost out of cigarettes and that provided enough of an incentive that I talked him into going up with me. I'm sure he wouldn't have gone alone. As a result of the trip, it was almost midnight before I got into bed and I was still sleeping

Passengers Elliott Bayley (left) and Deb King videotape an interview with a somewhat reluctant Brian Bell, one of the *Speer*'s watchmen. Bell is standing in the shade of the transversely mounted unloading boom, located just ahead of the ship's stern cabin. (Author's collection)

soundly when the alarm went off at 5:30 A.M. There wasn't much open in Silver Bay by the time we got up town. There was a dance going on at the local bowling alley, but from the looks of the raucous crowd we saw coming and going, it was mainly attended by teenagers. Our shopping opportunities were limited to the two gas station convenience stores that were open.

While we made the short trip from Two Harbors to Silver Bay, I managed to get through to my son Scott on the cellular pay phone. He's in Traverse City for the long Labor Day weekend. He was excited that I called because he wanted to hit me up for some tuition money for college. He's only taking two classes this fall for his first semester of college, but the tuition bill just about floored him. I had told him some time ago that I would reimburse him for his tuition and textbook expenses, and he was eager to see if I would make good on my promise. I did, gladly. At least I'm in the process of doing so. I've written a check and will mail it tomorrow when we go through the Soo. He sounded genuinely happy that I agreed to mail him some money, as the tuition and some other unexpected expenses he's had lately have pretty well drained his savings. He sounds good, though, like he's enjoying life and all the promise it holds for an eighteen-year-old. He's grown up a lot in the past year, and I enjoy watching his development.

We didn't get out of Silver Bay until around 5:00 P.M., after a nineteen-hour load. That's not uncommon there. In fact, I remember loads on the *James R. Barker* that took thirty to thirty-six hours. I guess they almost ran out of pellets before they finished loading us today. At the end, they had a couple of front-end loaders scrapping up pellets that previously formed the base for a mountainous pile of ore.

We should be back up to Lake Superior early next Saturday morning if all goes well. I'm expecting Erik Melander, my relief, will be waiting when we get in, so I'm starting to count the days until I get off. I hope the office doesn't change their minds now. Once you've got it in your head that you're getting off a boat, it's hard to reverse directions and enthusiastically leap back into things. As it is, Captain Craig, Mrs. Craig, and I will end up staying aboard the boat—as passengers—until it gets back down to the Soo on

Sunday evening. We have our cars at the Soo Warehouse, and there just isn't any easy way to get from Two Harbors or Silver Bay to the Soo. It will be a good chance to relax and catch up on my sleep before I get off. By next Saturday, I'll be ready for a break. This passenger stuff is wearing me out! Hopefully, it will get easier in the coming days. It's 9:00 P.M. now—bedtime.

Monday, September 2

Labor Day

Soo Locks

Today went a lot better than yesterday and we were out of the galley by 6:00 P.M. The passengers apparently partied a little last night and none showed up for breakfast this morning, which gave me a lot of extra time to get lunch ready. We had the whole crowd for lunch, but since we were going to be at the locks at suppertime, I suggested they might want us to set out a buffet in the passenger quarters, so they could eat whenever they wanted and not miss any of the sights. That went over well with them, so Tom and I spent about an hour late this afternoon putting together an outstanding buffet. There was enough food to feed the Polish army! Oh well, you never skimp when you're cooking on a steamboat, especially for passengers. We wouldn't want steamboat cooks to get a bad name.

We're taking quite a delay here at the locks. Both the *Gott* and *Blough* are ahead of us and there's a fair amount of upbound traffic, too. The captain on the *Gott*, J. R. Nelson, had some heart problems last night and they called the Coast Guard station at Portage Entry on the Keweenaw Peninsula to come out and take him off. That left them short a captain. The first mate holds a master's license, but he doesn't have much experience handling the boat, so the office arranged for Elden Brege to ride the pilot boat from the Soo up as far as Gros Cap at the entrance to the St. Marys River to take command. This is the third time that Captain Nelson has had to get off the boat because of heart problems. I guess he's planning to retire next year,

The *Speer*'s expansive deck is the perfect venue for an after-dinner stroll for Anne Lewis and Joe Ehlers as the ship threads its way between the Manitou islands and the Sleeping Bear Sand Dunes on northern Lake Michigan. Because the *Speer* has unusually narrow hatches, seen on the right of the photo, the deck wings of the 105-foot beam ship are exceptionally wide. (Author's collection)

but maybe he should hang it up now before he suffers a major heart attack out on the boat. I'm sure the office will take a careful look at his medical report before they let him return.

I walked up to the bow after work this evening and noticed that there's a Texas state flag flying from the forward mast, along with the fleet flag, the Canadian flag, a Michigan state flag, and Minnesota's state flag. The state flags represent the home states of the crewmembers on the boat, with the Texas flag there by virtue of the fact that the regular captain on this boat lives in Brownsville, Texas. I'm going to give Captain Craig a hard time over the fact that the Texas flag is flying over the Michigan flag, even though Captain Craig lives in Grand Rapids, Michigan. With the regular captain gone, I think that the Michigan flag should be flown higher up the mast in honor of the home state of the current captain and the resident steward.

Standing almost straight out in a stiff wind, five flags fly from the mast on the bow of the *Edgar B. Speer*. On the left is the fleet flag for Transtar, the corporation that owns the USS Great Lakes Fleet. To the right of the Transtar flag is the familiar Lone Star flag of Texas, home to the *Speer*'s captain. Below the Texas flag is the state flag of Michigan, while the Minnesota flag flies to its right. Many of the *Speer*'s crewmembers are from the two Great Lakes states. Above the Minnesota flag is the Canadian flag, flown as a courtesy by U.S. freighters that frequently cross into Canadian waters on their trips up and down the lakes. Similarly, Canadian ships on the lakes display the U.S. flag. Under the *Speer*'s mast is a shelter used by lookouts during inclement weather. (Author's collection)

Tuesday, September 3
Lake Michigan, Downbound

What a long day! I started this morning at a few minutes before 6:00 A.M. and it was 8:00 P.M. before I finally got out of the galley. I should say "we," though, because Tom Schroeder was there with me the whole time. Jake and Ken Ehlers, our passenger porter, took a little time off in both the morning and afternoon, but Tom and I stuck with it every minute to get everything done. Tomorrow's menu is a little easier, thank God!

The bad news is that some genius in the office has decided that we should anchor off Gary until the *Gott* is done unloading. The *Gott*'s only a couple hours ahead of us, so that means a delay of ten to twelve hours. The difficult-to-fathom part of the whole situation is that we won't be at the same dock at Gary as the *Gott*. We could both unload simultaneously and be on our way back up the lake. In that scenario the *Gott* would probably take a few hours' delay after we pass her, but we wouldn't lose any time at all. A net two-hour delay seems better than a ten- to twelve-hour delay. Maybe the office uses new math. None of the crew is happy about the delay, including the captain and our passengers. Several have commitments up north that they're going to miss because of the delay. That could mar what otherwise has been a near-perfect trip.

We received the September issue of the company newsletter last night and I finally got to see the pictures of Margy Kruger modeling logo clothing for our fleet. She does have her hair down in the photos and it looks fine, but not as nice as when she has it pulled back in a quasi-ponytail. I also got letters from my brother and Ralph Roberts, which was nice.

When we passed the *Columbia Star* in the river recently, Gary came out on the bridge wing and waved. I noticed there was another guy standing next to him holding a video camera. Gary wrote that his companion that day was Jack McCarthy, the son of John McCarthy, who was first mate on the *Edmund Fitzgerald* and one of the twenty-nine sailors who died that terrible night in 1975 when the ship sank into Lake Superior. Jack works for insurance underwriters that insure ships in the Oglebay Norton fleet. Gary said that McCarthy's wife gave him a copy of my *Steamboats and Sailors of the Great Lakes* a year ago. Gary wants to get him a copy of *Queen of the Lakes* and have me inscribe it to McCarthy. I'll be happy to do that, of course.

There's still no word on when Gary will be getting off the *C-Star*. He's got to be tired by now. Gary started sailing around April 25 or 26 and hasn't been off the boat since, except for two transfers, neither of which involved more than a day or two. I think he's expecting the worst, because he wants me to pack up his winter clothing and ship it to him when I get home.

Dick McDonald, the regular chief engineer on the *Speer*, returned from vacation and boarded last night at the supply boat. He's from Rogers City, and I remember him from years ago, because he married Marie Yeager, a girl I had a crush on when I was in elementary school. She was a lot older than I, but I thought she was gorgeous. I remember being devastated when she and Dick got married.

Wednesday, September 3
Gary, Indiana

Well, about an hour before we reached Gary, we received word that the *Gott* would allow us to go into the harbor first, so we could unload simultaneously. She's now a few hundred feet behind us, unloading into the trough as we unload into the hopper. We've been here since around 11:00 A.M.; it will be close to midnight before we finish. The *Gott*, however, should be out of here by 8:00 P.M.

It's about 3:00 P.M., an hour before I serve supper, and I've got all kinds of time on my hands. Our passengers left shortly after we docked and rode the South Shore Railroad into Chicago for a day of sightseeing. Tom Schroeder wanted to go into Chicago, so I gave him the afternoon off and sent him along to help the passengers find the train station. They won't be back until early evening, so it's almost like a day off for me. I'll put out some munchies up in the passenger quarters for their return, because they told me they were planning to have a late lunch in Chicago. I'll be able to relax

211

this evening, the first time in a week, and I plan to get to bed real early. We'll have two more busy days going up the lakes before things return to normal and I leave. There's been no official word from the office yet, but I assume that I'll be relieved at Two Harbors and move to the *Munson*. All plans are subject to change.

It's now 5:30 P.M. and I'm done for the day. Hooray! It's been a relaxing day, although interesting. Our passenger porter hasn't been worth a damn since the night we stayed up late for groceries. He worked about two hours this morning and then went to his room to sleep. He didn't come back out until about 4:00 P.M. I sent him up to vacuum and mop the passenger quarters, which took about fifteen minutes. When he returned he filled a plate with beef burgundy and sat down in the messroom. I guess the work made him hungry. Altogether he worked between two and three hours today.

First Mate Tom Lanthier takes up a position at the end of the *Speer*'s shuttle boom to make sure that it is properly positioned over the unloading hopper at U.S. Steel's sprawling Gary Works, in Gary, Indiana. Iron ore pellets discharged by the *Speer* will be carried to storage piles by a system of conveyor belts. (Author's collection)

Tom Schroeder isn't much better. When I talked to him yesterday about taking the afternoon off if we were in port, I said his baking, salads and other responsibilities had to be finished before he left. I don't need any extra work at meal times. Tom was agreeable and even spoke about working last night to get things done. I guess he changed his mind. He baked a pan of cinnamon buns this morning for coffee break and a banana cake that was the sole dessert for both lunch and dinner. He didn't frost the cake. When I went to get the relish tray out just before dinner, there were two empty sections on the tray and a note that read, "Green onions and fresh mushrooms." Five minutes before the crew came in for dinner I discovered I needed to clean green onions and mushrooms for Tom's relish tray. I'm not sure what planet he's from, but it's not mine. The guy just amazes me. I hope he doesn't hold his breath waiting for another afternoon off while I'm on the boat. He blew it.

I ran up to the captain's room the other evening to get a bunch of stamps out of his desk drawer so the passengers could put off mail at the Soo and I took some time to look around. He's got more electronics in his room than most video arcades! Surrounding his desk is a gyrocompass repeater, a Loran unit, a global positioning system display, and a big color monitor that's hooked into the ship's position plotting computer. It displays a chart of the area the boat's in and shows its position. The captain can sit at his desk or in his easy chair and see exactly where his ship is. Back in the old days—the 1960s—all a captain had was the compass repeater. Before gyrocompasses came out after World War I, ship captains relied on a marginally dependable magnetic compass to show him the direction the ship was headed in. Little is left to chance with today's electronics, yet ships still run aground with surprising regularity. That should come as no surprise to students of shipwrecks. Historically, most groundings have resulted not from a lack of adequate navigational data but from human error.

When my brother returned to work on the lakes as a mate a couple of years ago after an absence of close to fifteen years, he found a lot of new equipment in the pilothouses of the ships he worked on. These pieces included new navigational systems, computer systems that plot a ship's position on an electronic chart, collision avoidance radars,

Mark Thompson, the *Speer*'s steward—chief cook—grills skewered chicken and vegetables for the crew and a group of passengers. Cooks on Great Lakes ships have a reputation for turning out copious quantities of home-cooked food for their hungry crews. (Author's collection)

cell phones, fax machines, and loading computers. Gary joked at the time that when he left the lakes all they had in the pilothouse was a gyrocompass and a coffee pot. The growth in electronic technology has been rapid. It's hard to believe that fifteen years ago, the first microcomputers were just debuting. Today, computer technology has dramatically changed the way we do our jobs on the boat, from the engine room up to the pilothouse. Several of us on this boat even have notebook computers on board for our own personal use, such as keeping this logbook.

Friday, September 6

St. Marys River

It's 4:50 A.M. and I've already showered and made a pot of coffee. I must have slept exceedingly well last night, because I woke up a few minutes after 4:00 A.M. feeling refreshed. We're apparently at anchor someplace in the St. Marys due to fog. Drat! This will delay our arrival at Two Harbors, where our passengers will disembark. Don't get me wrong, they're great passengers, but all of us in the galley are tired of working fifteen-hour days. The second cook and passenger porter are fairly inexperienced and turning out six meals a day instead of the usual three has put a strain on all of us. Things were pretty ragged yesterday, but we managed to get through it. I think today will be better—the menu is simpler—but that remains to be seen.

When I finished work at 8:00 P.M. last night I put together my Soo grocery order to send it in the mail at the locks this morning. Next I finalized today's menu and removed the things I needed from the freezers. By then the day was pretty well shot and I didn't have the energy to write anything in this blasted log. Instead, I went up to the passenger quarters and lured Deb King away from her husband by proposing she come have a cigarette with me out on the afterdeck. She's a reformed smoker, but still enjoys the occasional cigarette. She's one of the fortunate few who can smoke once in a while without getting hooked again.

We sat on the swing out on the deck that adjoins the passenger quarters and smoked a couple cigarettes. The evening was as pleasant as the conversation. Deb's a doctor at the clinic in Two Harbors, in family practice with Sarah Nelson, another passenger. Deb's married to Mark Johnson, a tall Nordic type who owns a big car dealership in Two Harbors. Sarah's husband Joe Ehlers has a travel agency in Duluth. The other couple, Anne Lewis and Elliott Bayley, are an attorney and electrical engineer-entrepreneur, respectively. Elliott's company manufactures power-generating windmills. They're all delightful, and it's been fun to have them aboard. The only fly in the ointment was that the captain wanted us to hold separate meal hours for the passengers, which proved to be a *tremendous* amount of work. It's not that preparing a second meal after each of our regular meal hours is the problem, it's the extent to which it cuts into our preparations for the next meal. By the time we're done with breakfast, for example, I've only got about an hour to get lunch ready— or two lunches, to be precise. After lunch, only two hours

215

are left to cook two dinners. The next time I cook for passengers, I'll handle the situation differently. Fortunately, the meals went well. The crew's happy and so are the passengers. Only twenty-four hours remain; even with the fog delay, things should be back to normal by noon tomorrow. After the schedule of the past week, putting out three meals a day for the crew will seem like a walk in the park.

First Mate Tom Lanthier called personnel yesterday to confirm whether I would still be relieved at Two Harbors. Dick Johns didn't have an answer for him, or for me. He hemmed and hawed before admitting he did not know where my relief was. Amazing! When he spoke with me on the boat last week he was quite definite that I would be relieved at Two Harbors by Erik Melander. Now the situation appears to be up in the air. I don't know if I should start packing and cleaning my room. If we ran this boat the way they run the personnel office, we'd spend much of our time wandering aimlessly around the lakes, unsure of which port to go to or how to get there. I was planning to write a letter to my brother today to let him know I was leaving the *Speer* and transferring to the *Munson,* but now I'm not sure what to tell him.

Several crewmembers expressed some dismay about my departure, though I've assured them Erik's a good cook. They'd rather stick with a known commodity. That's some indication of the number of second-rate cooks out here on the lakes. There's probably a fifty-fifty chance the next cook who climbs up the ladder won't be as good as the one who's descending. I have mixed emotions about leaving the *Speer.* This is a comfortable boat, it's got a great galley, and I've made some friends among the crew.

On the other hand, I miss the gang on the *Calcite II* and visiting Rogers City occasionally. For the past couple of days, I've been looking forward to getting off, but that's largely due to the stress of having passengers aboard. The thought of a couple days between boats to sleep in and relax was—and is—appealing. Once our passengers disembark, I'm sure I'd be happy here. I guess I'm just worn out. I've been out here over a hundred days now and though I hate to admit it, I could use a break. It's so nice to have money rolling in steadily that I hate to take a vacation. There's too much uncertainty about what will happen during the balance of the season.

When Dick Johns was on the boat, he mentioned that there's still talk in the office that two of the small boats, probably the *Calcite II* and *Myron C. Taylor,* may lay up at the end of October. If that happens, it's unlikely I'll get much work the rest of the season because the two displaced cooks would have a first crack at relief jobs. With that possibility looming in the hazy future, I'd just as soon work every day I can right now.

Tuesday, September 10
S.S. *John G. Munson*
Rogers City, Michigan

I got off the *Speer* at Two Harbors late Saturday afternoon and signed on the *John G. Munson* at noon today at Calcite, after two days of luxurious rest at home. Jake Gajewski and I rode the bus from Duluth to St. Ignace, a trip that took from 8:00 P.M. Saturday until 6:00 A.M. Sunday. I then caught a limo—actually a minivan—from St. Ignace to the Soo to pick up my car and finally arrived home in Rogers City at about 9:30 A.M. My joints still hurt from the ride. I can't sleep sitting up and there's no way a six-foot-tall guy can lie down and sleep on a seat less than four feet wide. The best I could do during the overnight trip was doze off occasionally in some awkward position. The arduous trip left me feeling as though I spent ten hours in a boxing ring with George Foreman.

The final day of my stay on the *Speer* was a busy one. I stayed up talking with the passengers until midnight the night before, so I was a little groggy all day. I still managed to get out three meals, clean the galley, and pack up and clean the room that had been my home for three weeks. Jake was battling health problems and the captain thought it best that he go home and see his own doctor. Jake and I caught a ride into Duluth with the passengers. That was pleasantly convenient, since the transportation opportunities out of Silver Bay are extremely limited. They dropped us off at the

217

bus station after stopping at their favorite downtown Duluth restaurant for a couple of drinks and an introduction to the owners of the trendy establishment.

I developed a real liking for Deb, Mark, Sarah, Joe, Anne, and Elliott during their stay on the *Speer*. They were fun to have aboard, and despite all the extra work, I hated to see our passengers go. We all exchanged addresses and they made me promise to visit them in Duluth in the not-too-distant future. I'm going to do my best to keep that promise. It constantly amazes me how close you get to people after only a week together on a ship.

I spent a quiet Sunday with my mother recuperating from my marathon bus ride. Yesterday I ran errands all day. I joined the Calcite Credit Union, stocked up on cigarettes and toiletries, searched for a car for Scott, and even made a quick trip down to Alpena. There I picked up some under-wear and a couple pairs of slacks at Wal-Mart and enriched the owner of the local used book store by purchasing a few volumes. I picked up books on Hemingway's boyhood, life in a lumber camp, a journal about an 1840 trip around Lake Superior, and an interesting volume on early steamboats. A three-volume history of Michigan tempted me severely, but it was priced at seventy dollars and I didn't have that much cash with me. Fortunately, the bookstore didn't take credit cards, so I managed to escape without blowing my allowance on the set. If it's still there when I get off the *Munson,* I'm not sure I'll have the willpower to pass it up a second time. As I leafed through the pages, I was attracted by sections that described daily life for early settlers at places like Detroit and Mackinac. That's the sort of thing I'm interested in as background for my planned historical novel set in Michigan, so I see the seventy dollars as a business investment. Perhaps I can talk the guy in the bookstore down a little. I've basically quit buying new books, preferring instead to borrow them from the library, but I love to add old books to my small, steadily growing collection.

It's just after 1:00 P.M. now and I'm enjoying an un-expected free afternoon. The regular cook, Mike Deragon, wants to work through dinner tonight, so I don't have any-thing to do until tomorrow morning. I'll go out in the galley later on and snoop through the refrigerators and freezers to see what I've got to work with. He has stuff thawing for

218

me to make spaghetti and corned beef tomorrow, but that doesn't sound too exciting to me. After a casual inventory, I'll put together a menu for a few days. I'm only going to be here seven days, while Mike attends the wedding of one of his kids down in North Carolina. He'll return a week from now at Calcite or the Soo, depending on our schedule.

I just took some time and looked around the galley, and then made a few additions to the grocery order that Mike readied to be put off at the Soo tomorrow. The boat's pretty well stocked, though there seems to be a shortage of fresh vegetables and a few of the other items I use regularly. I didn't order much; by the time we take on groceries at the Soo on the downbound leg of our trip, I'll only have four to five days left before I get off. I don't want to stick Mike with a lot of stuff he doesn't use.

The galley on this boat is massive, with miles of counter space and more cabinets and cupboards than they have on the thousand-footers. It should be a comfortable galley to work in, though I'll be leaving about the time I'm familiar working in it. I develop new routines for each boat I work on, which usually takes three to four days. Until then, I feel as though I'm cooking in someone else's kitchen. Oh well, the week I'll put in here will make it easier for me if I ever return, and I imagine I will.

The steward's room is quite nice. Not as large as the one on the *Speer*, but big enough to hold all the basics—desk, recliner, etc. Mike also has an air-conditioner built into one of the portholes, and he's left that for me as well as his television and VCR. All the comforts of home!

The *Munson* is a beautiful boat. She's of the same vintage as the AAA-class boats, like the *Callaway, Clarke,* and *Anderson,* but she has many frills that they don't have. In design and outfitting, she's more like Inland Steel's *Sykes* and *Ryerson,* widely acclaimed as the best-looking freighters ever built on the lakes. When the *Munson* was launched, she was the flagship of Bradley Transportation Lines grey fleet. They spared little expense for her. It'll be fun to look around when I have some time.[16]

---

[16]The *Munson* was launched on November 28, 1951, at Manitowac Ship Building in Manitowac, Wisconsin. Originally a few inches over 666

It's now 6:00 P.M., Mike Deragon is gone, and this boat's galley is mine for the next week. There are a couple of crewmembers on here who sailed with me before and Deragon said he'd heard I was "a good cook." I'm always a little leery when a cook says something like that to me—I'm always afraid that they're trying to sucker me into saying something stupid. It's better, and smarter, to be meek.

Two other boats have joined us at Calcite. A little while ago, the *Middletown* slowly steamed into the slip next to us and the *Charles A. Wilson* sits just outside the slip on what's called the powerhouse wall.

We were also visited by Herb Nelson, vice president of our union—the American Maritime Officers. Herb is the father of Cam Nelson, an oiler on the *Speer.* Herb's a favorite of mine, and he's done many favors for me over the years, including helping me secure my first cooking job. I had a chance to talk to him a little today about my interest in running the steward's school that the union sponsors each winter in Toledo. I was asked to do it several years ago, but my son Scott came to live with me and I spent the winter in Traverse City. When I returned to sailing last year, I wrote the school director and expressed an interest in handling the steward's school. A cook from American Steamship ran the school for several years and he had first dibs on the job.

---

feet long, she was lengthened, or "stretched," in 1976 and now measures 768 feet. When she was launched, she was the largest self-unloader on the Great Lakes, second only to Inland Steel's *Wilfred Sykes* in overall length. Powered by a 7,700 horsepower steam turbine engine, her boilers were originally coal-fired, but she was converted to oil at the same time she was being lengthened. The *Munson* replaced the *Carl D. Bradley* (1927) as the flagship of the Bradley Transportation Company of Rogers City, Michigan, a subsidiary of U.S. Steel. The fleet was the first on the lakes to be made up entirely of self-unloading ships. Their primary mission was to haul limestone from U.S. Steel's Calcite Plant at Rogers City to steel mills and stone docks around the lakes. Many of the docks called at by the Bradley boats were not equipped with shoreside unloading equipment, which is why the fleet's founders decided to operate self-unloaders. In 1983, management of the grey boats of the Bradley fleet was fully integrated with the red boats of U.S. Steel's Pittsburgh Steamship Division when the USS Great Lakes Fleet was formed. The *Munson* is named for a former president of Michigan Limestone and Bradley Transportation who went on to become U.S. Steel's vice president for raw materials. John G. Munson died the same year the ship bearing his name was launched.

The *Calcite II* passes its bigger and newer fleetmate, the *John G. Munson,* in the St. Clair River. Both ships were once part of Bradley Transportation Line's "grey fleet," operating out of the Port of Calcite at Rogers City, Michigan. While the Bradley ships have since been absorbed into the USS Great Lakes Fleet, the *Calcite II* and *Munson* are still crewed mainly by sailors from the Rogers City area. (Author's collection)

Things have changed a little this year, though, and they may be looking for someone new to run the school. Herb said he would tell Harry Crooks, the school director, about my interest and I'll follow up with a personal letter to Harry. Running the school would be fun and would keep me out of the unemployment line for two to three months this winter. The extra money would be nice and I'd still have six to eight weeks to go south once the school ends. I don't expect to be called back to work next year until June 1. This year was a fluke and may not be repeated. Running the school would certainly be better than sailing into January or February. The money's not quite as good, but the working conditions are a whole lot better. I've given a lot of thought to what's needed in the steward training program and I think I could make some significant improvements. Maybe we could even turn out a few stewards who actually know how to cook.

I also learned today that the officers in the Inland Lakes Management fleet—the old Huron Cement fleet—have walked off the job in an effort to gain union representation. They've been non-union for many years; several years ago they rejected a vote to affiliate with our union. Now that management of the fleet is being transferred to a tug-barge company and their company has launched its first tug-barge cement carrier, the officers apparently see things in a different light. Motivated by a deep concern for their futures, they've now decided it might be prudent to join the AMO. They're picketing at the LaFarge cement plant in Alpena, the fleet's home port. Herb Nelson thinks the company will cave in and allow a unionization vote in the immediate future. If that doesn't happen I may walk the picket line for a short time when I get off here.

Time to work on a menu for tomorrow. Alas, tomorrow morning I will once again have a crew to feed.

Wednesday, September 11
St. Marys River

We finished loading at Calcite about 8 o'clock last night and sailed up to Cedarville to take on the rest of the load. We got out of Cedarville around 10:30 A.M., and are now headed for Duluth.

The second cook here cooks breakfast, an old tradition on the grey boats, so all I did this morning was worry about lunch. That went quite well, though I spent an inordinate amount of time stumbling around the galley looking for pots, pans, cutting boards, bread, and so on. The big seller at noon was a tuna salad sandwich, even though I also offered an open-faced prime rib sandwich. Like almost every boat I've been on, the crewmembers here prefer a bowl of soup and a sandwich at noon. That's no surprise, I guess; that's the lunch of choice for many Americans or at least it was until fast food restaurants became popular.

I've got my menus planned for the entire seven to eight days that I'll be here. I made them up last night and between 6:00 and 7:00 this morning, based on what Mike left me and what's ordered from the Soo. I added a few things to his grocery order, but we won't have that stuff until we're downbound from Duluth on Saturday afternoon. The boat's pretty well stocked up, but there's a definite absence of fresh vegetables, like cauliflower, mushrooms, acorn squash, asparagus, and green beans. That's too bad, because this is the time of year that we get great fresh vegetables. Fortunately, a couple crewmembers brought surplus sweet corn and tomatoes from their home gardens. The tomatoes are firm and sweet—I used them this noon on sandwiches and the second cook put several platters out on the tables. We'll have the sweet corn tonight.

I've sailed with a couple of guys on this ship and many others I knew when I lived in Rogers City twenty-plus years ago. Ralph "Levy" Lewandowski, the captain, remembered me, as did Harry Goebel, the first mate. The chief engineer here is my cousin Jack, who brought his wife Ada on for a trip. I spent a little time talking to them during lunch and look forward to a more extended conversation later on.

Quite a few of the guys also know my brother Gary. Several went to school when he did and others sailed with him on the grey boats at the start of his career. Everyone here's friendly and talkative, quite a difference from the greeting I received when I went on the *Speer.* Of course, I'm somewhat of a known commodity here, since I'm from Rogers City and have sailed with several crewmembers before. The guys on the *Speer* didn't know what they were in for when I showed up and I'm from Rogers City (the guys on the red boats don't have much good to say about the crews on the grey boats). I guess it's sort of a geographical bias and it works both ways. I'm not sure I'd want to be an outsider and get assigned to one of the grey boats. I probably wouldn't feel that I was being welcomed with open arms.

It'd be easy to feel like an outsider on the grey boats—hell, there are times when I do. Most of the crewmembers have sailed together for years—many crewmembers have over thirty years on the boats. They also know everyone in Rogers City and frequently talk about people in town. A sailor who wasn't from Rogers City wouldn't know those people or even care about them, so he'd be left out of a lot of conversations. The guys on the grey boats also like some foods that aren't found on the red boats, like fresh and smoked Polish sausage from Rygwelski's Market in Rogers City, raw chopped beef with lots of onion and pepper in it, and pickled bologna. They're a regular part of the menu on the grey boats, but an outsider probably wouldn't think they were so special. Most outsiders are loath to even try chopped beef, especially after all the warnings against eating meat that hasn't been thoroughly cooked. (I've never heard of anyone getting sick from eating chopped beef. We've been eating it in our family as long as I can remember, and whenever my sister and I go home during the holidays, we make sure Mother gets a couple of pounds for us.) Based on my experience, I think crews are slow to accept anyone they don't know. The newcomer has to prove himself before they welcome him into the crew. Most outsiders who end up on the grey boats don't stick around long enough to get over that threshold. That's too bad, because it promotes a schism between the two branches of the fleet when there isn't an iota of difference between sailors on the grey boats and those on the red boats.

Keith Adams, the second cook, is bending over backwards to please me. I think he'd do all my work for me if I'd let him. That's interesting, because I've heard *nothing* good about him from anyone in the fleet. Most people I've run across describe him as lazy and dirty. The guys in the galley here also received advance warning that I'm a demanding steward. Mike Deragon asked me if I was hard to work for. The question surprised me and I collected my thoughts for a couple of seconds before I answered. I responded by saying, "Most of the porters and second cooks I've worked with would probably say that I was difficult to work with. I work hard and I expect the porter and second cook to work hard, too." Apparently, word that I'm demanding spread to most of the galleys in the fleet. That's okay. Fear is sometimes an effective motivator. Regardless, Keith was helpful this morning and did a fine job. I hope he keeps it up for the next week. Tom Burke, the porter, normally works as a deckhand, but he, too, seems to be doing a fine job. Tom's from a long line of Great Lakes sailors—his father retired a few years ago as a captain in this fleet and I've sailed with his brother Jim, who's an engineer.

We're not going to be into Duluth until about 8:00 in the evening, which is too bad. It would be nice to have some time to go up the street, perhaps look up Anne Lewis and Elliott Bayley. Chances are I'll stay on the boat, as I normally do. The steel mill at Lorain, where we'll unload the iron ore pellets we'll take on at Duluth, is in a shabby neighborhood, so I probably won't go up the street there either. After Lorain, it's back to Calcite, and there's a good chance that Mike will be back then. That'd be okay with me. I'm looking forward to a couple of weeks off.

I'm lobbying hard to get back to the *Calcite II* on October 1 when Bobby Bauer goes on vacation. I wrote the fleet manager a letter on the pretext of sending him a copy of the menu I used when we had passengers on the *Speer*. In the same letter I asked if he would put in a word for me to personnel to try to get me back on the *C-II*. I also wrote a note to Mike Gapczynski, who'll be going back on the *Calcite* as captain in the next few days, asking him to put a little pressure on the office to get me back over there. I'm pretty sure Mike will follow through on that, especially if the crew hears that I'm available when Bobby gets off. It would be good to be back with them again. I don't think I've ever enjoyed a crew more, not even when I was on the *James R. Barker*, my home for four or five years.

Returning to the *Calcite II* would definitely be like going home. With the prospect of teaching at the union school this winter, it would also be nice to be on a boat like the *C-II* that's going to lay up before Christmas. I could spend the holidays at home before I headed to Toledo in time to organize everything before the students begin classes in early January.

The steward school has been a sore point with many cooks around the lakes for years. The old adage is that if you can't cook when you get to the school, you won't be able to cook when you leave. When I went through the program, there was absolutely no instruction in cooking. When you cooked, you prepared things you already knew how to cook or you had another student help you. I think anyone graduating from the school should have a grounding in all the basic cooking techniques. They should be forced to demonstrate their competence by being required to prepare dishes they are not familiar with. Students in the school also need more training in calculating and controlling food costs, ordering and inventorying, and preparing dishes that are low in fat and cholesterol. When I attended the school, we participated in a week-long program at Riverside Hospital in Toledo on nutrition. This area needs to be strengthened even further. There were people watching their fat and cholesterol intakes on every boat I've been on, so it's critical that cooks prepare dishes that will fit into those diets. I, for one, think there should be a low-fat, low-cholesterol entree offered at every meal. It would be fun to control the curriculum and instruction at the school, and try to improve the education of stewards on the lakes. At the same time, the workday at the school would afford me lots of opportunities to write and research in both Toledo and Detroit. I'd also be closer to Meredith and Scott, with lots of free time on the weekends to visit them.

We lost one of the crewmembers last evening. The guy came back to the boat just before it left the dock at Calcite and stumbled and fell when he got to the top of the boarding ladder. He fell five or six feet to the deck and hit his head. By the time I saw him, he had a lump the size of a lemon, was weak-kneed and staggered. They sent him to the local clinic to check him for serious injuries. The word this morning is that when he took a blood alcohol test, his blood alcohol level was five times the legal limit. It's unlikely he'll return soon; his route back to the boat may include a stop at an alcohol rehab program. Had he fallen in the opposite direction, he would have plummeted about fifteen feet to the concrete apron on the dock. A fall from that height would have left him paralyzed or dead.

Heavy drinking was once part of life on the boats, but those days are over. There are few heavy drinkers left; those who overindulge and get caught receive little sympathy from most of their shipmates. The general sentiment on the boat today was, "He should have known better."

It's now 6:00 P.M. and I finished work at 5:30. I don't know what to do with all the time I have on my hands. I only worked a little over eight hours today, a far cry from the fourteen to sixteen I put in on the *Speer*. I'm tired today, but only because I didn't sleep well last night. By the time I got done working on the *Speer*, I barely had the energy to crawl back to my room, and my legs and feet never quit aching. They'd be sore when I went to bed at night and they'd still be sore when I got up in the morning. This should be an easy week, but I'm glad it's only a week.

I really do need a week or two off to recuperate before I go back out to finish up the season. I feel sorry for my brother

Gary. He's been on the boats since late April, and it now looks as though he may not get a vacation at all. If he sails until lay up, he'll have worked almost nine months without a break. He'll make a lot of money, but he'll probably sleep for a whole month when he gets home.

You may have noticed that I haven't mentioned the weather much lately. When you're working on an air-conditioned boat like the *Speer,* the weather is largely irrelevant. Many days I worked all day in the galley and had no idea what the weather was like outside. Actually, the weather has been hot and quite humid for the past week or so, even up on Lake Superior. That's in the process of changing, though. This evening it feels like fall outside. It's too cool to be outside in my shorts and shower sandals. A big low pressure system is moving into the Great Lakes region, which will produce heavy rain and lower temperatures. It's awfully early for cold weather to be setting in. Let's just hope that it's only temporary. The weather in September and the first two or three weeks of October can be marvelous or miserable. I'd prefer the former, especially if I have a couple of weeks off once I finish on the *Munson.* I'll definitely turn the air-conditioner off before I go to bed tonight. I almost froze to death last night.

Thursday, September 12
Lake Superior

It's 5:30 A.M. and we're in the midst of our first fall storm of the 1996 shipping season. It's nothing too serious, but we've been rocking and rolling ever since we left Whitefish Bay yesterday evening. We're taking the route up along the north shore of the lake, instead of the direct route down the middle. The captain called back at suppertime last night and told us to secure everything in the galley before we shut down for the day, because the forecast called for ten-foot seas. On a thousand-footer like the *Speer,* with about twenty feet of freeboard, ten-foot waves are little cause for concern. If the smaller *Munson* encountered ten-foot seas, however, it would have waves breaking over the deck, since it has only about eight feet of freeboard. On the *Calcite II,* which is smaller still, older, and has even less freeboard, the captain might anchor somewhere rather than battle ten-foot seas.

The word from the office is that the *Calcite II* and *Myron C. Taylor* will both lay up at the end of October this year before the bad fall storms descend on the lakes. They're too old and too ripe—some would say "rotten"—to be out in bad weather. They also lose so much time anchoring for weather in the late fall that they become inefficient. Of course, a lot will depend on how much cargo the company has to move before the end of the season. If the customers are pressing for more shipments, it'll be hard for the office to justify laying up two boats that early. My hunch is that both will still be out well into December, the usual scenario.

I'm serving pizza for supper tonight, and if I get everything prepped this morning, I may ask my cousin Jack to give me a guided tour of the engine room after lunch. I imagine that the engine room is just as elaborate as the galley, so I don't want to miss it.

This is probably a good time to say a few words about the men who work in the engine room. The engine department is headed by the chief engineer. The chief is basically a day worker, except that he's available when the ship is in the rivers or in a maneuvering situation should something go wrong. The chief is primarily a supervisor, so you seldom see him with a wrench in his hands. That varies, though, depending on the chief. I've seen some who never got their hands dirty working on machinery and others who willingly pitch in whenever there's a major repair project. Generally, the chief assigns the work to be completed for the rest of the engine staff, and personally supervises major projects, such as emergency repairs. When the fuel on the *Calcite II* was contaminated earlier this summer, Chief Engineer Bob Lijewski spent a lot of time in the engine room ensuring that the watch engineer and oiler changed oil filters often enough to prevent damage to the generator. When the first assistant engineer had problems getting a mooring winch to work properly, Bob stood by and gave him advice on what to try next.

Much of the chief's workday is taken up with paperwork, preparing orders for needed parts, keeping various records, and filling out reports. When the boat takes on bunkers, or fuel, it's also common for the chief to personally oversee the operation.

Below the chief is the first assistant engineer, who is a day worker. The first does most of the repair work around the ship outside the engine room, including everything from solving an electrical problem with the ship's incinerator, to getting the mooring winches to work properly, to repairing electrical fixtures, to correcting plumbing problems, to maintaining the ship's emergency generator and testing it weekly. He's the boat's maintenance man and the list of problems that need to be corrected is literally never-ending. While much of the repair work in the engine room can be done by watchstanders, "the first" is usually involved in all major projects, like replacing fuel pumps or cylinder liners on the diesel-powered boats. Because problems occur any time day or night on a ship that's operating around the clock, the first assistant generally gets quite a bit of overtime. It's not uncommon for the first to make more money in a season than the chief. On thousand-footers, there's also a second assistant engineer, referred to as the "day second," who works along with the first assistant. On smaller boats, if the first needs a second pair of hands on a project, he's usually assisted by the handyman.

There are three other assistant engineers in the engine department who serve as watch engineers in the engine room—a second assistant, senior third assistant, and junior third assistant. They stand watches, just like the mates do, working four hours on and eight hours off. They run the main engine, generators, and various other machinery that keep the ship moving. Much of their time is spent in the engine control room observing the myriad of gauges that monitor most of the critical machinery functions. Each watch engineer also has a primary responsibility for certain machinery they perform maintenance on while they're on watch. One takes care of the ship's generators, which are large diesel engines, while another is responsible for the boilers. On a diesel boat, small boilers supply hot water for the ship, but on a steamer massive boilers produce steam to drive the engines. Boiler water is tested frequently and chemicals are used to remove minerals in the water that would cause scale to built up in the boilers and reduce their efficiency.

Second Assistant Engineer Iggy Donajkowski stands by in the diminutive engine control room of the *Calcite II* while the ship maneuvers at a dock. The captain and mates can operate the throttles from the vessel's pilothouse, but an engineer is always available in the engine control room when the ship is in restricted waters in case there is some sort of equipment malfunction. (Author's collection)

An oiler or qualified member of the engine department (QMED) work with each of the watchstanding engineers. The oilers and QMEDs are unlicensed seamen, but they've passed a Coast Guard exam to get their rating, similar to the able-bodied seamen in the deck department. They regularly make rounds of the engine spaces, checking the status of the various machinery. In addition, each oiler or QMED also has specific equipment they're responsible for maintaining on their watch. For example, one cleans the strainers on the fuel lines or the fuel-water separators if it's a diesel-powered ship. The unlicensed crewmen in the engine room spend a lot of their time cleaning equipment and mopping the decks throughout the engine spaces. Many people have an image of engine rooms as grimy and dirty, everything coated with a layer of black oil—the black holds of days past. That's not the case anymore in a well-maintained engine room and most engine rooms I've seen are well-maintained. The constant rounds of scrubbing and mopping actually keep things quite clean.

This ship also carries a handyman. His primary responsibility is to maintain and operate the self-unloading system. When those duties don't fill his workday, he's assigned to other activities in the engine room, such as assisting the first assistant engineer, stowing supplies, or moving barrels of lubricating oil. Other fleets have a conveyorman, whose only duty is to maintain and operate the unloading system. In such cases, there's usually also a wiper on the engine room staff. The wiper is an unrated seaman, so virtually anyone can fill the position. The wiper cleans, paints, empties trash barrels, assists when fueling, and the like. In this fleet, a temporary wiper is usually assigned to each boat for about one month a year. A wiper was assigned to the *Calcite II* earlier this summer, and he spent most of his time painting a storeroom in the engine room. People in the handyman and wiper positions are usually day workers.

In order to be eligible to write the Coast Guard exam to be rated as an oiler, a sailor must have six months' experience as a wiper. After three years as an oiler, an individual may write the Coast Guard exam to become a third assistant engineer. Many engineers today are graduates of maritime academies, rather than having worked their way "up the hawsepipe." Jack Thompson, the chief engineer on the *Munson*, worked his way up through the ranks to become an engineer. His son Steve, however, attended the Great Lakes Maritime Academy for three years and received a license as a third assistant engineer when he graduated and passed the necessary Coast Guard exams.

In the past we heard a lot of discussions—arguments, really—about the relative merits of deck and engine officers who come up through the hawsepipe versus those who graduated from maritime academies. Mates and assistant engineers right out of maritime academy programs often came aboard not knowing how to perform a lot of the practical day-to-day tasks on the ship. The freshly graduated mates, for example, often are not proficient at running deck winches, because they didn't receive such training in their academy programs and they never worked as watchmen or wheelsmen. Academy-produced engineers often have simi-

231

lar shortcomings: few gain any experience operating a lathe, cutting threads on a new length of pipe, or adjusting a steam mooring winch. The academy-produced mate and engineer's knowledge tends to be more theoretical than practical, which makes them the target for a lot of criticism from the crewmembers they work with aboard ship.

On the other hand, there are many things that academy graduates understand better than hawsepipers. The mates from the academies are generally better prepared to use sophisticated electronics found in today's pilothouses, like LORAN, and the complicated collision avoidance radars. In the engine room it's not uncommon for academy graduates to be better schooled in electrical systems than those who have risen up through the ranks. It's also likely that they're better prepared to operate the computers increasingly installed in the engine rooms of ships for use in maintaining inventories, ordering parts, and the like. My view is that there are some things that hawsepipers are better at and there are some things that academy graduates are better at. The differences seem to disappear after a few years on the job. Then it's merely a matter of raw intellect and the individual's personal work ethic that determines how good a mate or engineer they will be. Not too many years ago, it was relatively easy to tell the academy graduates from the hawsepipers just by appearance and demeanor. That's not the case anymore. The people who manage to struggle up the hawsepipe to the officers' ranks today are just as sharp as the academy graduates.

Friday, September 13

Duluth, Minnesota

We arrived here to unload around 4:00 A.M., and when we're done we'll shift to the Duluth Missabe & Iron Range Railroad's dock to load taconite. Like our fleet, the DM&IR is owned by Transtar. Both were previously owned by U.S. Steel, now USX; the nation's largest steelmaker still controls over 40 percent of the stock in the fleet and the railroad.

We'll probably have company from the office today. The second cook says that Jerry Walls usually visits the boat when it's in Duluth and takes sweet rolls and cookies back to the staff. I rather enjoy seeing people from the office. It's a chance to find out the latest scuttlebutt. The person I'd really like to see is Fred Cummings, the fleet manager. I'd like to get his reaction to the job we did with the passengers on the *Speer*, and twist his arm a little about getting back to the *Calcite II*. Unfortunately, he didn't receive my letter yet.

I'm not at all impressed with galley operations in this fleet. One of the problems is that there's no one in the office with any background in food service, so the stewards get little direction. As a result, the way galleys are run from one boat to another varies significantly, and the office's expectations are vague. It seems the only time a steward hears from the office is if food costs are too high. Although I've been with the fleet for more than a year, nobody has ever told me what range of food costs I should shoot for.

The galley here on the *Munson* is the best I've ever worked in. It's spacious with more than enough counter space and it's well equipped. The only thing I don't like about the layout is that the steam table, which was added a few years ago, is located in the messroom instead of in the galley itself. As a result, I can't use it to hold food during the meal hour. Instead, I have to keep everything in pots on the stove and worry constantly about something burning. The steam table was put out in the messroom to hold leftovers for the crew after meal hours. The galley is locked up when dinner is over. That's standard operating procedure on most of the boats in the fleet, though I've only done it at a few docks where dock workers who come aboard the ship to eat are known to snoop around in the storerooms and lockers. I've rarely encountered a problem with crewmembers taking things out of our coolers or storerooms without permission.

Like the *Speer*, the galley here on the *Munson* is disorganized. Cooler space, in particular, isn't well used and items seem to be stowed haphazardly. I guess I'm a little obsessive-compulsive about keeping things organized, probably as a result of the years I spent with George Rydberg on the *James R. Barker*. There, everything had its place, and it had better be there when George went looking for it.

233

Saturday, September 14
Lake Superior, Downbound

We finished loading and left Duluth around 9:30 P.M. last night, which means we'll be getting groceries at the Soo at a bad time, about 1:30 or 2:00 in the morning. Geez, I hate to have my sleep disrupted. By the time I get groceries put away, I'll be sweaty and my heart will be pumping as though I'd just ridden the exercise bike for an hour. It'll be tough to get back to sleep. I'd almost prefer that we got groceries at 4:00 A.M. because I'd just stay up afterward. Oh well, we've got a lot of water to cover before we get to the supply boat. Since the lake is still a little bumpy, we could easily get delayed.

I'm struggling a little with my menus. I'm going to have steak tonight. I usually serve grilled chicken breasts or chicken kabobs with it, but I don't have any chicken breasts. I'll have to see what kind of fish I can find to run as an alternative to the steak. I also don't have much in the way of fresh vegetables—no cauliflower, broccoli, green beans, mushrooms, or asparagus. Hell, I don't even have any frozen vegetables, except for a lonely bag of stir-fry vegetables the last relief cook left here. The best I can do is to cook some fresh carrots. Fortunately, we've got lots of those. I'll be very glad when I get some of my own groceries aboard, as it'll certainly make menu planning easier.

We should be at the steel mill in Lorain, Ohio, around noon on Monday, and back up to Calcite at noon on Wednesday. My guess is that the regular cook will be back then. His son is getting married today, so that gives him plenty of time to get back to Rogers City from North Carolina. I should have some time off then, though I still don't know how much. I'm sure I'll be off until the end of September, but if I don't return to the *Calcite II* when Bobby Bauer goes on vacation, I could be off until the end of October. That's too much time off. If I can't go back to the *C-2*, I think I'll call the union hall and try to ship out with another fleet, though there isn't usually much of a demand for relief cooks in October.

I just finished a busy lunch and am taking a break while the second cook and porter sweep and mop the floors in the galley, messroom, and dining room. This morning I made a double batch of taco pie, steak subs, tuna salad subs, stacked ham sandwiches, stacked turkey sandwiches and cheese soup. The taco pie was the hot entree at lunch; many crewmembers ordered seconds, even though my portions were very generous. The tuna and steak subs also went well. A lot of the guys chose both a sub and some taco pie. I said something to the second cook about the crew enjoying Mexican food, and he replied that Mike Deragon doesn't do that sort of thing because he's "just a steamboat cook." He seemed to be offering the insight as an excuse for Mike not offering a big variety of foods. I think that's just a cop-out for sheer laziness or lack of interest in cooking and Mike's lack of pride in his job. For sixty thousand dollars a year, he should be able to keep the crew happy.

We're taking the long way around to the Soo because of the weather. Fairly strong winds are out of the north, so we paralleled the north shore until we passed Isle Royale and the Keweenaw Peninsula. Then we put the wind and seas on our port stern quarter and headed down for the Soo. It looks like a typical November day outside—grey as slate and the temperature is only around fifty degrees. I hope this weather breaks by the time I get off the boat. After sailing for four months, I deserve a little nice weather when I'm off.

Because of our detour, it now looks as though we won't be at the *Ojibway* supply boat until around 4:00 A.M. That's not a bad time in my book. I'll go to bed early, get up for groceries, take a shower, watch the overnight news on CNBC, and maybe do a little writing.

Sunday, September 15

Soo Locks

Sault Ste. Marie, Michigan

It's 2:30 A.M., and we're just pulling out of the Poe Lock. In another half hour the *Ojibway* will come alongside and lower a couple skips of groceries onto our deck and we'll spend a busy hour stowing everything. Getting groceries in the middle of the night is usually a killer, but I was tired after putting in a long day yesterday. I managed to fall asleep at 7:30 P.M., so I've had close to a full night's sleep already. I'll try to get another hour of shut-eye once we're finished with groceries, but I'll survive even if I don't.

Now it's 5:45 A.M. and I'm up for the day. I managed to sleep a little after groceries, and I feel well rested, which is pretty amazing since I was up from 2:30 until almost 4:00 A.M.

Ada Thompson got off at the supply boat this morning. Charlie Horn, Jack's maternal uncle, and his wife came up from Rogers City to give Ada a ride home. Charlie was chief engineer here on the *Munson* until he retired a few years ago after a long career on the lakes. A few years later, Jack became the *Munson*'s chief.

Charlie had a brother who was also a sailor. Paul Horn was working as an oiler on the *Carl D. Bradley* when it sank in a storm on Lake Michigan on November 18, 1958. Young Paul Horn was one of thirty-three sailors who died that black night, most of them from Rogers City. Had he survived, it's likely Paul, too, would have gone on to become a chief engineer.

Jack's son Steve is the third generation from the Horn/Thompson family to work on the lakes. A graduate of the Great Lakes Maritime Academy, Steve is an engineer in this fleet. Steve will be a chief someday; I imagine at some point he'll get assigned to the *Munson*, following in the footsteps of his father and great-uncle.

There are also some sailors on the Thompson side of Jack's family tree—my brother Gary and I. As I've said before, sailing is often a family affair in Rogers City.

The *Gott* followed us across Lake Superior yesterday, and our captain said that Captain J. R. Nelson is aboard again. It was just a few weeks ago that the Coast Guard evacuated him from the ship with heart problems. Apparently the company isn't completely convinced that Nelson should be back out. Elden Brege, who replaced Nelson, is reportedly still aboard—just in case.

It's now shortly after lunch and I'm taking a break before going back out to start supper. I'm tired and a nap would be nice, but I'll tough it out until after supper, and then go to bed early tonight.

It's still grey outside today, but the winds have subsided.

The marine forecast this morning called for strong winds out of the east and northeast, with seas reaching twelve feet. Fortunately, the forecast was wrong or we'd probably be at anchor in the St. Marys. At this point, I'd prefer not to have any delays. I'd also prefer not to be out on the lake in twelve-foot seas!

This is the end of the pay period, and I had to turn in our time sheets this morning. I worked 152 hours in fifteen days, an average of just over 10 hours a day. A person on the beach with a normal forty-hour-a-week job would have worked eighty hours during the same period. No wonder I'm tired. I won't be tired when my paycheck comes, however. I'll make well over three thousand dollars for the fifteen-day pay period, the most I've *ever* made. That'll be a nice paycheck to deposit, even after Uncle Sam takes his share.

Monday, September 16
Lake Erie, Eastbound

We should be at the U.S. Steel/Kobe mill in Lorain around noon. While I've visited Lorain hundreds of times on boats, it'll be my first trip up the Black River to the steel mill. All the other times I've been to Lorain I was on thousand-footers that unloaded at the taconite pellet terminal located at the mouth of the river. From there the pellets are loaded onto smaller boats for the short trip over to Cleveland and up the Cuyahoga River to LTV's steelmaking complex. It seems like an inefficient process to a lot of people, unloading pellets and then reloading them on other ships, but it actually saves LTV millions. Ships small enough to make it up the serpentine Cuyahoga can't carry more than about 25,000 tons of ore. The thousand-footers that bring the ore down from the lakehead, however, can load 60,000 tons or more, with operating costs that are only a little higher than those of the smaller River-class boats. The economies of scale in having a thousand-footer carry the pellets on the sixty-hour trip down the lakes more than offset the added costs of transshipping the ore at Lorain. Mills like the one at Lorain and the LTV plant at Cleveland were built around the turn of the century, when even the largest ships on the lakes could negotiate the Black River or the Cuyahoga.

If a steel mill were built today, it wouldn't be up a narrow and winding river, but at a port that could be served directly by thousand-footers, to save money on pellet delivery. The Bethlehem Steel mill at Burns Harbor, Indiana; the U.S. Steel plant at Gary, Indiana; the LTV and Inland Steel mills at Indiana Harbor; and the National Steel facilities at Zug Island on the Detroit River are all served directly by thousand-footers. The Rouge Steel mill that supplies steel to the Ford Motor Company's manufacturing plant in Dearborn, Michigan, on the other hand, is located at the head of navigation on the Rouge River and can't be served by thousand-footers. Lacking even a transshipment facility, ore for Rouge Steel must be brought down from the upper lakes and delivered to the mill by ships no longer than about 800 feet. That obviously adds to their production costs.

Other steel mills served by the Great Lakes shipping industry are in even less advantageous locations. ARMCO Steel, for example, located in Middletown, Ohio, between Dayton and Cincinnati, is far inland from the lakes. Iron ore to feed the furnaces at ARMCO is brought down from Lake Superior on Oglebay Norton ships that offload their cargoes at Ashtabula or Toledo, Ohio. From there, the ore is shipped overland by rail to the ARMCO plant, adding greatly to the steelmaker's cost of obtaining raw materials.

It's mid-afternoon now, and we're unloading. The first assistant engineer and the wiper are putting new filters in the ventilation system over the stoves and ovens, so there's nothing I can do in the galley right now.

When we came into the river this morning, the *James R. Barker* was unloading pellets at the transshipment terminal, and the *American Republic* was loading for the trip over to Cleveland. Dan Culligan, first mate on the *Barker,* was out on deck when we went by, and I talked to him for a minute or two as we passed. We were only about thirty feet off the *Barker* as we went by. Captain Brian Laffey was also standing out on the deck behind his room, just below the pilothouse, and he gave me a big hearty wave, as he always does. It was good to see both of them, but I missed seeing my old buddy "Big George" Rydberg, the steward on the *Barker.* He was probably taking his morning break when we went by, or maybe he'd gone up to use the phone on the dock. I'm hoping the *Barker* will still be there when we go out around 7:00 this evening, but I think I heard someone say they were supposed to be unloaded by about 5:00 P.M.

The old railroad ferry *Lansdowne,* which was tied up on the waterfront in downtown Detroit as a floating restaurant for many years, is now located just above the Black River bridge, at the defunct American Ship Building yard here in Lorain. She's been partially repainted since her Detroit days, but I didn't see any activity around her. I'm surprised they can't find some use for her. My sister Liz, brother-in-law Gordon Dickson, and I had dinner on her one evening a few years ago. The food was excellent, but there weren't many customers on her that night.

The captain called back just after lunch to say that the office had called to report that Mike Deragon will be waiting when we get to Calcite, as I'd expected. Several crewmembers have already expressed their regrets that I'm leaving so soon. Captain Lewandowski said he hopes I can come back when Mike takes his vacation in November. That'd be fine with me, but I'd really rather be back on the old *Calcite II.*

Supper's over now. I need to go back into the galley and pull stuff out to thaw for tomorrow, but I'll wait until after the guys have the floor mopped. I also need to prepare a grocery order, but I can't find the requisition forms anywhere. I'll conduct a more extensive search when the second cook and porter leave the galley. The order forms for the Soo Warehouse are huge, about twenty-by-thirty inches and they don't fit into standard desk drawers or file cabinets. Many cooks have special hiding places where they keep them. I haven't discovered Mike's spot yet. If I can't, he'll have to do the grocery order when he gets back tomorrow.

Fred Cummings, the fleet manager, called me this afternoon on the cell phone to thank me for the job I did on the *Speer,* and to tell me that he'd talked to Dick Johns in personnel. I am going back to the *Calcite II* on October 1. That's great news.

When Tom Burke, the porter, called his wife in Alpena this afternoon, she said that Canonie, a tug company from

Muskegon, has taken over operation of the Inland Lakes Management fleet—the former Huron Cement fleet. Apparently, Canonie's first act was to fire all the crewmembers, officers and unlicensed seamen alike, and advertise for replacements.[17] Some of the guys who used to sail for Inland Lakes might apply for their old jobs, purely out of desperation, but other than that Canonie will probably discover that with regard to deck and engine officers, the only applicants they'll get are likely to be a few bums none of the other companies will hire. They're definitely not going to find enough officers to sail all the Inland Lakes boats. Hell, the other shipping companies on the lakes can't even find enough mates and engineers to cover vacation reliefs.

The takeover by Canonie, a non-union company, and the unexpected firings make for interesting developments in the continuing saga of the cement fleet. Regardless of the results, there's going to be a lot of bad blood. I'll drive down to Alpena Wednesday and walk the picket line to support the Inland Lakes sailors. They're in tough straits right now, and they need to know that sailors all over the lakes support them. I wouldn't want to be in their shoes.

A few years ago, the contract between our union and Interlake Steamship expired, and talks between the union and the company broke down. James Barker, president and Interlake's majority stockholder, put out the word that he was going to take the company non-union. We were told that the boats would be laid up and we could either sign personal contracts with the company or pack our bags and get off his boats. A lot of us were terrified and damned mad. Barker thought he could get enough officers to crew three of the ten boats the company was then operating, but I doubt that would have happened. Had we taken Barker's non-union jobs, all of us would have lost our pension benefits with the union, and we would have been permanently blackballed. Since the union controls almost all of the jobs on the lakes,

---

[17]That bit of information turned out to be inaccurate. The licensed crewmembers actually walked off the boat when the company refused to hold a timely union representation election. Several later told me they feared that if a representation election wasn't held before the end of the sailing season, the company would have tried to replace them over the winter months when the boats were laid up.

that wasn't a reassuring prospect. Before Barker's magic deadline passed, he and the union settled and averted the nightmare. Like many of the Interlake sailors, I respected Barker right up until he issued that ultimatum. After that, I didn't like him and I sure as hell didn't trust him. Others felt the same way. For all of Barker's business acumen, he made a tactical error when he threatened the officers who crewed his ships.[18]

Tuesday, September 17

Detroit River

It's 4:30 A.M., and I'm up, showered, and dressed. Some would probably say that I've got "channel fever," because I'm getting off tonight, but I had my six hours of sleep and woke up refreshed at 3:30 A.M. I actually lounged in bed for awhile after waking up, which always feels good. It's something I don't allow myself to do too often. I'm glad I slept well last night, because this will be a long day. In addition to preparing three meals, I've got to pack and clean my room—or, more accurately, Mike Deragon's room—before we arrive at Calcite this evening.

One of the sailors I've enjoyed getting to know while I've been on the *Munson* is John Yarch, a veteran wheelsman. John's from Rogers City and grew up just a couple houses down from where my dad was raised. After his father died and his mother remarried, John bought the house he had grown up in. He and his wife live there yet today. That, my friends, is consistency. John's been just as consistent in his career—he's been sailing for this fleet since 1954, more than forty years! This will be his last full season on the lakes. He'll come out next spring just long enough to collect his

---

[18]While in Duluth waiting to board the *Roger Blough* in late November, I discussed this incident with a senior staff member in our fleet office. He told me that when Barker tried to break the union, he contacted all the other shipping companies on the Great Lakes and asked them to follow his lead. For one reason or another, saner heads prevailed at the other companies and they all declined Barker's invitation to declare war on the union. That's reassuring.

241

vacation pay, and then he'll go down the ladder for the last time to go home to his house on First Street in Rogers City's "Polish Town."

I wish I could spend more time with John. He's a soft-spoken, pleasant fellow, and tells some wonderful stories about sailing "in the old days." After lunch yesterday, we talked about vacations. John told me that when he started sailing there were no vacations. You went on the boat at fitout, and you didn't get off until it laid up at the end of the season. Later, according to John, sailors got ten days of vacation a year, which had to be taken between June and August when college students were available to sail relief. The office was pretty hard-core about that policy, too. John's wife was pregnant during that period, and scheduled to give birth in mid-September. John begged the office to let him take his vacation in September, so he could be home when his wife delivered. I remember those days well, because I grew up with the sons and daughters of many sailors who couldn't get off the boats to be home for major events in their children's lives. And the shipping companies wonder why their crews eventually unionized!

Looking back over the years I've sailed, I missed a lot of things that went on in the lives of my children, though I did manage to schedule my vacations so I could get home for most of the major events. I was sailing when my first book came out, though. I arranged with my publisher to have copies of the books shipped to Meredith and Scott in Traverse City. As soon as possible after the publication date, I called Meredith to get her impressions of the book. Her first words were precious. "Geez, Dad, it's a *real* book!" she exclaimed. I would have loved to have been there to see the look on her face when she opened the books.

But I digress. Even though John Yarch has more than forty seasons out here on the lakes, he's not the senior sailor in the fleet. That honor goes to George Sobeck, second cook on the *George A. Sloan,* but not by much. John started sailing on November 29, 1954, but George had signed on the articles for the first time on November 21, 1954. Interestingly, John later married George's sister.

George is from another of Rogers City's sailing families. His brother Dick is captain on the *Sloan,* and his brother

John is an oiler on the *Calcite II*. Together, the three Sobeck boys have spent more than a hundred years out here on the lakes.

George's career almost ended in 1958. He was a porter on the *Carl D. Bradley* that season, but took emergency leave in mid-November when his father died. While George was home for the funeral, the *Bradley* broke in half and sank in a killer storm on Lake Michigan. The sailor who had taken George's place on the *Bradley* went down with the ship. The following week, George was attending the funerals and memorial services for thirty-three of his former shipmates.

Another fellow I've enjoyed getting to know during my brief stint here on the *Munson* is First Mate Harry Goebel, who's also nearing the end of a long career out here on the lakes. Harry's wife called the boat Monday and left a message for him to call her as soon as possible. All of us who sail dread getting such calls, because it usually means we're in store for some bad news, but when Shirley talked to Captain Lewandowski she made it clear that it wasn't an emergency—she just wanted to talk to Harry as soon as possible. When Harry nervously called his wife on the ship's cellular phone a little while later, she informed him that she had bought him a car at an estate auction—a 1951 Ford that had been in storage for a couple of decades! Harry's a car nut, and he'd asked Shirley to bid on the old Ford for him, although he thought it would sell for a lot more than he was willing to pay. For one reason or another, the car actually sold for thousands less than its appraised value, and Harry is now its proud owner. That's all he's been able to talk about since his conversation with Shirley. He's anxious to get home tonight and take a look at the antique auto. Restoring the old Ford to pristine condition will give Harry plenty to do in his retirement and keep him out of Shirley's hair.

Shirley's call to the boat brought good news for Harry, but that's not usually the case. When a sailor gets a phone call from home, it's almost always bad news, as our families know not to call the boat just to chat. I was sailing with a deckhand from Buffalo, New York, on the *Elton Hoyt 2d* in 1989 when he got an emergency call telling him that his mother had been killed when the garage next to her home exploded. We later learned that her neighbors had been manufacturing illegal fireworks in the garage when it blew up. The deckhand's mother was working at her kitchen sink when the explosion occurred. We were on our way down Lake Michigan when the news came and the captain arranged for a Coast Guard boat to come out from Frankfort to take the crewman off. Following an old tradition on the lakes, we took up a collection to give the deckhand some traveling money for the long trip home.

My brother was also sailing when our father died. His boat was actually in at Calcite when Dad got sick and had to be taken to the hospital. Gary ran back down to the boat and told them he was going to take a trip off. Dad's condition improved a little over the next couple of days and Gary rejoined his boat the next time it came in. A week or so later, Dad took a turn for the worse and the doctors didn't expect him to live. We hurriedly called Gary's boat to let him know the situation. There weren't any cellular phones on the ships in those days, so you had to call WLC, the marine radio station in Rogers City. The station would contact the boat on the radio and patch your call through. Conversation during those radio transmissions was a little difficult, because only one person could talk at a time, and you had to say "over" to let whomever you were talking to know it was their turn. Gary's boat was on its way up the St. Clair River at the time, and the captain arranged for the pilot boat at Port Huron to come out and pick him up to go home. My sister Liz, who worked at Chrysler in Detroit, met him in Port Huron a few hours later and they made the long four-hour drive to Rogers City. Unfortunately, by the time they arrived at my house, Dad had already died.

Back in the days before radios were installed on ships, which took place between the 1920s and World War II, many sailors arrived in port to find out that friends or loved ones had died and been buried while they were out on the lakes. There was simply no way to contact the sailors in those days. Today, it's hard to imagine what it must have been like before radio. When you were out on the lake you were totally cut off from civilization.

Well, I've got lots of work to do. This will have to be all until I get over to the *Calcite II.*

Saturday, October 5
Lake Huron, Downbound

Hooray, I'm home! I came back aboard the *Calcite II* in Rogers City at about 10:00 last night. It's great to be with the gang again. They seemed as glad to see me as I was to see them. That's not to cast any aspersions on the crews on the *Speer* or *Munson,* but this is *my* crew, at least for this year.

I took seventeen days of vacation after leaving the *Munson,* and I enjoyed every minute of it. I even accomplished everything I had hoped to do during that time. I bought a car for son Scott—his high school graduation present—spent time with Scott, Meredith, and my mother, picked up artwork for *Graveyard of the Lakes* from Ralph Roberts, and relaxed a little. It was the best vacation I've had in years, even though it was on the short side.

Rumors persist that the *Calcite II* and *Myron C. Taylor* will lay up around November 1, so I didn't want to take a whole month off, and then get laid off a couple weeks after returning to work. Besides, I wanted badly to come back to the *C-2.* I knew Bobby Bauer was going on vacation around October 1, so it was either come back or let someone else have *my* boat.

I even had a quasi-date while I was off—miracle of miracles. Old friend Sally Schalk Zapata and I went to an Italian restaurant for supper one evening. The ambiance at the place was mediocre and the food was disappointing, but they served some sensational bread, the company was great, and I enjoyed the evening immensely.

The day after I got home from the *Munson,* I went to Alpena to do a little shopping. I spent some time on the picket line with the officers from Inland Lakes Management—the old Huron Cement fleet. The officers want union representation, something they're legally entitled to, but the company seems to be delaying a representation election. The fleet management recently changed when the Andrie brothers from Muskegon took over. They run a non-union tug company, Canonie, and were chosen to manage Inland Lakes' new tug-and-barge. Later it was announced that the Andries would also take over management of the ships in

245

the cement fleet. Fleet personnel are afraid that all the ships will eventually be replaced by tug-barge units. By joining our union, they'd have the option to ship out with other Great Lakes companies if their jobs are eliminated by the move to tugs and barges. Few have any interest in working on tugs, and it's unlikely there will be enough jobs to accommodate all of them. The new tug is crewed by only eight men and there's talk the number will soon be reduced to six.

Dennis Myatt, who was at the maritime academy when I worked there, has been sailing as a mate on the cement boats for a number of years. We had a chance to get reacquainted while walking the picket line. Dennis is also a Vietnam veteran and married to a Vietnamese woman. They spent last winter visiting her family in Saigon, the first time either had been back since Vietnam fell to the communists more than twenty years ago. Dennis said there are communist police on virtually every corner in Saigon, but they never hassled him during his stay. He and his wife are looking forward to going back again, and may even move there once Dennis retires from sailing. While Japan and other Asian countries are currently investing heavily in Vietnam, it's still extremely inexpensive to live there.

While in Alpena, I also ran across Captain Bob Massey, whom I haven't seen in about a dozen years. When I first met Bob, he was running a marine salvage and construction business in Alpena and I was a reporter for one of the local radio stations. I spent quite a bit of time with Bob over the next four to five years; I even worked for him on a couple of occasions. Bob salvaged the *Nordmeer, Pewabic,* and *Monrovia,* which all sank off Alpena and Thunder Bay Island. During the time we spent together, he taught me a great deal about diving, salvage, shiphandling, navigation and being a man. We always worked and played hard. I have nothing but good memories of those special days. Bob's still knocking around the waters of Thunder Bay. He bought a forty-foot boat from the Coast Guard last year and he's got himself a little marine towing business. Unfortunately, by the time I tracked Bob down, it was almost time for me to go back on the boat, so our visit was brief. I'll look him up again when I get off the boat, though—now I know where to find him.

Sunday, October 6
Lake Huron, Upbound

We docked on the back side of Zug Island at Detroit at about 6:00 this morning. We were unloaded and on our way back up to Calcite before lunch. We'll be there about 9:00 tomorrow morning, which is a lousy time for those of us in the galley. I'm going to let Geno and Steve Kandal, our porter, take off when we get in. I'll cover lunch and dinner myself; it's not going to be very busy anyway. The only customers we'll get at Calcite will be the watchstanders, five to six people at the most. If I have time, I'll run up to my mother's in the afternoon and check my mail. If I can't manage to get away, it won't be any major loss. Heck, I just spent more than two weeks at home.

One guy I miss here on the *Calcite II* is Jerry Macks, normally the first mate. Jerry got put off a couple of weeks ago when Dick Sobeck, the new captain, discovered that Jerry's merchant marine document—his sailing card—had expired back in June. Jerry was operating on the assumption that he could continue sailing on his mate's license, but when Dick checked with the office, word came back that Jerry would have to get off until he got his card renewed. That's been taking six to eight weeks, so it'll be awhile before Jerry is back out on the lakes. I guess Jerry was quite upset when he had to get off. I'm sure the people at the Coast Guard office in Toledo will be *very* familiar with Jerry before this is over. If there's any delay in renewing his sailing card—and it's likely there will be—they'll get an earful from brother Macks. He's not one to mince words. In their defense, however, Jerry should have renewed his sailing card before the start of the season. We receive constant communications from the Coast Guard, the company, and our union about the need to make sure our sailing cards are renewed. A number of guys invariably ignore that advice and end up with an expired card. It even happened to the captain of a boat here on the lakes.

Don Dehring has gone first mate in Jerry's absence. He's another good friend, and I enjoy chatting with him after his 4-to-8 watch, but he doesn't tell colorful stories like Jerry Macks. Jerry is a storyteller *extraordinaire*.

247

Speaking of Don Dehring, it's almost eight o'clock and Don will be coming in for dinner in a minute or two. Time for my dinner, too.

Tuesday, October 8
Detroit River

I was too tired to write anything last night, and I'm not in much better shape this evening. I haven't gotten a good night's sleep since I came back on the boat. One night I had insomnia—chocolate induced—another night I stayed up late to watch the presidential debate. Last night I turned the light out at a few minutes after 9:00 P.M., thinking it was going to be my chance to catch up on my sleep. I fell asleep fast enough, but woke up at about 1:30 A.M. with indigestion, undoubtedly the result of eating my own cooking. I didn't have dinner until about 8:00 P.M., and I guess I shouldn't have eaten that big piece of my pizza spaghetti casserole. I don't know if it was the pepperoni, Italian sausage, onion, or green pepper, but something upset my stomach, which caused me to toss and turn from 1:30 until it was time to get up at 5:30 A.M. I should have taken a nap this afternoon, but I was so tired I was afraid I'd have a hard time waking up and getting dinner ready. Tonight, friends, I *will* get at least eight hours of sleep!

We were at Calcite from about 1:00 yesterday afternoon until 10:00 P.M. last night, so everyone managed to get home for at least a little while. I gave the second cook and porter dinner off, but I still managed to get home for an hour or so in the afternoon.

The *George A. Sloan* was leaving Calcite when we got there, and the captain on the *Sloan* told Dick Sobeck that the office has scheduled them to take a load of coal into the LaFarge cement plant in Alpena. To do that they'll have to cross our union's picket line at the plant, something other union fleets refused to do. One of the fleet's managers from Duluth will supposedly make the trip into Alpena, "to make sure things go okay." We interpret that to mean that he'll be on the boat to threaten any of the crewmembers

248

who express reluctance to cross the picket line. I imagine someone has notified the president of our union about the scheduled trip. My guess is the union will encourage the office to change their plans. I'd hate to have one of our ships be the first to break the picket line.

Yes, there is a picket line out on the waters of Lake Huron off Alpena. Striking officers from the cement fleet have been going out to the junction buoy at the entrance to Thunder Bay in small boats anytime they receive word that a ship is bound for the cement plant. I only know of one ship from a unionized fleet that was scheduled to go into Alpena. An Oglebay Norton boat was headed there with a load of coal, but company officials changed their minds when the ship got to Thunder Bay, and it continued to Calcite and unloaded there. Since then, trucks have been hauling the coal from Rogers City to the cement plant at Alpena, an expensive operation.

I think there's a good chance that if the *Sloan* goes into Alpena with a load of coal, our union will ask the officers to walk off the ship without unloading it. That could tie the ship up until the strike is settled, and that prospect may force the office to reconsider their plans.

Apparently, several of the strikers crossed the picket line and returned to work on the cement boats. All three are now in operation—the *Alpena, Iglehart,* and *Townsend.* That's not good news. Most of us thought it would be impossible to find enough officers to crew the three ships. I'm sure my friends walking the picket line in Alpena are devastated. If Inland Lakes Management and LaFarge have all three boats back in service, there is little incentive for them to talk to the strikers. Word is they have been offering up to one thousand dollars a day for officers willing to cross the picket line and go to work.

There was heavy boat traffic on the St. Clair River to-day, including a lot of Canadian freighters headed north in ballast, probably to load grain. The three Canadian ships that have been laid up most of the year at Point Edward, Sarnia, Ontario, have apparently been put into service for the fall grain movement. We also passed the *Columbia Star,* my brother's boat, just above the Blue Water Bridge at Port Huron. It was mid-afternoon, though, and there was no sign of Gary. He's on the 8-to-12 watch, and was probably napping. There was a good sea running out of the north at the time we saw the *Star;* I got a couple of good pictures of her throwing up tons of spray as her blunt bow drove into the waves.

Wednesday, October 9
Goderich, Ontario

We got our official notice today: We're scheduled to lay up around October 31 at Fraser Shipyard in Superior, Wisconsin. We could, however, run as late as November 9 or 10, depending on weather conditions, cargoes, and other factors. That's surprisingly early to take a boat in for the season. Supposedly, the *Myron C. Taylor* will follow us in around November 1. Either cargoes are dropping off as we near the end of the shipping season, which would be an unusual phenomenon, or the company figures they lose too much money trying to run the small boats during the heavy weather period in the fall.

It's not good news for me. With a nine-day lay up, I'll be done between November 9 and November 19. Anyone going on vacation in November will already be off, so I'll be unemployed until December 1. If I teach at the union school, though, I'll have to be off the boat by Christmas, so it may not even be feasible for me to take a relief job during December. Who's going to want to come and relieve me a day or two before Christmas? As the song says, "If it wasn't for the bad news, there'd be no news at all."

We're loading salt at Goderich, Ontario, on the east shore of Lake Huron, a couple hours north of Sarnia. It's the first time I've ever been along this shore, and I'm struck by how much it reminds me of the eastern shoreline of Lake Michigan. It has the same type of bluffs running along the beach. We're loading salt at a mine here. They've got a strange loading system that must have been designed by Rube Goldberg. We're only taking a little over ten thousand tons, but it's going to take us twelve to sixteen hours to load it. I would have liked to have gone up the street and looked around a little. Goderich seems to be an attractive little town, and there's a P&H freighter tied up farther inside the harbor. There's also a pilothouse off a freighter in a little park just across from where we're loading. Unfortunately, it's cold and rainy, and I'm exhausted from a long day in the galley. All I want to do is curl up in bed.

Thursday, October 10
Lake Huron, Upbound

It's the middle of the afternoon, and I'm taking a break. I got a lot done this morning, and thought I would take a little nap this afternoon, but the boat is rolling so badly that I couldn't fall asleep. We left Goderich shortly after 6:00 this morning and we're crossing Lake Huron on a line from Goderich to Thunder Bay Island in the face of fairly strong north-northwesterly winds. The seas seem to be running from six to eight feet, enough to bounce this little tub around pretty good. We're not riding well at all. There's no steady rhythm to the boat's movements. She goes up and down, then rolls a little and shudders as additional waves hit the hull and interrupt the boat's motion. There's also a lot of vibration, as though we're running in shallow water. Hopefully, it'll let up as we get closer to the Michigan shoreline. This old bucket isn't in any condition to be taking heavier seas than what we have right now.

We got a report this morning that the *Sloan* was around Pte. Aux Barques, at the tip of Michigan's thumb, on her way up to Alpena with coal. They should arrive there sometime tonight; we're all anxious to hear what happens.

Interestingly, the company—actually, the same guy from the office riding the *Sloan* to make sure the crew takes it into Alpena—also got tough with the crew here. He put out the word that he wanted the mud shoveled out of several of the ballast tanks before the boat lays up. The contract between the unlicensed union and the company, however, includes a clause that says the crewmembers don't have to work in the tanks except when the boat is scheduled for a five-year Coast Guard inspection. That's another year away, so most of the guys don't want to go into the tanks. It's a cold, dirty job, especially this time of the year. When the

251

A stiff fall wind on Lake Huron billows up the tarps used to cover the hatches on the *Calcite II*. The tarps prevent water from leaking through the joints in the ship's telescoping hatch covers and getting into the cargo hold. Most newer ships have single-piece steel hatch covers that do not require tarps. (Author's collection)

captain relayed that message to the office, he was supposedly instructed to tell the crew to get to work in the tanks "or else." They can file a grievance, but long before it would be settled they'd have finished with the tanks. I guess it's fair to say that there's no "spirit of cooperation" between this company and its unions right now. I'm sure that if the *Sloan* unloads its coal at the cement plant in Alpena, the company will consider it a major victory over our union. I hope our union doesn't let them get away with it, or the office will be on the muscle the rest of the year.

I sent a grocery order up to the pilothouse to be faxed into the Soo Warehouse yesterday, so we could get them when we reach Cedarville around October 12, and the captain summarily chewed me out. They picked up groceries the last time they were at Cedarville, on October 1, and we normally wouldn't have placed another order for two and a half to three weeks. Bobby Bauer must have been visiting another planet when he did the last grocery order, because there was hardly any meat or milk when I got on. We'll be lucky if the milk lasts until we get to Cedarville and I'm already being forced to become creative with my menu planning. Except for one strip loin, a standing rib roast, and twenty-five pounds of ground chuck, I'm out of beef. The only pork I have is a half a box of ribs, half a box of smoked pork chops, and three hams, and I already served ribs, smoked chops, and ham earlier this week. There's just enough chicken for one meal, but there are three whole frozen turkeys. I guess it's fair to say that there's plenty to eat here, as long as no one is too concerned about variety. There will be a load of groceries waiting for me when we get to Cedarville Saturday or Sunday.

Dinner's over now, we're riding a lot smoother, and I'm looking forward to a relaxing evening. I'll watch a little television, including *Seinfeld,* my favorite show, and struggle with menus for the next couple of days. A bunch of the guys tried to talk me into sitting in on a low-stakes poker game this evening, but I didn't bring much cash with me when I came aboard, and I'd like to hold onto what I have. I also value my evenings. I put in a long day and I look forward to kicking back and relaxing at the end of the day. The *Sloan* is due at the cement plant in Alpena right about now—6:00 P.M.—and we hope that we'll get word of what transpires there. We're also supposed to get an itinerary tonight, the first we've had in awhile. We've sort of been running trip to trip, but the office now has a schedule for us that covers the next week or two. The captain talked to someone in the company's traffic department this afternoon. It doesn't sound as though we're going to get back to Calcite anytime in the near future. We're apparently going to spend some time down on Lake Erie, and then load coal at Ashtabula for the cement plant in Alpena. Drat! I hope that trip gets cancelled. The person in traffic also told the captain that since the company has a tremendous amount of cargo to move during the balance of the season, many in the office were surprised by the decision to lay up the *Calcite II* and *Taylor* so early. Many of the crewmembers still think the boat will be sailing long after October 31. That's a distinct possibility and it would please me greatly.

253

Friday, October 11
Green Bay, Wisconsin

We're just entering the Fox River at Green Bay, on our way up to the Fort Howard Paper Company with our load of salt. It's been quite windy all day, and the captain is a little worried the wind may have blown enough water out of the river that we might not be able to reach Fort Howard. If that happens, we'll have to find someplace to anchor to wait until the wind dies down and the water flows back into the river.

It's an hour or so later now and we're almost to Fort Howard. No problems so far; we'll be tied up in another thirty minutes. I stood out on deck while we were going up the river and through the city of Green Bay. There's lots to look at along the banks of the river, but much of my attention this evening was focused on the deckhands, who were busy removing the tarps from the hatches. The leaf-type hatch covers on this boat will allow water to get into the hold if it's raining or if we happen to take seas over the deck, God forbid. In order to prevent the cargo hold from flooding, the hatches are covered with tarps when we're carrying cargo. The huge tarps are stretched over the hatches, and then the ends and sides are wrapped around wooden battens held in place by the hatch clamps. Removing the tarps at each unloading dock and putting them back on after the boat is loaded is a major project and lots of extra work for the deckhands. It gets even worse when snow and ice form on top of the tarps. It's no wonder that shipowners and their crews were quick to embrace the single-piece steel hatch covers when they came out. Not only are they safer than the telescoping covers, but they also eliminate a lot of work for the crews on the boats. Today only a couple of old boats still have leaf-type hatch covers. This is the second one I've been on. I finished out the season last year on the *Kinsman Enterprise*, which is the same vintage as the *Calcite II*, and has leaf hatches. The only other U.S. boats I'm aware of that have telescoping hatches are American Steamship's *John J. Boland*, Oglebay Norton's *Frantz*, and our *Taylor*.

On our way up the river here we passed two cement

boats that are operated by Inland Lakes Management, the Alpena-based company that's being struck by our union. The first was the old *Lewis G. Harriman,* which hasn't run for a number of years. Like many of the old cement boats, she's being used as a storage barge for cement, augmenting what can be stored in the silos at the cement terminal. I don't ever remember seeing the *Harriman* before. She's tiny, even compared to the *Calcite II.* She can't be much over 400 feet long.[19]

The second cement boat we saw was the *J. A. W. Iglehart,* which was unloading at the LaFarge terminal here. The *Iglehart* left Alpena yesterday, crewed by officers who are strikebreakers, or "scabs" in the parlance of the American labor movement. Because they willingly crossed the picket line and took the boat out, Inland Lakes Management will be less likely to bargain with our union and the officers who went out on strike. That's too bad. My thoughts this evening are with my buddies who are on the picket line in Alpena, and who face a bleak future because their company has found crews for the *Alpena, Iglehart,* and *Townsend.*

Saturday, October 12
Lake Michigan

We left Green Bay during breakfast this morning and are now steaming across northern Lake Michigan on our way to Cedarville to load stone. We were supposed to be in there at 3:15 A.M., but we're still getting a pretty bumpy ride, so we could easily lose some time. That'd be just fine. We've got groceries coming at Cedarville, and I'd just as soon not

---

[19]The *Harriman,* launched in 1923 as the *John W. Boardman,* is actually only 350 feet long. I later learned that the *Harriman* had been towed from Milwaukee to Green Bay in late September to serve as a storage barge for cement. It hasn't run since 1980, and was used for storage in Milwaukee until LaFarge Corporation completed work on its new cement terminal there. With the *Harriman*'s arrival in Green Bay, the Canadian cement barge *Metis,* that we saw on June 13, was no longer needed, and it was towed from Green Bay to Windsor, Ontario.

Third Mate Ron "Pootzer" Buczkowski uses a portable radio to give "distances off" to the captain, who is up in the pilothouse maneuvering the ship out the Fox River at Green Bay, Wisconsin. The *Calcite II* has just gone through one of the numerous bridges that cross the river and Buczkowski is letting the captain know that the stern has cleared the structure. To the left of the *Calcite II* is the *Samuel Mitchell*, a small cement carrier built in 1892 that is used today only for cement storage. (Author's collection)

have to get up at 3:15 A.M. My days are long enough when I get up at 5:30 A.M.

Green Bay—the bay, not the city—was fairly calm when we came out, but it grew rough just as soon as we poked our nose through the Rock Island passage. In fact, it was at 4:00 P.M., and I was just starting to serve dinner when we began to roll quite a bit. I thought for a few seconds that portions of dinner were going to end up on the deck, but it never got that bad. My big concern was for the barbecue grill out on the fantail that was loaded with filet mignon at the time. The engineers built the grill from half of a fifty-five-gallon oil drum and one of its legs keeps falling off. I was afraid all the rolling would cause the leg to fall off and the grill would topple, dumping those gorgeous steaks onto the deck. Geno ran out and pulled the steaks off the grill, just in case, but it managed to stay upright until the boat settled down a little. I put the roll bars on the stove tonight, just to make sure that the pots and pans with leftovers from dinner don't slide off onto the deck if we start to roll again. That's the first time this season I've felt a need to use the roll bars, so I guess the fall sailing season is officially upon us. From here on out it may only get worse. If our orders hold, we'll be off the lake around the end of the month, thereby missing the "gales of November." We don't have any trips scheduled after October 23, although we're likely to lose a day here and there because of weather, so we'll probably be out here until the end of the month.

After writing in this log last night, I went out into the messroom and talked with the guys coming off the 4-to-8 watch. Butch Kierzek told a story about an engineer in this fleet who is infamous for stealing things from the boat, especially from the galley. Among the items he regularly took when Butch sailed with him were jars of peanut butter and cans of solid white albacore tuna. The galley crew put a fresh container of peanut butter out on the table in the messroom or the officers' dining room, and it would be gone in the morning. One cook quit putting full containers of peanut butter out. When a jar of peanut butter was empty, he'd fill it half way from a fresh container. This engineer was only interested in taking *full* jars. As Butch tells it, the boat was in at Calcite and all the guys were waiting to race down the ladder and get home. Among them was the larcenous engineer, whose jacket front was noticeably bulky. He also held one forearm across the bottom of his jacket, as if to prevent something from falling out. The engineer started down the ladder just ahead of Butch. When he was partway down, he lost his balance and moved the arm that was across the front of his jacket. Two glass jars of peanut butter slipped from his jacket and smashed to pieces on the dock. Rather than act embarrassed, the engineer launched into a tirade about how some deckhand had put jars of peanut butter in the pockets of his jacket. With his arm firmly holding the front of his jacket to prevent the loss of any more of his larder, the engineer stormed home.

Earlier in the evening, several of us laughed about how hard it was to get dinner ready when we started rolling coming out of Rock Island passage. John Buczkowski, the 8-to-12 watchman, said that back in 1991 or 1992, the *George A. Sloan* ran into heavy seas in the same spot. The captain nosed out of Green Bay onto northern Lake Michigan and discovered twelve- to fifteen-foot seas. Without hesitating or notifying the crew, he ordered the wheelsman to put the wheel hard over to return to the sheltered waters of Green Bay. At about the same time, three crewmen who bunked up forward headed back along the deck to have supper. Partway down the deck, one of the three, a veteran sailor, saw from the wake that the ship was turning. Eyeing the size of the seas, he knew the boat was going to roll and if they stayed out on deck they would likely get wet. Hollering to the others, he took off at a dead run for the forward cabin, the others in close pursuit. By the time they reached the cabin, the boat was already rolling badly as it wallowed in a trough of the sea partway through the turn. For a minute or two, the boat stalled in the trough and began to roll violently, first to starboard until the fence that runs the length of the deck was awash, and then, after shuddering to right herself, she'd roll to the port side.

When the rolling started, John Buczkowski, who was standing watch up in the bow, ran down the stairs to a refrigerator that was used by the guys who lived up forward. John remembered that the hooks that were supposed to hold the refrigerator to the bulkhead weren't latched. As he passed the crew's recreation room he was startled to see several recliners tumbling end over end across the room, smashing against the bulkhead. When the ship rolled the other way, the chairs reversed their courses and tumbled across to the other bulkhead. When John reached the re-frigerator, it was just in time to see the door swing open and all the contents fly out—pop, jars of pickles, plates of food. The contents of the refrigerator were still in midair when the heavy refrigerator began to slide across the room, as if in pursuit of its airborne contents. The mélange crashed into the bulkhead on the other side of the room. When the ship rolled the other way, the refrigerator, pop, pickles, broken glass, and other debris slid back across the room, slowly at first, and then picking up speed as the ship's roll became more pronounced. John quickly retreated from the room, and, like most of his shipmates, spent the next couple of minutes trying to stay upright. "It's the only time I ever walked on the bulkheads [walls]," remembered John.

Listening to Butch and John, it struck me how much time sailors spend reminiscing about events that occurred years ago on boats they were on. We are inveterate storytellers. I must hear up to twenty stories a day from other crewmembers. I've been known to tell a few stories myself. I've worked in many professions during my lifetime, but I'm not sure I've ever worked with people who are so prone to talk about events from the past. I'm not sure why that's the case, but we even have a name for the stories. They're called "sea stories." The way to tell the difference between a fairy tale and a sea story is that a fairy tale begins with "Once upon a time" while a sea story begins with "Now, this is no shit." The stories told aboard ship are often embellished. The storyteller isn't lying, at least not most of the time; he's merely trying to make marginal improvements to the story, to make a good story even better.

Most of the time, the storyteller claims to have been a witness to the event he's telling his shipmates about. If he wasn't actually present, that's easily forgiven as long as the story is told well. Many times the same sea stories—the "classics"—will be told on different ships, even in different fleets. If all the sailors who claimed to have witnessed some of those events had actually been present, the audience would have had to have been large enough to fill Tiger Stadium . . . and any ship with all those people aboard would have been seriously overloaded. A shipmate on the *Kinsman Enterprise* gave an authoritative, supposedly firsthand account of the stabbing of the chief engineer on the *James R. Barker* a few years ago. He didn't know at the time that I *was* on the *Barker* when the stabbing occurred, and I didn't let on to those sitting enthralled in the messroom that the storyteller was giving them, at best, a secondhand account of the event. Heck, he told the story real well.

I'm convinced some of the better sea stories have been around for generations, surviving after the sailors and ships involved were long gone from the lakes. Stories like that get updated about as often as General Motors changes the styling of its cars.

The mate just called back to tell me that we're going to make a haul—turn—shortly, and he thinks we might do some rolling. I'd better get out into the galley and make sure everything is secured. I've cleaned up galleys after a ship rolled and everything came off onto the deck and I don't want to do it again if I can help it. That's no sea story.

Monday, October 14

Columbus Day

Lake Erie, Eastbound

God bless old Christopher Columbus, the most famous of all sailors. Thanks to him, today was a double-time day for those of us sailing on the lakes—sixteen hours of pay for eight hours of work. Double-time pay somehow makes the day's work much more bearable. The television newsman at a Toledo, Ohio, station just said that it's probably not politically correct to honor Columbus as a hero anymore. His image has been tarnished by the sad plight of the Native Americans that resulted from European exploration and colonization. Thousands of Native Americans died of diseases caught from the Europeans; thousands of others were killed. From Columbus to Custer, Europeans, and those of European heritage, progressively destroyed the Native American cultures in the Americas.

I have a hard time holding Columbus responsible for the plight of the natives he encountered on his explorations of the Western world, however. Hell, even the doctors in that era didn't understand how diseases were transmitted or why American Indians died from microscopic organisms that the Europeans were largely immune to. What's more, Columbus's voyage to the Americas was an absolutely awe-inspiring undertaking. Given the risks of any voyage on the Atlantic in the tiny sailing ships of that era, especially when the predominant opinion of the day held that the earth was flat and Columbus and his shipmates were likely to sail off the edge of the world and into eternity, Christopher Columbus deserves to be honored for the single most significant voyage of discovery in the history of the planet. His trip more than five hundred years ago set in motion an unprecedented migration from Europe to the Americas. No, he didn't discover the Americas. Asians had done that thousands of years earlier, probably migrating across a land-bridge between Alaska and China during one of the ice ages, then fanning out across the continents and to the islands of the Caribbean, where Columbus discovered them. No, Columbus didn't discover the Americas, but he was the first European to discover the continents. A Johnny-come-lately, perhaps, but his epic voyage of discovery changed the face of the planet. Those of us who sail the inland seas of North America find it easy to admire Columbus's achievements as a master mariner who sailed into uncharted waters. What happened to the Native Americans—or those who emigrated here from Asia in the days before Columbus—is a separate issue that will be debated eternally.

It's a magnificent Indian summer day, one that a sailor like Columbus would have appreciated. I even managed to get outside to sit on a hatch for half an hour before starting dinner. We were in the St. Clair and Detroit Rivers most of the day, so we were able to take advantage of the warm and sunny weather. There was quite a bit of boat traffic in the river, mainly Canadian freighters heading for the grain ports along Lake Superior. It was a great day for sightseeing and I took lots of boat pictures.

Shortly after we left the mouth of the Detroit River around suppertime and sailed out onto Lake Erie, we met the *George A. Sloan,* headed in the other direction. The captain was in the dining room when the *Sloan* approached, but he went to the phone and called the pilothouse to tell the mate on watch not to blow a salute unless the *Sloan* blew one first. Apparently, the last time we went into Calcite, Captain Sobeck blew a salute to the *Sloan,* which was leaving port, but they never returned his salute. The *Sloan* passed us a few minutes later. We didn't blow a salute and neither did they. I guess we're unofficially snubbing each other. I suppose the captain's feelings got stepped on when his salute off Calcite wasn't returned. Our captain sure as hell isn't going to give in, and the captain on the *Sloan* apparently is just as stubborn.

While the weather was splendid today, the joints in my shoulders, elbows, wrists, and knees are aching. That usually indicates a change in weather is forthcoming. I don't think it's going to get any nicer out, so we're probably in for some typical blustery fall weather. Drat.

Tuesday, October 15
Fairport, Ohio

It's another beautiful Indian summer day, despite my aching joints. The deckhands are working in their t-shirts and it's warm enough in the messroom that we turned the fan on for the first time since I've been back.

We arrived here at the mouth of the Grand River shortly before 2:00 A.M., and finished unloading our cargo of stone at about 8:00 A.M. Then we backed out of the river and turned around, so we could come back into the salt dock where we're now loading. It's a long, slow process, between twelve and fifteen hours, but with the weather the way it is, nobody is complaining.

As we discharged our cargo of stone this morning, the sandsucker *F. M. Osborne* unloaded directly across from us. Other than in pictures, it was the first time I'd ever seen the boat, which is somewhat of a fixture down here along the Ohio coast. The boat looks like a miniature lake freighter, with cabins fore and aft. Its deck is a hopper that is filled with sand that the boat sucks off the bottom of the lake with a suction pipe dragged alongside. The sand settles to the bottom of the hopper and the water sucked up with it rises to the top and eventually flows overboard. It's identical to the setup on the old *Massey D*, where I spent a lot of time on back in the 1970s, although the *Osborne* appears to be a little bigger.[20]

---

[20] Built in 1910 as the carferry Grand Island, the vessel was converted to a sandsucker in 1954. In 1958 it was lengthened 40 feet and renamed

With its self-unloading boom swung out of the way, a shoreside loading rig pours bluish-white road salt into the cargo holds of the *Calcite II* at a dock in Fairport, Ohio. Passing the 605-foot *C-2* is the 114-foot *Emmett J. Carey,* a tiny dredge that sucks sand off the bottom of Lake Erie. Fully loaded, her deck is almost awash. Sand dredged up by the *Carey* and other "sand-suckers" is used primarily in construction and manufacturing. (Author's collection)

I made pizza for supper last night for the first time since my return. It went over well, as usual, and the crew put away fourteen and one-third pizzas between dinner last night and when I came into the galley at 6:00 A.M. this morning. That's the most pizza the gang here on the *Calcite II* has eaten all season, but it still falls more than a whole pizza short of the record set last year on the *George A. Sloan.*

I went out on deck to watch the loading for awhile and the guys waxing the top edges of the hatch coamings with beeswax. That's a bit of technology that goes back many years. They do it so the hatch covers will slide easier.

Captain Sobeck talked to the office today about the *Sloan*'s trip into the cement plant at Alpena. Apparently,

---

LESCO—probably an abbreviation for Lake Erie Sand Company. The 150-foot ship was given its present name in 1975.

there were no problems. The strikers and our union officials supposedly said it was okay for the boat to unload its cargo. They were even willing to allow crewmembers to get off the boat and pass through the picket line if they wanted to go uptown. I can't figure it out. Why are they being so cordial? My only thought is that the strike is against Inland Lakes Management, while the *Sloan*'s cargo was being delivered to LaFarge. To take action against companies doing business with Inland Lakes Management could be construed as a secondary boycott, which would be illegal. Regardless, it must hurt when the strikers see ships crewed by AMO members hauling into the cement plant.[21]

Wednesday, October 16
Lake Erie, Eastbound

We were delayed leaving Fairport last night, because the tug-barge *McKee Sons* was on its way into the river there as we were ready to leave the dock. As a result, it was after 11:00 P.M. when we left Fairport. We arrived at Toledo at about 10:00 A.M. this morning. We docked on the west side of the Maumee River, just below the I-280 bridge, within sight of downtown.

---

[21]When the cement plant in Alpena was owned by Huron Cement, the boats were also owned and operated by the company. When the plant was sold to LaFarge, however, that company couldn't own a majority interest in the ships, because they're a French corporation and vessels they owned would be prohibited from operating in trade between U.S. ports. To get around the law, LaFarge sold the boats to a U.S. bank and then arranged for some former officials from Huron Cement's marine division to set up Inland Lakes Management and charter the boats back. Inland Lakes Management is really a paper corporation. The only asset it has that's worth anything is its contract with LaFarge to haul cement. It's generally assumed that LaFarge controls the fleet operations. That became evident when they ousted the old fleet managers and brought in the Andries. Despite the obvious connections, LaFarge and Inland Lakes Management technically remain separate entities Our union's action is against the fleet, not the cement manufacturer. If we could bring a strike action against LaFarge, we'd be in a much stronger bargaining position, and the problems in Alpena would probably be settled quickly.

I went up the street as soon as we finished lunch, which was a big mistake. I was driven by my addiction to make the trip because I'm almost out of cigarettes. I remembered there was a gas station that sold cigarettes not too far from the dock, so I decided to go up. Just getting from the boat to the dock was a hassle and I should have given up at that point and taken an afternoon nap. Since the boat couldn't get up against the unimproved dock, I had to ride ashore in the workboat. That's bad enough, but my old buddy Jimmy Atkins was operating the workboat, which added another negative element to the equation. Jimmy may be an excellent driver when in his pickup or on his Harley, but he operates a boat about the same way I do brain surgery—clumsily. Jimmy ran the boat up on some rocks just offshore and for a few seconds I thought both of us were going for a swim in the muddy Maumee. Despite Jimmy, I still managed to exit the boat and skate over some slime-covered rocks before I reached the safety of the shoreline. That proved an omen of things to come.

After a mile walk to the gas station I remembered from my days at the union school in Toledo, I discovered it didn't carry my brand. I should have gone back to the boat then and there, but I decided to walk farther downtown in quest of my cigarettes. Another half mile or so of trudging along the pavement brought me to the heart of downtown Toledo, into the midst of bank buildings, law offices, restaurants, upscale retail stores, and hotels—everything except a store selling cigarettes. So that the trip wouldn't be a total failure, I stopped at an ATM machine and got some cash, thinking ahead to Conneaut and Ashtabula, where they have lots of cigarettes at bargain basement prices.

I gave up and looked around for a taxi to take me back to the boat. I saw a few, but they all had passengers in them, so I started hiking back. As I walked out from the boat, I met a lot of truck traffic heading for the dock where we were unloading. I fully intended to catch a ride back with one of them to avoid the long, hot walk down the gravel road. The only traffic I encountered on my return trip were the same trucks I saw on my way out, but this time the trucks were headed in the other direction. Hot, sweaty, and dirty from the dust kicked up by the convoy of eighteen-wheelers that passed me I then braved another ride in the workboat. Jimmy made three passes before he got the boat close enough for me to get in; when he tried to maneuver the little aluminum boat alongside the hull of the *C-2*, I nearly dove for the painter that we tied the boat to. Once I got it hooked onto the bow, I immediately scrambled up the ladder hanging over the side of the ship. Another second or two in the workboat with Jimmy and he might have managed to tip us over. The mate, watchman, and wheelsman standing around on deck all got a chuckle out of my little adventure in the work-boat. I told them that letting Jimmy run the workboat was analogous to allowing a three-year-old to play with a loaded bazooka. It almost makes a guy want to give up smoking. I'm rationing my few remaining cigarettes, but I'll be back up the street on another shopping trip the first chance I get.

John Sobeck, the oiler on the 4-to-8 watch, went through the 1995 and 1996 engine room logs this morning and compared anchor time for the first sixteen days of October. By this time last October, the *Calcite II* had lost more than 138 hours due to weather—almost six full days. This year, we've lost only about 19 and a half hours for weather, and another 2 hours due to an equipment malfunction. What a difference a captain can make! Last year, the *C-2* had a rookie captain. I don't know if the weather was much worse last year, or if he was just overly cautious, but during the first sixteen days of October last year the boat was at anchor a third of the time. This fall, we've got an experienced captain. Dick doesn't take many chances, but he keeps us moving whenever possible. If Dick had been here last year, maybe the office wouldn't be planning to have us lay up so early.

According to Chief Engineer Bob Lijewski, the office is now talking about laying up the *C-2* around November 4. The chief didn't know whether that means we'll get another cargo or two, or whether the brass merely expects us to lose some time along the way. The weather was sensational again today, in the seventies, but a cold front is supposed to move through on Friday. That could bring some high winds that could easily cost us time. Most of us hope that we get a few more trips. The first week of November is just too early to lay up. The guys without enough seniority to bump someone off another boat may be off until late April of next year, almost six full months. If that happens a lot of sailors' wives will be

266

tearing their hair out before the first warm winds of spring blow over the Great Lakes.[22]

Thursday, October 17
Lake Erie, Westbound

We got into Fairport early this morning, spent the day taking on another load of salt, battened down the hatches, and headed back for Toledo at about 4:00 P.M. We should be in there about 4:00 A.M. tomorrow morning, and will head for Cleveland as soon as we unload. Time is of the essence because there's a storm moving onto the lakes; if we don't get into Cleveland before it hits, we may have to anchor someplace for a day or two.

The temperature today was in the seventies again, but it may well be our last day of Indian summer weather for the year. We received a storm advisory from the National Weather Service office in Cleveland early this morning. An intense low pressure storm system developed last night in Kansas and Nebraska and it's expected to be centered over Lake Superior by Friday morning. According to the weather bulletin, we can expect southwest gales to develop on Lake Erie tomorrow morning. Since we'll be running along the south shore of Lake Erie on the trip from Toledo to Cleveland, we should get some protection from the winds and seas. Captain Sobeck still hopes to reach Cleveland before the weather deteriorates too much. We'll be loading coke breeze at Cleveland, which takes about thirty-six hours, so the storm may well blow itself out of the Great Lakes region before we finish loading and depart for Green Bay. That would be nice. None of us wants any delays right now. If we spend too much time at anchor, we'll probably get orders to go directly to the lay-up dock.

One bit of good news today: we got orders for a few more trips. Instead of going to Superior to lay up after unloading

---

[22] As it turned out, some of the crewmembers didn't go back to work until the *Calcite* fitted out in early June 1997, exactly six months after they'd gotten off the boat in 1996.

at Green Bay, we'll go to Calcite to load for Detroit, and then back to Cedarville to pick up a cargo of stone for Gary. Once we unload at Gary, we'll slide over to nearby South Chicago and load coal for the power plant on Lake Charlevoix. These trips may add another week or so to our season and keep us running through about November 1. If that happens, we'll have the *C-2* laid up and head for home about November 12. Most of us have our fingers crossed that the weather won't be too bad and the office will see fit to add enough additional trips to keep us busy until around December 1. Right now our future remains uncertain.

We are all pleased to make a trip into Calcite. During the season, most of us accumulated a lot of "stuff" on the boat that will be a nuisance to haul home from Superior— televisions, VCRs, air-conditioners, dorm-size refrigerators, books, and spare clothing. The chief engineer even has his treadmill aboard. Most of us will charter a bus for the trip from Superior to Rogers City after the boat is laid up. Imagine what a production it would be to try to pack stuff like that for a bus trip. Now we'll lighten up our loads when we hit the dock at Rogers City. We'll be lean and mean from then on, each of us down to a sea bag or two filled with essentials we'll need for our final trips.

At breakfast this morning, Butch Kierzek and Iggy Don-ajkowski laughed about a cook they once sailed with who took the concept of leftovers into a new dimension. If he had hamburgers, meatloaf, or swiss steak left after a meal, he put it into a big galvanized bucket he kept in the boat's walk-in cooler. When he accumulated enough meat in the pail, he used it to concoct a steamboat-sized batch of goulash! Needless to say, his goulash was not popular with the crew. If they didn't eat it, he saved it a few days and put it back on the menu. The crew quickly learned to ask for a heaping plate of goulash, and then stealthily dump it into the trash can when the cook wasn't looking. Lunch that day was a peanut butter and jelly sandwich.

Butch said another cook he worked with saved cake that was leftover from dessert, allowed it to dry out completely on the counter, and then carefully scraped the frosting off. He crumbled the cake up, added raisins and a little liquid to the stale crumbs and made cupcakes. Doesn't that sound good? Steamboat haute cuisine. Bon appetit!

Chief Engineer Bob Lijewski will get off in Cleveland tomorrow so he can be home for his son's wedding on October 26. He probably won't be back until we arrive at the lay-up dock. John Bellmore, now the first assistant, will take over while Bob is gone, and we'll get a new third assistant, although we don't know who will be assigned to the *C-2*.

Jimmy Atkins, my porter for a time during the summer, is a deckhand again. He was one of the few crewmembers who wasn't happy to hear that we'd been assigned a few additional trips. Jimmy, a bachelor, doesn't want to work any longer than necessary and is ready to go home now. At supper, the guys in the messroom kidded him about coming up with a scam to get off before lay up. The general consensus is that Jimmy will start limping a bit tomorrow, a little more the day after, and by Sunday he'll be hobbling around the boat and complaining constantly about his leg or foot. I think it's more likely that he'll develop a back problem. He's supposedly had back problems a couple of times in the past, usually when he worked as a deckhand. I think he's on the verge of a relapse. While we kidded Jimmy about coming up with a scam, he just smiled. He's a sly devil.

One of the guys who called home today reported that the fall colors are at their breathtaking peak in northern Michigan right now. We haven't seen much in the way of color down here. With a storm and high winds just over the western horizon, most of the leaves will probably be stripped off the trees back home before we get there. Damn, I missed the entire summer out here and now I'm missing the fall colors. I'd rather miss winter.

Friday, October 18
Lake Erie, Eastbound

What a dramatic change in weather! I awoke this morning to a grey, rainy, windy, fifty-degree day and things haven't improved any. For the first time this season, I closed all the doors to the galley, messroom, and dining room because it was so cold I got goose bumps. I'm afraid that from here on out, it's going to get worse.

We bailed out of Toledo around 9:00 this morning and headed for Cleveland. With the weather conditions rapidly deteriorating, the captain wasn't sure we'd be able to make it into Cleveland. He thought we might have to go into Sandusky, Ohio, home of the Cedar Point amusement park, and anchor until the storm passed. That alternative wasn't necessary and we are going into the harbor at Cleveland right now. We'll load for the next thirty-six hours, so the storm should be history by the time we're ready to leave for Green Bay.

Captain Sobeck and I are planning to go to the Rock and Roll Hall of Fame right after lunch tomorrow. We'll be pressed for time because I'll have to be back by 3:00 P.M. to prepare supper, but it's the best we can do this season. I'm kind of kicking myself for not visiting the hall of fame when we came here regularly during the summer. It was open until 9:00 P.M. then, but now it closes at 5:00 P.M., so it's either run up in the afternoon, or miss it entirely. The captain wants to buy some t-shirts for his grandchildren and I think I'll get shirts for Meredith and Scott, and a coffee mug for my collection. It should be an enjoyable afternoon. The captain thinks maybe we'll see Elvis there. He reportedly frequents the place during the off-season, when there aren't so many tourists around. At least that's what the captain says, and he never stretches the truth.

Sunday, October 20
Cuyahoga River, Cleveland

Although we finished loading our cargo of coke breeze around noon today, we're sitting here at the dock waiting for Lake Erie to calm down. It's our third grey, rainy day in a row, but there isn't much wind at the dock. Apparently there's still quite a sea running out on Lake Erie, which is why the captain decided to sit here awhile before heading for Conneaut. The 1,000-foot *Presque Isle* couldn't make it into Conneaut this morning; if they can't

270

get in, neither can we. We still haven't seen anything of the *Buffalo* either. She called yesterday morning to report she was two hours from the mouth of the Cuyahoga, on her way from Lorain to the LTV steel mill up the river. At the last minute, the captain of the *Buffalo* decided the seas were too risky to try to get into Cleveland, so they anchored someplace. I thought she'd pass us this morning, but she hasn't appeared yet.

The boat is a mess. Coke breeze all over the deck has mixed with the water that's lying everywhere. We mop the deck in the galley twice a day, but it's dirty five minutes later. I don't know how soon we'll be able to get the mess off our deck. It's unlikely we'll clean the boat during the short trip to Conneaut, so we'll live with the mess for awhile.

I managed to talk to Meredith, Scott, and my mother on the phone today. Meredith was getting ready for a visit

While the *Calcite II* loads at a dock on the Cuyahoga River at Cleveland, the tug *Delaware* tows Erie Sand Steamship Company's 620-foot *Richard Reiss* backward down the narrow, winding river. Once the *C-2* finished loading, she too used a tug to back down the river to Lake Erie. (Author's collection)

271

tonight by her uncle—her mother's brother—who's passing through Kalamazoo. Scott is in Traverse City for the weekend, the first long trip he's taken in the minivan I bought him while I was on vacation. He loves it and the freedom it gives him. For the past year, he's been without access to a car. He managed to get by, mooching rides from friends, but it was certainly inconvenient. Now he has his own wheels, and he's happy.

My mother informed me this morning that my uncle Lawrence Thompson died on October 12. He was extremely ill when I came back on the boat, and they didn't expect him to live more than a day or two. He had several heart attacks recently and one of his legs was amputated. Thompsons don't die easily. They cling to life with great tenacity, probably longer than they should.

After Uncle Lawrence was cremated, his ashes were buried on the grounds of the Norway Pines Hunting Club, outside of Rogers City, which he belonged to most of his life. He was a great outdoorsman, who fished and hunted every chance he got. His love of the outdoors was a legacy passed on to him by his father, my grandfather, who was never happier than when he was in the woods, or on a river or lake with a fishing pole in his hands. My dad also inherited that love of the outdoors, but for some reason he quickly lost interest in hunting and fishing. He spent his time in the outdoors camping with his family or roaming the backroads of northern Michigan, enjoying the scenery and the occasional glimpse of a deer. My time in the outdoors has been spent in similar pursuits, mainly camping and canoeing; I haven't hunted in about twenty years.

On a lighter note, Captain Sobeck, Don Dehring, and I went to the Rock and Roll Hall of Fame yesterday afternoon. We stayed there a couple of hours, which isn't enough time to do anything more than just walk through the six-floor museum dedicated to rock and roll. It's an incredible place and I would love to return this winter with Meredith and Scott to spend an entire day. Yes, we saw Elvis. Even though it was drizzling when we got to the Hall of Fame, he was sitting on the edge of a planter out in front, greeting people as they arrived. Nice fellow that Elvis.

Monday, October 21
Conneaut, Ohio

We finally got in here at about 6:00 this morning, after running checked down most of the way from Cleveland because the lake was pretty choppy. We finished unloading about 4:00 P.M., but the deck gang has to hose down the cargo hold before we can leave. Once all the coke breeze has been washed down onto the belts, they'll start the unloading system and run the tailings off into a railroad car. It's nasty stuff, and we can't dump it into the lake, like we could if we were cleaning up after a stone, coal, or sand load. As soon as the deck gang's done, we'll head for Ashtabula to load coal for Green Bay.

It was another grey, rainy day, except for about an hour this afternoon when we saw patches of blue sky. The sun even peeked through a couple of times. That didn't last long, though, and it quickly clouded over again.

I didn't feel well this morning. I was sore all over and felt tired, despite a good night's sleep. I took a two-hour nap after lunch and felt a little better by the time I got up. I guess I'm okay now, but I'm planning to get to sleep early again tonight. I've worked about 150 days now without missing any work due to illness. That's common on the boat. I only know of one guy here on the *Calcite II* who missed part of a day because he wasn't feeling well. I doubt there are many workplaces around the country that can boast that kind of a record. We work through a lot of minor illnesses and aches and pains that might keep workers on the beach home in bed for a day or two. If I'd been working a normal job this morning, I'd have called in sick, taken a couple of aspirins, and gone back to bed.

When the captain called the traffic department yesterday, he told Ilona Mason that he, Don, and I had gone to the Rock and Roll Hall of Fame. In the course of the conversation, Cap told her that we both bought a few souvenir t-shirts. According to Captain "Honest Dick" Sobeck, Ilona asked if I'd gotten her one, and Dick said he didn't think so, but that I had bought shirts for three of the other women in the Duluth office. He knows I'm planning to ask Ilona out on a date when I get to Duluth, and he's "helping me out" in his own unique way. He's quite an agitator and loves to stir things up whenever he has a chance. Since he calls the traffic department and talks to Ilona almost every day, there's a good chance she won't be talking to me by the time I reach the head of the lakes.[23]

I've never met Ilona, though I did see a picture of her in one of our fleet's monthly newsletters. After making trips with me on the *Speer* and *Munson*, Jerry Walls, our fleet operations manager, decided that Ilona and I should get together. He thinks we'd enjoy each other's company. When I was home on vacation, Jerry tracked me down at my sister's in Detroit to talk to me about an article he's writing for our next fleet newsletter. It was during that telephone conversation that he told me he was lobbying Ilona on my behalf. He also told me why he thought I would enjoy going out with her. According to Jerry, Ilona doesn't normally date sailors, especially someone from our fleet, but he thought she might make an exception in my case. Of course, with all the help Dick Sobeck's giving me, I'll call to ask her out and she'll hang up on me.

I'm getting a little nervous about the article Jerry Walls is writing for the next issue of the fleet's monthly newsletter. It's the first in a series Jerry's doing on people in the fleet with interesting hobbies and backgrounds—and it's going to be about me. It's primarily going to be about the books I've written, and a little bit about jobs I held before I decided to go sailing. I suspect that I'll get a lot of flak from the guys on the boat when they see the blurb. It'll probably give Captain Sobeck all sorts of new ammunition to keep things stirred up. Ah, anonymity is such a wonderful thing.

---

[23]The fleet's traffic department actually schedules the ships, based on the needs of our customers. There are many factors that must be taken into consideration when scheduling, including the cargo size, the location of various ships in the fleet, which is taken from the "morning reports" faxed into the office every morning by each ship in the fleet, size restrictions of ships that can reach the customer's dock, and the potential for a backhaul cargo. The traffic department staff also must make sure that each ship gets to a fuel dock regularly, and that they visit the Soo, Calcite, or Cedarville every two to three weeks so they can pick up groceries. During the sailing season, someone from the traffic department is on duty seven days a week.

Wednesday, October 23
Northern Lake Huron

We've had a bumpy ride most of the day. I was awakened just before 3:00 this morning when the ship rolled so badly a couple of times that I rolled over in my bed. It leveled out some after that, and I managed to get back to sleep, but with six- to eight-foot seas hitting us on our stern quarter all day, we pitched and tossed steadily. The seas flattened out just before supper, when the wind died and I thought we were home free. Not so, I'm afraid. Just about the time dinner ended, a squall hit us from the west accompanied by strong winds and rain. Fortunately, we're close enough to shore that the seas don't build too much before they hit us, but it's like driving a '52 Dodge three-quarter-ton truck with bad shocks down a rough road. We're about to make a run for the Straits of Mackinac right now, where we'll anchor until the weather quiets down.

A bunch of us are planning to pull a major practical joke on Jimmy Atkins. Jimmy's been trying to buy a new Harley-Davidson motorcycle for several months now, but the best he could do was put his name on a waiting list. If someone who's ordered a bike from the dealership backs out, Jimmy can buy one. While we were down on Lake Erie, Jimmy received a message that someone had backed out, and he'll be able to get his Harley. Of course, Jimmy is stuck out here on the boat, so it's going to be a little tough to get to the dealership to pick the bike up right away. The good news is that we'll probably lay up in another week to ten days and Jimmy has been anxiously counting the days until he can purchase his new hog.

Jimmy's frequently pulled practical jokes on shipmates so we thought it was time to get even. At supper tonight, the guys kidded Jimmy about coming up with some excuse to get off the boat to pick up his bike. Jimmy remained calm and nonchalantly remarked that we'd be laid up before long, so he'd get his bike then. Thinking quickly, I said, "Don't be too sure of that, Jimmy. The office told me today to stock up on groceries." Jimmy knows the office has been bugging me to carry only enough groceries to last until November 9 or 10, by which time we'd be finished laying up this old

275

bucket. As the implications of my statement sank in, Jimmy developed a distinctly sick expression. A few minutes later, he came into the galley and quietly asked me if what I'd said was true. I said, "Sure, Jimmy, the office told me to buy all the groceries I wanted, and not to get caught short." Jimmy rattled off several obscenities, ending with, "I've got to get off this damned boat!"

Once Jimmy left the galley to go forward to his room, the rest of us quickly put together a plan guaranteed to drive Jimmy mad. We're going to put together a fake fax message from the Harley dealer to Jimmy, informing him that he has forty-eight hours to purchase the bike or lose it to someone else on the waiting list. We'll do it when we're going to be out on the lake for a couple of days, so it'll be impossible for him to contact the dealer. We're all sure that Jimmy will invent some scheme to get off the boat—probably a faked back or leg injury. We'll let the captain in on the prank, so he'll refuse to let Jimmy leave, on the pretense that no relief deckhands are available. Jimmy will definitely be hard to live with at that point. Oh, it's going to be such fun!

I'm back to good health, by the way. I felt so good yesterday that I did two loads of laundry last night, which is why I didn't enter anything in my log. If we lay up as scheduled, I'll only have to do laundry one more time before I get off, a day or two before I head for home. I don't like to travel with a lot of dirty laundry in my seabag.

Friday, October 25
Straits of Mackinac

Around 2:00 this afternoon, when we were eight hours from Rogers City, our orders were changed. Instead of going to "Dodge," we're on our way to Cedarville and should be in there about 9:00 this evening. Needless to say, most of the guys on the boat are extremely disappointed. It doesn't bother me, since we wouldn't have gotten into Calcite until 11:00 P.M., which is way past my bedtime. The Calcite trip wasn't cancelled, just postponed until after we run down

276

Lake Michigan. Perhaps when we finally get to Calcite it'll be at a better time for those of us who work in the galley.

There was no installment in this logbook last night, because I made my first-ever trip to a casino. John Sobeck, Gene Schaedig, Don Dehring, and I went to the Oneida Casino in Green Bay while the boat was unloading coal at the Fort Howard Paper Company dock. After three hours on the slot machines, I left with $7.25 more than I had when I got there. At that rate, I was working for just over $2.40 an hour, well below minimum-wage standards. It could have been worse—the other three guys all lost money. Don and Geno only lost a few dollars, but John, the inveterate gambler in the group, lost a tidy bundle. He was pretty bummed out all day today, but plans to attempt a comeback at the casino in Hessel tonight. If I'd have lost as much as he did, I'd probably swear off gambling forever. Of course, that's easy for me. I don't enjoy gambling, because I don't like to lose money. I didn't enjoy my time at the casino and I'm not sure I'll go to one again. Maybe because I took so many statistics courses in graduate school, I have a hard time justifying participating in an activity where the deck is stacked against you. Face it, my gambling friends, in the world of casino gambling, the casino is going to win in the long run. You may win a battle or two, but the casino will win the war. That message was obviously lost on the thousands of people who took time out from their Thursday evenings to visit the casino in Green Bay. The place was packed with people of all sizes, shapes, and ages, including lots of ladies who must have been my mother's age. I was a bit overwhelmed with all the people, the commotion, the noise, the smoke, and the relentless sound of quarters and nickels dropping into slot machines.

For me, the most interesting thing about last evening wasn't the casino or the gambling at all, but the fact that the casino was run by the Oneida tribe of Native Americans. How in hell did the Oneidas get to northern Wisconsin? As I remember, the Oneidas were from New York State. Weren't they one of the Five Nations of Iroquois that lived around the Finger Lakes area in the northern part of the state? Nobody I met last night could tell me how the Oneida got to Wisconsin, not even our cabbie, who seemed to be an expert on virtually every other topic we brought up on our taxi ride from Fort Howard to the casino. I'll have to check it out. As an aside, I find it slightly unsettling that so many Indian tribes are now running casinos. I guess they've been real moneymakers for the tribes, but it seems so alien to their heritage. As one of the guys put it, we stole from them for hundreds of years and now they're getting even.

I went to bed about midnight last night, but couldn't fall asleep. I'm sure I tossed and turned for at least an hour, so I was a bit tired when I got up at 5:30 A.M. It would be nice to go to bed early tonight, but we're not going to be into Cedarville until about 10:00 P.M., and I've got groceries coming. Since the Soo Warehouse was sending a truck down with some stuff for the engineers, I faxed them a small order. It's only been two weeks since we last got groceries, but we're starting to run out of things, such as milk. It looks now as though my next grocery order will be around the second of November, when we pass through the Soo on our way to the lay-up dock in Superior. The cupboards will be almost bare by then so I'll get just enough supplies to get us to Superior and through nine days of lay up. I should have menus planned by then for the entire lay-up period, so I'll order exactly what I need and no more. I don't like to get rid of a lot of excess groceries at the end of the season. Some stuff will go to the Salvation Army, or somewhere, though. I've got two cases of canned crinkle-cut carrots that were sent to us with our fitout order in April. I haven't used any of them, nor did either of the other cooks who were here during the season. I've also got about three cases of canned cranberries that Bob Bauer ordered for some reason known only to Bob. When I serve cranberries to the crew here, it's unusual if they go through more than about two cans during a meal. At that rate, the three cases would last well into the 1999 shipping season. Unfortunately, with no heat on the boat during lay up, the cans could freeze and burst if we don't get rid of them somehow. Of the stuff I've ordered during the year, though, there won't be enough to fill more than about a shoebox. That's the result of the fact that I'm somewhat obsessive about coordinating my grocery orders and my menus. I'm ready for bed right now, but I have to stay up until we get the groceries aboard. Oh well, I'd rather be doing this than feeding quarters to a slot machine at a casino.

Saturday, October 26
Lake Michigan, Downbound

I'm worn out. Two days in a row without getting enough sleep has done me in. On top of that, I had an extremely busy day. Supper, for example, included prime ribs au jus, chicken cordon bleu, and orange roughy Florentine, along with baked potatoes, long grain and wild rice, and asparagus with Hollandaise sauce. Putting a meal like that together will tire you out, even if you're well rested. Tonight, my friends, I will get a good night's sleep, aided by the fact that we go off daylight saving time during the night, which means I can get an extra hour of sleep if I want. The only problem is that I'm so accustomed to getting up at 5:30 in the morning that my body's internal clock will undoubtedly wake me tomorrow at 4:30 A.M. That'll be okay, though, as I'd love to be able to stay in bed for an hour before I have to get up.

It was around 10:30 last night before we finally got our groceries aboard. After that, I spent some time talking with April Bellmore, the chief's wife, and Val Peacock, the handyman's wife. This is the first time that I've really had a chance to talk with them since they made trips with their husbands during the summer. They're a riot, especially when they're together, and they were both feeling their oats last night.

Val and April weren't the only wives who made the trek from Rogers City to Cedarville to meet the boat last night. At the Cedarville plant, they don't let anyone drive down to the dock until the boat is tied up, and when they started letting cars through the gate last night it looked to us like a caravan headed for the boat. There must have been seven or eight cars, plus the grocery truck from the Soo Warehouse.

I also talked for a few minutes with Jane Bruski, the wife of one of our deckhands. Jane, too, traveled with her husband Frank during the summer and she spent a lot of time chatting with us in the galley when he was working. Jane's now working at a restaurant in Rogers City, so she's not always able to meet the boat. She told me she's bragged a lot to her new bosses about the food on the *Calcite II.* I'll have to stop and eat at the restaurant someday during her shift.

279

After chatting with everyone, it was around midnight before I got to bed, and I still couldn't fall asleep right away. I groaned when the alarm went off at 5:30 A.M., and I didn't move around too fast for the first hour or so I was up. When the sun rose in the eastern sky, I was glad I was up. We were in the Straits of Mackinac at first light, and I saw the first reddish glow of the sun rising behind the Mackinac Bridge. The sunrise brought a beautiful, brisk autumn day, and a call from the mate on watch in the pilothouse that we were going to pass my brother's boat just west of the straits. I went out on deck with my camera, accompanied by a couple friends, to watch the *Columbia Star* pass. We blew a salute to the *Star* as she went by, she saluted us in turn, and Gary came out on the bridge wing long enough to wave. Ships salute each other in passing, and brothers wave—it's the way of the Great Lakes shipping industry. There *is* a touch of the romance of the sea in this job, though it often gets buried by the day-in, day-out drudgery of loading, unloading, hosing decks, shoveling the tunnel, repairing equipment, pumping ballast, and cooking three meals a day. It's not like working on the ships in television shows like *Adventures in Paradise* or *The Love Boat*, but life on the lakes *is* different than working in an office or factory. We're separated from our families and friends, we roam all over the lakes like nomads, and we live with the risk, though a small one, of being shipwrecked. It's definitely not your basic 9-to-5 job, with the morning commute from the suburbs, an evening trip to K-Mart to buy toilet paper on sale, and dinner on Sunday with the in-laws.

Sunday, October 27

South Chicago

We got into Gary about 11:00 this morning, finished unloading by 3:30 in the afternoon, and arrived at the coal dock here on the Calumet River shortly after 6:00 A.M. It'll take us about eight hours to load and then we'll head north for the power plant on Lake Charlevoix. The weather forecast isn't good, though. They've got gale warnings posted for Lake Michigan with winds out of the northwest, so we'll probably try to sneak up the Wisconsin shoreline to stay in the lee of the land. If the winds have gone down by the time we get up around Green Bay, we'll cut across the lake. If not, we'll anchor someplace.

The *Speer* unloaded on the other side of our slip at the U.S. Steel plant at Gary today. Lynn Sternberg, who's cooking there now, came over to see me. Sitting in my room and talking for the better part of an hour, Lynn filled me in on the trials and tribulations he's had this season. Lynn is supposed to be the permanent steward on the *Edwin H. Gott,* but he and the captain have had an ongoing feud that ended with Lynn chasing the captain down the dock at Two Harbors. After that, the office transferred Lynn to the *Speer.* He's supposed to return to the *Gott* around the first of November, when Bobby Bauer's vacation ends and he comes back to the *Speer.* Lynn expects that will lead to further problems between himself and the captain.

While on the *Speer,* Lynn's also had a difficult time with Tom Schroeder, the porter there now. Tom was the second cook on the *Speer* when I was there. Lynn said he's given Tom a number of verbal reprimands because he wouldn't follow his instructions. That surprises me a little. When I worked with Tom, we did not get along and he kept repeating how much he enjoyed working with Lynn. "I'll be glad when I'm back with Lynn," he said again and again. Apparently, the honeymoon is over. They even had a big argument earlier today when Tom asked to take the day off to go into Chicago and Lynn said no. Lynn said that Tom has changed dramatically since he sailed with him last year, and Lynn doesn't particularly want to work with him again.

Lynn also had some serious problems with another porter he worked with this season. The porter, who once worked as a steward, drank heavily and kept telling Lynn he wanted his job. Lynn said he caught the porter rifling through the drawers in his room on two occasions. When he confronted the porter about what he was doing, he reportedly told Lynn he was looking for some drugs he had hidden in Lynn's room. Lynn threw him out of his room and spent several hours literally tearing the room apart looking for the stash of drugs. To get caught with drugs on an American ship means instant revocation of your merchant marine document, and federal drug charges. Lynn didn't find anything and he wondered if the porter was telling the truth or not. On other occasions, the porter kept asking Lynn how he was feeling. When Lynn wanted to know what was going on, the porter said he'd spiked Lynn's drink with LSD. While he just about worried himself sick, Lynn didn't have any reaction to the LSD, if there was any in his drink. Lynn didn't report the incidents with the porter to the office for reasons I won't go into. I suppose when the office reads this, they'll be on the telephone to me asking for details.

Monday, October 28
Lake Michigan, Upbound

Things keep getting crazier and crazier. The office called this afternoon and alerted us that we may go directly to lay up after unloading on Lake Charlevoix tomorrow. Four boats are ahead of us at Calcite, including the 1,000-foot *Presque Isle,* which takes up to twenty-four hours to load. If that's not enough, the Calcite quarry people told the office today that they don't have enough of the size stone we're supposed to be hauling to Detroit to give us a full load. If the Duluth office gang can't come up with an alternative plan in the next twenty-four hours we'll head this old girl for the barn. I think most of the guys in the crew are in shock right now. They were extremely quiet at dinner tonight.

This morning, Geno and I worked out a plan to get most of our major lay-up jobs finished before we get to Duluth. If we head for lay up tomorrow, those plans are right down the toilet and it's back to the drawing board. Steve, the porter, will go home with the forward-end guys— the deck department—within twenty-four hours after we tie the boat up at Superior, so only Geno and I will be here during lay up. Because of that, I hoped to finish most of the major cleaning while we were still on the run. If we lose our last scheduled trip, we simply won't have time to do that. God, I can't believe the season could be ending this early.

Tuesday, October 29
Off Mackinaw City

When I got up this morning we had just docked at the power plant at Advance, Michigan, on Lake Charlevoix, and were starting to unload what we thought was our last load of the year. Before we finished unloading, however, the captain called back to say that our orders had been changed and we were going to Calcite for a load after all. Instead of taking it to Detroit, though, it's destined for Duluth; after unloading we'll shift over to the Superior side of the harbor and lay up. Most of the guys on the boat were pretty excited, because with the *Presque Isle* loading ahead of us at Calcite it looked as though we could have a twenty-four hour delay before we start loading. This would give everyone time to haul any unneeded gear home and visit with their families before heading for lay up.

The weather threw a wrench into the works. A fast-moving storm struck the lakes region. Winds picked up before we reached the Straits of Mackinac, and they were predicted to increase to between fifty and sixty miles an hour out of the southeast. The captain decided it would be dangerous to continue on toward Rogers City, because there was a good chance that the southeasterly winds would keep us out of the harbor. If that happened, we would be forced to spend the night beating into the teeth of a vicious storm. This boat's getting a little too old for confrontations with major fall storms, so the captain decided to anchor between Mackinaw City and Cheboygan, about fifty miles short of home. With luck, the winds will die down by morning and we'll continue on to Rogers City. There's even a chance we'll still have to wait for the *Presque Isle* to finish loading before we can get into the slip at Calcite.

It'll have been seventeen days since we've been into Calcite, so it will be good to get home. I called my mother on the cell phone and she said I had quite a pile of mail waiting for me. I'm also doing laundry tonight, so I can haul some of my stuff home before we head for the lay-up dock. It should only take us about nine or ten days to get up to the head of the lakes, unload, and lay up this old crate, so we don't need a lot of gear with us.

It was fun coming out of Lake Charlevoix just after lunch today. Though the crowds were a lot smaller than during the summer season, there were enough observers on hand to make it interesting. An elementary school class waited along the piers as we came through, and Tom Flanner and some of the other deck guys threw Halloween candy to them, which went over real big. When we cleared the bridgekeeper's office on the way out, the captain blew a long salute—three longs and two shorts—to signify that we wouldn't pass that way again until next season. The bridgekeeper returned the salute and taped our passage with a video camera. I asked one lady standing along the riverbank if she knew Larry Grooters. When she said she did, I told her my name and asked her to tell Larry I said hello. Larry is the pastor of the church I attended when I lived in Charlevoix. I haven't seen him in four or five years, but if he gets my message he'll at least know I'm alive and well, and still working on the boats. Larry was fascinated by the big boats. He always got excited whenever he saw one coming through the channel at Charlevoix. Every time we go through there, I hope to see Larry and some of my other Charlevoix friends, but I've yet to see a familiar face.

Wednesday, October 30

Off Mackinaw City

It's 9:30 in the morning and we're still at anchor. During the night, six other boats joined us, including our fleet's *Myron C. Taylor,* American Steamship's *St. Clair,* Algoma Central Marine's *Agawa Canyon* and *Algoway,* a Russian freighter, and an unidentified tanker. The Russian and one of the Algoma boats left a short time ago to head down Lake Huron, but the rest of us are staying put. There are reportedly fifteen- to eighteen-foot seas out on the lake, and the wind, which died off during the night, may kick up to about fifty miles an hour this afternoon, accompanied by the year's first snowfall. We may not be able to make the short trip down to Rogers City until tomorrow.

John Sobeck, the 4-to-8 oiler, apparently was not too busy on watch this morning. He used the computer in the

284

chief's office in the engine room to make up *Geno's Special Cookbook*, which he presented to Geno at breakfast this morning. When Geno opened it, all the pages were blank. We all got a chuckle out of that, including Geno.

It's now 2:30 P.M. and we're sitting in the bay between St. Ignace and Mackinac Island. The winds were fluky all morning and then shifted to the northwest. They began to blow like crazy around noon. Within a period of thirty minutes, we went from about a two-foot chop to bouncing around in six-foot seas. It quickly became apparent that if the wind continued to increase from the northwest, our anchorage wasn't safe, so the captain hauled up the hook and headed for our present location. The *Taylor* followed along not far behind us. Geno, Steve, and I hung around the galley until we got into the bay around 1:00 P.M., because we were worried that we might roll quite a bit when the old man hauled her around. Fortunately, although she wallowed a little, there wasn't any bad rolling. We're in a protected location now. We should be safe here until this storm blows itself out.

When we left our old anchorage, we headed straight into the wind until we were abreast of this bay before we made our haul. While we headed northwest, we steered on the middle of the Mackinac Bridge, and I saw cars going across. It was obvious they were inching along. The winds up there must have been fierce. I'm surprised they were still letting cars cross.

When the guys on the 8-to-12 watch came back for lunch, they told us that the two ships that had pulled up their anchors and headed down the lake were actually on their way to DeTour, at the mouth of the St. Marys River. That's reassuring, as I'm not sure it's safe to be out on Lake Huron today.

It's supposed to snow today, but so far there's been nothing but cold rain. The temperature dropped about ten to fifteen degrees when the wind shifted to the northwest; it's simply a nasty day out there. Maybe we'll go to Calcite tomorrow. Nobody seems to be in a big hurry right now. Ordinarily in a situation like this, most of the crew would try to second-guess the captain, arguing that we could have safely made it to Rogers City this morning. There's none of that going on, though. Nobody wants to risk having to swim the last stretch home.

I just finished with supper, and the captain told me he doubted we'd be going anywhere tonight. There's no sign that the winds are going to let up, and it may well continue to blow tomorrow. When we go to Rogers City is anybody's guess. At least the television reception is pretty good where we're sitting.

Thursday, October 31
Halloween
Off St. Ignace

Well, we've lost over forty-eight hours now, and it looks as though we may stay at anchor here until early tomorrow. It's still blowing very hard. Once last night and again early this morning, we started to drag our anchors as the wind and seas tore at the boat. We started the engine, pulled up the anchors, and moved to a new position. We're now close to the shore, just northeast of the city of St. Ignace, with Mackinac Island directly off our stern.

We're not the only ones sitting here. The tug-barge *Joseph H. Thompson-Joe Thompson, Jr.* and Oglebay Norton's *David Z. Norton* are anchored just off downtown St. Ignace. The *Myron C. Taylor* and an unidentified tug-barge are anchored between us and the *Thompson* and *Norton,* almost on the beach. A news report on a local radio station said seventeen freighters are anchored in the St. Marys River waiting for the weather to break.

Not everyone is sitting tight, however. The 1,000-foot integrated tug-barge *Presque Isle* finished loading at Calcite this morning and headed for Gary. The guys on the 8-to-12 watch in our pilothouse saw her sneak along the shore, and then head under the Mackinac Bridge and into Lake Michigan. When the captain came back for supper tonight, he said the *P.I.* was encountering fifty-mile-an-hour winds off Green Bay. She's obviously beachcombing along the Wisconsin shore on her way down the lake to stay in the lee of the land for shelter from the wind and waves, but I bet they're still getting a pretty good ride. The westerly winds are taking them almost broadside—the worst possible situation. Even though the *Presque Isle* is 105 feet wide, I imagine she'll roll some.

The first snow of the year fell today. Snow squalls have been sweeping through all day, but no snow accumulated on our deck because the wind blows it away. Looking out toward St. Ignace, it appears as though the ground is covered with snow. The temperature this morning was about thirty-three degrees and I don't think it rose much throughout the day. Temperatures tonight should dip into the low twenties, so the kids are going to have to bundle up when they go trick or treating.

We had a little Halloween celebration at dinner tonight. We had pizza and pop, and we passed out three candy bars to each of the guys. The crew seemed to be in good spirits, although I think everyone is getting bored.

I had a message yesterday to call Jerry Walls, our fleet's operations manager, and I finally got through to him late this afternoon on the cell phone. Jerry wanted to let me know that if we're up in Superior next Tuesday, we're going to have a bunch of bigwigs from Transtar's corporate office in Monroeville, Pennsylvania, for breakfast, including the company president. Jerry doesn't want us to do anything special, but he doesn't want us to feed them Spam either. They'll tour the boat and talk with the chief engineer about some of the work planned for lay up this year. I'm glad Jerry warned me, so I can make sure the dining room is squared away and all of us wear clean, starched whites. We tend to get a little lax during lay up. We wear jeans and t-shirts a lot of the time if we're doing heavy cleaning, and we normally shut down the officers dining room and feed all the crew in the messroom.

Somebody from the Duluth office also called the old man on the cell phone today. The person asked Dick how long it would take us to get to Calcite from where we're anchored because they hoped we could beat a Canadian boat into the dock. Captain Sobeck supposedly responded with "We'll load after them." He's handling this weather delay well, and he's not about to pull out of this anchorage until he knows we can travel safely down the shore. He doesn't want to take on any fifteen- or twenty-foot waves during the last trip of the season. Good for him. We've got some captains in this fleet, as in all fleets, who would gladly haul up anchor and race for Calcite to make a few points with the office. That's one reason so many ships have gone down in storms on the lakes—some captains lacked the good sense to stay put in bad weather.

Friday, November 1
Lake Huron, Downbound

It's early afternoon now and supper's in the oven, so I'm killing time. At 10:00 this morning, we lifted anchor and headed for Rogers City, despite the fact that the winds were still blowing a steady twenty-five miles an hour from the west, with gusts up to forty miles an hour. The old man said we'll try to make it into Calcite. So far, the ride hasn't been bad at all. I bet we'll slide into the harbor at Rogers City with little difficulty. We should be there around 3:00 P.M.

On the way out of anchorage at St. Ignace this morning, we blew a long salute to our *Myron C. Taylor*, which was still at anchor. They're on their way to Manistee, Michigan, on the west shore of Lake Michigan, and with winds out of the west, it's going to have to calm down considerably before they have any chance of making it in there. They could easily stay at St. Ignace for another day or two. I'm sure they're getting cabin fever as bad as we were. We were at anchor for more than sixty hours, and the *Sloan* came in just a few hours behind us.

First Mate Don Dehring and I have been kidding each other lately about how much weight we've gained this season. Don got in the best shot of the season at breakfast this morning, dealing me the coup de grace. I was wearing a t-shirt that has drawings of all the 1,000-foot freighters on it and Don said the shirt was stretched so tight the boats looked like they were 1,200 feet long! With the end of the season fast approaching, I'm not sure I'm going to be able to top that. Maybe next year.

We'll have quite a crew change at Calcite. Chief Engineer Bob Lijewski, First Assistant Tom Brege, and Third Assistant John Wysocki are all supposed to be coming back, along with Jimmy Atkins, who will go back as a deckhand, and Al Gapczynski, who will relieve Dick Sobeck as captain.

Oiler Andy McGinn chats with First Assistant Engineer John Bellmore in the wood-paneled officers' dining room aboard the *Calcite II*. Today, fire prevention regulations prohibit the use of wood in ship construction. (Author's collection)

Dick will now go over to the *George A. Sloan* as captain. The *Sloan*'s supposed to sail until early December. The other guys who are getting off are all temporary reliefs, except for John Bellmore, who has been sailing as chief engineer since Bob Lijewski got off a couple of weeks ago for his son's wedding. John scheduled vacation for the month of November to be off for deer hunting season, and he decided to take it, even though we'll have the boat laid up and be home before the opening day of hunting season. I don't blame him for wanting to miss all the hassles of laying up the boat.

We arrived at Calcite around 3:30 in the afternoon on our last trip of the year. There was enough stuff hauled off the boat in the first thirty minutes to fill a rather large moving van, as everyone "lightened up" before going to the lay-up dock. I let Geno go home shortly after we got in, and Steve was busy changing linens for the four new officers coming aboard. He and I stayed through the dinner hour, even though we only served one person. No one else was interested in eating.

I went to my mother's for a few hours and sorted through a huge stack of mail that had piled up during the past four weeks, including the company newsletter containing the article about me. Actually, it's quite good, and I'm pleased with Jerry Walls's work. The facts were 99 percent accurate and I appreciated Jerry's more subjective comments. Even the photo he took of me on the *Speer* turned out well. Here's the article:

> Unsurprisingly, we have many uniquely talented individuals working at the Fleet, and we would like to introduce someone who fits that description—Steward Mark Thompson. Mark joined the Fleet in September 1996 when he started cooking on the M/V *Gott*. He comes to us with sailing experience—previously working as a cook for Interlake. In addition to being a consummate chef, Mark has accomplished notable achievements in academics and public service.
>
> Mark has a bachelor's degree in political science from Lake Superior State University in Sault Ste. Marie and a master's in public administration from Michigan State University. He taught political science at LSSU and he also taught a graduate class in public administration at Western Michigan University. He has written 2 books and worked at the Great Lakes Maritime Academy as the assistant to the superintendent. Two of his more illustrious jobs include 4 years service in the U.S. Army, Special Forces, with a couple of years in Vietnam, and service in the Michigan state legislature as a representative.
>
> For those who have the opportunity of being shipmates with Mark, you will notice that he runs a galley which maintains a high standard of efficiency and quality. He's a good conversationalist with a quick wit and someone who's always interested in "your story." You see, Mark is still writing, and it seems as though he has found a way to combine the best of both worlds. He can pursue his academic interests of research and writing without leading the economic life of a teacher—which is just above the poverty line.
>
> So, if you see Mark out on "the boats," don't hesitate to say hello and strike up a conversation. But choose your words carefully—they might end up in a book!

Not bad. My only concern is that nobody on the boats and none of the people from the Duluth office will *ever* talk to me again.

I managed to talk with both Meredith and Scott on the phone while at my mother's, which is quite amazing. They're so hard to catch at home. Their mother is going to be at Meredith's place in Kalamazoo this weekend, and Scott is going to go over there after he finishes work on Saturday. He's still thrilled with his car, and even sent me a note thanking me for my generosity.

It's now a little after 9:00 P.M. I've pulled out the meats I'll need for meals tomorrow, and I'm almost ready to call it quits for the day. Loading is going better than usual, and we should be out of here around 9:45 P.M., which may put us at the grub boat at the Soo at about 6:00 in the morning. There's a good possibility, though, that we'll be delayed by the weather. It's been snowing all evening and the wind is howling.

Saturday, November 2

Whitefish Bay, Lake Superior

When I looked outside at about 5:00 this morning, I couldn't figure out where we were. We should have been almost to the Soo, but we definitely weren't in the St. Marys River. I saw land on one side of the boat, but not on the other. Around 6:00 A.M., I suddenly realized what had happened. The captain had decided to hug the shoreline on the way up the lake, going almost all the way to the Mackinac Bridge before he cut through Round Island Passage between Mackinac Island and Round Island. When I first looked out we were probably somewhere near Cedarville, and by 6:00 A.M. we reached DeTour and the mouth of the St. Marys. It took us almost six hours longer to get to the Soo that way, but with the wind howling and the heavy snow squalls, it was clearly the prudent approach.

I gave Don Dehring, the first mate, a hard time about our roundabout trip when he came in for breakfast after standing the 4-to-8 watch. I accused him of not knowing how to get to the Soo, and following the shoreline because they knew it would eventually lead them to DeTour, which they would recognize because of the bar adjacent to the ferry dock. Everybody got quite a laugh out of that, including Don, but it wasn't as clever as Don's comment the other day about the 1,200-footers on my t-shirt.

There was a time, not many years ago, when boats in the grey fleet seldom ever went up onto Lake Superior. The markets for the stone and coal carried by little boats like the *Calcite II* and its predecessors in the grey fleet are located largely around Lakes Michigan, Huron, and Erie, in the major urban areas and industrial centers. The only reason we're up here now is to go to the Superior, Wisconsin, shipyard, although one of the small boats in our fleet occasionally hauls a load of stone or salt up. That's unusual, though. It's more likely that such a cargo would be backhauled by one of the larger boats taking ore down the lake, like the *Munson, Callaway, Clarke,* or *Anderson.*

I was pretty feisty this morning. Geno and I gave John Sobeck a bit of a hard time. He stops in the galley every morning at 7:15, after waking the guys for the 8-to-12 watch in the engine room. That's when he always teases us about something. This morning he complained that our Halloween decorations were still up. I planned to take them down, but hadn't gotten around to it yet. Geno had some free time, so as soon as John left for the engine room, he removed the witches, vampires, and bats and stowed them away for next year.

We were sitting around talking after breakfast when John noticed the Halloween decorations were gone. "What happened to the Halloween decorations?" he asked. "We took them down yesterday," I answered, "after you gave us such a hard time about having them up yet." John thought for a moment and then asked, "That was this morning, wasn't it?" Don Dehring immediately replied, "No, they were gone last night when I came back to the boat." John paused for a moment and then remarked, "I could have sworn they were up this morning." Everyone present swore he was wrong. He sat quietly after that, pondering the possibility that he'd been caught in some sort of a time warp. We spouted off reasons why he might have become confused about when he had complained about the decorations

The *Calcite II* takes on its last load of groceries and supplies for the 1996 season when it passes through Sault Ste. Marie on its way to lay up in Superior, Wisconsin. Ships in the USS Great Lakes Fleet are normally supplied from the fleet's warehouse complex at the Soo throughout the sailing season. Supplies are delivered to the passing boats by the "grub boat" *Ojibway,* on the left, which hoists the provisions aboard using a crane. (Author's collection)

still being up after Halloween. Most of the explanations revolved around the prospect that he had breathed in too many fumes down in the engine room, or enjoyed too many beers at Greka's tavern before returning to the boat last night. He left the galley a few minutes later, thoroughly confused.

We put off our excess groceries at the supply boat when we went through the Soo, took on a few needed supplies, and got our laundry back. I took some pictures of the guys bringing the groceries aboard from the supply boat. The last time we got supplies at the Soo was on our first trip down the lakes after leaving the lay-up dock in Superior back in early May. The next time they'll see us will be at the start of the 1997 shipping season.

We went through the MacArthur Lock, the one closest to the viewing stands at the locks, and, despite the fact that it was bitterly cold and snowing, a few hearty tourists watched us pass through. I took a picture of them as they took pictures of us. Turnabout *is* fair play.

Whitefish Bay was pretty choppy when we arrived. While we were between Paradise and Whitefish Point, Michigan, the old man hung a left turn, we ran in close to the beach and anchored. I guess the captain heard a radio call from a boat that had gone around Whitefish and immediately encountered winds blowing up to forty miles an hour and twelve-foot waves. Smart move on the captain's part! Of course, when Don Dehring and the other guys on the 4-to-8 watch come back, I'll accuse them of getting lost.

Sunday, November 3
Lake Superior, Westbound

We hauled up the anchor about 11:00 last night and headed out across Lake Superior. The lake's still a little rough, but we're riding well. We should arrive in Duluth about 7:00 in the morning. We'll be unloaded by noon and then everyone will pitch in to clean up the cargo hold and unloading tunnel before we shoot across to the shipyard at Superior. I think we'll be in there about suppertime. The next twenty-four hours will be extremely hectic, creating a lot of frayed nerves and patience worn thin before we tie up at the shipyard.

There's a big flap going on right now over how the deck guys are going to get home. Usually, they charter a bus for the ten- to eleven-hour drive to Rogers City. The deckhands, however, being the rebels they are, decided they wanted to charter an airplane from Alpena to pick them up and fly them into Rogers City. One of the watchmen didn't like the bus arrangements that a wheelsman made, so he announced he was going to contact another bus company. With that, the wheelsman dropped his efforts to arrange transportation. At this point, the deck department guys don't know how they'll get home, and they won't have much time to make arrangements during the next twenty-four hours. Flaps like this are apparently not at all unusual at lay up.

294

Second Mate Mike "Redneck" Westbrook stands by a mooring winch as the *Calcite II* slowly enters the MacArthur Lock at Sault Ste. Marie, Michigan, on its way to its lay-up dock in Superior, Wisconsin. The locks at the Soo move ships around a falls in the St. Marys River. Ships on their way to Lake Superior are raised twenty-one feet, while ships downbound for Lake Huron are lowered twenty-one feet. (Author's collection)

The bus trips home are rather infamous. It's common to have beer on the bus and a couple of guys always get smashed and make asses of themselves. One year, the bus company was so disgusted with some of the sailors' behavior aboard their charter bus that they called the fleet office and informed them that they would never charter to groups from this fleet again. I don't tolerate drunks well, so I hope that everyone in our group is well behaved. If things get out of hand, I'll simply get off the first chance I get, and wait for the regular White Pine bus heading south.

The guys in the deck department should have everything at their end of the boat laid up and be on their way home sometime Tuesday morning. Steve, the porter, will go with them. Butch Kierzek and Larry Post from the deck department will stay to help with the engine room lay up. Once the deck guys head home, that will leave thirteen of us on the boat, exactly half the normal complement. It makes for a lot less work for us in the galley, but it seems we always get a lot of extras at mealtimes during lay up, mainly workers from the shipyard and people from the office. Since they don't announce their intentions to freeload in advance, it's easy for the cook to get caught short.

Captain Al Gapczynski and Don Dehring got word from the office today that they'll both go to the *Philip R. Clarke* when they get off the *C-2*. They'll catch it around the seventh of the month at Calcite, so they will have a couple of days at home before they go back out. I think it'll be Don's first foray onto one of the red boats, but he doesn't seem too concerned about it. Having Al going over there as captain is probably reassuring to him.

I'm nervous about calling Ilona Mason to ask her to go out with me. I've never met her, never talked to her, and have only seen her in a photo, and it wasn't a particularly good one. Maybe nervous is a bit of an understatement. It might be more accurate to say that I'm *terrified*. Aw, what the heck, everybody says she's a nice lady, so it shouldn't be too painful to call and ask her out on what I hope will be a *casual* date. Gosh, I hope she's got a good sense of humor.

Monday, November 4
Duluth, Minnesota

What a busy day! When I woke up at 5:00 A.M., we were just outside the piers here at Duluth. After I showered and dressed, I went out on deck for a couple of minutes to get a look at Duluth. The Queen City of the North is beautiful, day or night, but I prefer the night scene. The steep hillside on which Duluth is built is covered with a thousand points of light at night. I don't think there's a prettier city on the lakes.

We arrived at the Hallett dock just before 7:00 A.M., and finished unloading in the early afternoon. We're still sitting at the dock, though, while the deck crew hoses down the unloading system and the tunnel. We should be leaving here for the shipyard at about 10:00 P.M. tonight.

We had lots of company from the office throughout the day, including the fleet president, the fleet manager, the director of engineering, and a few others. All stopped in the galley at one time or another. Fred Cummings, the fleet manager, talked with me for quite awhile. It's actually the first face-to-face conversation of any length we've had since I came with the fleet more than a year ago. He was complimentary about the job I did cooking for the passenger group on the *Speer*, and said I got rave reviews from them and from Captain Craig. Fred pretty much guaranteed me that I would be cooking for passengers again next summer.

Well, I did it. I called Ilona Mason and asked her to go out for dinner . . . and she accepted, though there was a brief moment of hesitation there when I thought she would say no. God, I'm thankful she didn't do that. It took me three trips to the phone in the engine room to work up the courage to actually call her. She was pleasant to talk to, at least after the first awkward minutes. We concluded we weren't really going out on a date—we're just getting together to talk about the future of the Great Lakes Fleet.

Tuesday, November 5
Fraser Shipyard
Superior, Wisconsin

Well, we're back where the season started almost exactly six months ago. We arrived at our lay-up dock and the captain signaled "Finished With Engine" on the engine order telegraph at 0040 this morning, or 12:40 A.M. civilian time. The deck crew was still cleaning the unloading tunnel at that time. In fact, they worked until late morning before they turned the rest of the job over to the port services crew. Some of the guys worked twenty-one hours straight. It's not easy work, either. Much of the spilled stone in the unloading tunnel had to be shoveled into wheelbarrows and wheeled to a sump where it was pumped overboard. In the cramped confines of the tunnel, it's backbreaking work, and the deck crew was showing some wear and tear this morning.

Things were a little frantic in the galley. We fed the crew and then had the bigwigs from the fleet office and Transtar come in to eat en masse. There were ten in all, including the captain and chief engineer. Geno and Steve waited on them, while I turned out eggs, pancakes, and French toast as fast as I could. It went smoothly, but it was hectic for awhile, and all three of us were glad when it was over. We shifted to local time at midnight last night, which meant that we got an extra hour of sleep, which we were thankful for.

The deck crew and Steve, the porter, left around noon for the long bus ride to Rogers City. Most of the guys stopped in the galley to say goodbye, and it was hard to see them go. They've been good shipmates, and they treated me exceptionally well throughout the season.

I called Ilona right after lunch, and our business meeting is set for tomorrow evening. She's going to pick me up here at the shipyard at 6:30 P.M., and we're going to go to dinner at Grandma's, a restaurant and watering hole down at Canal Park, the entrance to the Duluth harbor. She picked the restaurant and it was a good choice. It's an old established place with a good reputation.

A bunch of the guys are heading for the casino in Duluth tonight, including Geno, John Sobeck, Bob Lijewski, John Wysocki, and Larry Post. Butch Kierzek just got up after working half the night. He says he's too tired to do anything but lounge around the boat this evening. Iggy Donajkowski, the second assistant engineer, has security tonight, so he's on call in case there's any problem down in the engine room. Tommy Brege, the first assistant, is wandering around the boat, talking to anyone who will take the time to listen. Joe Fairbanks, an oiler, is working from 4:00 to 12:00 in the engine room; he'll be relieved at midnight by Andy McGinn, who will keep an eye on things until 8:00 A.M., when the rest of the engine crew will start another workday. The engineers "broke watches" last night, meaning that they'll all work days until they're finished laying up the boat. The phone company hooked up a telephone for us in the engine room this afternoon. Many of the guys have already taken the opportunity to call home, and I'll do that too in a few minutes. Then I plan to kick back, watch the election results filter in, and hope that I'll be pleased with the outcome.

Wednesday, November 6
Superior, Wisconsin

It's just after lunch, and I've got some time to kill so I thought I'd bring this logbook up to date. It's a cold, rainy day in Superior, and the weatherman predicts snow before the weekend. Because of the weather, Jerry Walls was the only one from the office desperate enough for a free meal to make the wet trek down to the boat.

Jerry Walls certainly lives up to his reputation as one of the real chow hounds on the fleet's payroll. For lunch he had a bowl of cream of broccoli soup, a fried ham and Swiss cheese sub, potato chips, and a side order of fettucine carbonara. He topped that off with a large piece of Geno's rich oatmeal cake and a tall glass of cold *skim* milk. By the time he got around to drinking the glass of milk I suppose he figured his arteries had reached the cholesterol saturation point! I kidded him that what he needed after a lunch like that was a little nap. He said, "You mean a captain's nap?" Napping after meals is a common pastime on the boats, but I found it interesting that the office labeled the phenomena a "captain's nap." I wonder if the captains know they are namesakes of the afternoon siesta on the boats. (They do now!)

We fed twenty-one people at lunch today, far more than we ever serve during the shipping season. We usually don't get more than fifteen or sixteen crewmembers for any meal, because there are always guys on watch and others who are sleeping. In addition to Jerry, we'll have Fred Jeffries and his port services gang for lunch everyday while we're here. Like Jerry, they can put away some chow.

The chief engineer is going to invite all the women in the office to have lunch on the boat Friday. I'm going to fix prime rib and something with shrimp in it in their honor. As one of the guys said this morning, it never hurts to suck up to the office a little. I've been doing my share of that since we've been here. I sent a large tray of fried cinnamon buns, fruit-filled sweet rolls, and pecan rolls back to the office with Jerry for their afternoon coffee break.

Of the gang who went up to the casino last night, only John Wysocki came back with more money than he left with.

The chief, Geno, John Sobeck, and Larry Post all lost money, though they aren't eager to tell us how much. Lots, I think, at least in a couple of the cases. No one plans to go back tonight.

I spent a quiet evening on the boat. Butch Kierzek and I chatted for awhile out in the messroom, and then I retired to my room and watched the election results come in. Bill Clinton easily won a second term. That pleased me, even though I was a Republican when I was a member of the Michigan House of Representatives back in the early 1970s. Over the years, I've become convinced that the Republican Party is most responsive to the interests of big business and the wealthy. As a result, much of what they do runs counter to the needs of working stiffs, like me. I'm deathly afraid that if we had a Republican president and a Republican Congress, they'd do what they could to cripple organized labor. Without the protection of labor unions, and given today's cutthroat corporate mentality, American workers would be driven back into the dark ages. Fringe benefits like pensions, medical insurance, and paid vacations could quickly become a thing of the past. I hope that Clinton has a highly successful second term, even though he's going to have to work with a Republican-controlled Congress. It'd be nice to see a little progress made toward resolving some of the major problems confronting our country, like health care.

Thursday, November 7

Superior, Wisconsin

Boy, am I tired today. Ilona Mason and I had a nice dinner last night and talked for hours, but I made the mistake of ordering a cup of coffee and a glass of kahlua while she enjoyed dessert. I couldn't fall asleep until about 1:00 in the morning. That makes for a short night's sleep when you get up at 5:30 A.M.

Ilona is a special lady, and I can see why Jerry Walls takes an interest in her well-being. She's attractive, extremely bright, a great conversationalist, and fun to be with. We talked steadily from the time she picked me up at 6:30 P.M. until she dropped me off at about 10:30 P.M. In fact,

I talked so much I grew hoarse. Our lives have followed parallel paths to an unusual extent, and we definitely have a lot in common. She's planning to come to lunch tomorrow, along with almost everyone else from the office, but I doubt that I will have much of an opportunity to talk with her then.

Two guys from the office showed up at the boat right at the end of our lunch hour today and asked if we could make up sandwiches for ten to twelve people attending a meeting back at the office. Fortunately, I made pizza for lunch and we had lots of leftovers. Earlier I'd shaved large piles of roast beef and ham I planned to use for sandwiches tomorrow. In about fifteen minutes, I put together a platter of pizza, a dozen assorted roast beef and ham sandwiches, some sliced pickles, stuffed olives, potato chips, and brownies. John Thibodeau from the engineering staff stuck his head in the galley later in the afternoon to say that the lunch was great. As I said previously, it never hurts to suck up to the office staff.

John paid a visit to the boat to let the chief know that at their luncheon meeting, the fleet bigwigs decided not to make any major expenditures on the *Calcite II* this winter. That was disappointing news for all of us. Some in the office advocated putting a lot of money into repairing the old tub before the 1997 season, and that bolstered our hopes that she would be around for quite a few more years yet. That's uncertain now. She's getting pretty ripe in her old age, and the decision to forego major repairs may indicate that they expect her to see only limited service in the future, maybe operating only six months a year, like this year. That's not good news. Now I almost wish I had sent them cold sardine sandwiches and a couple chunks of pickled bologna.

Quite a few of the crew went up the street tonight. Some were going shopping at Miller Hill Mall in Duluth, while several others, including Geno and John Sobeck, were talking about taking another crack at the casino. I'm going to lie low, do a load of laundry, and start making some preparations for lunch tomorrow. If I don't, I'm going to have to race around in the morning in order to get everything done. I'm basically going to be doing two separate lunches, one for the crew and the port services workers, and a second for the women from the office. I'm going to feed the ladies prime rib and cherry-mustard chicken breasts, and that's a little heavy for the crew. They'll have a lighter lunch and then enjoy the prime rib at supper.

I managed to get in touch with Anne Lewis and Elliott Bayley after I got back from my dinner with Ilona last night. They're two of the six passengers who made the trip on the *Speer* last summer. I called Anne's office in the afternoon and left a message on her voice mail that I was in town and hoped to see "the *Speer* gang." By the time I talked to her at home last night, she had called Joe, Sarah, Deb, and Mark and planned a dinner get-together for Sunday evening. Elliott and Anne are going to pick me up at the shipyard, and we'll start off by having drinks at their house, and then probably go to dinner. I'm sure it'll be fun, and I'm looking forward to getting their impressions of their trip now that some time has passed.

Friday, November 8

Superior, Wisconsin

I'm exhausted. It was a long, busy day. I was up at 5:00 A.M., and never slowed down until about 5:30 P.M. I'm stiff across the top of my shoulders and I've got the beginnings of a headache. I planned to go out tonight, but I don't think I've got the energy.

Our dinner for the office staff went extremely well. I thought everything was perfect. I don't think Geno and I could have done a better job. I stayed in the galley until after everyone was done eating, so I missed what went on during the meal, but those present said everyone had a good time. When I did make an appearance, after the chief called for me to come in, all of the people from the office introduced themselves. It was nice to finally put faces with the names I've heard. They all seemed friendly and pleased with the meal. Several asked for my recipe for "cherry-mustard chicken breasts." Ha! There isn't a recipe and there wasn't such a dish until I put it together today. It's my standard honey-mustard chicken breast recipe, but I added some dried tart cherries and a little cranberry juice to make a red sauce. I thought it was excellent and will make it again.

Margy Kruger was a surprise attendee this noon. She's been on vacation all week, but got back into town last night. She was down in New Orleans with her former sister-in-law, Dianne, who accompanied Margy on her trip aboard the *Speer* back in August. Margy said the weather along the Gulf coast was wretched when she was down there—in fact, it was colder there than it was up here for most of her stay. Now she gets to look forward to the long winter in Duluth! That ought to make the weather she had in New Orleans seem absolutely balmy.

Bob Jackson, the fleet's personnel supervisor, called the boat late this afternoon with boat assignments for those of us who want to continue working. Butch Kierzek and Larry Post are going to the *George A. Sloan*. Tom Brege is going on the *Callaway*, while John Wysocki will be getting on the *Gott*. I'm going on the *Roger Blough* on about the nineteenth as second cook. The office definitely did some juggling to keep me working, as I have no seniority in this fleet in unlicensed positions. I'm pretty excited about going on the *Blough*. She's one of the most distinctive ships on the lakes and her new captain is my friend Bill Craig, who was on the *Speer* when I was there this summer. I don't know who the cook will be. It's normally Al Chesky's boat, but everyone here says he takes his vacation at the end of the season. At this point, I'm scheduled to get on in Two Harbors, but Bob Jackson wants me to call him after I get home. I haven't given much thought to how I'll get to Two Harbors, but I may ride the bus up as far as Duluth and have someone from the office run me up there. There's no good way to get from Duluth to Two Harbors. About all you can do is take a cab and that's pretty expensive. If Gary happens to get off the *Columbia Star* at about that time, I'd consider driving up and having Gary drive the car home. I'd be afraid to bring my car up otherwise. If something happened and I got off the boat somewhere other than Two Harbors, getting the car would be a major headache.

I managed to get in touch with Harry Crooks, the education director for our union, this afternoon, and was ecstatic to learn that I've been picked to run the union's steward school this winter in Toledo. That's *very* exciting news.

Earlier today, I faced the prospect of being laid off for the next six months. Now I'll have a week off before I go to the *Blough,* and probably no more than a month off after the school ends in early March. That's not bad. I should still have time—and now the money—to run down to Louisiana for three or four weeks in the spring. Life is good.

Several *bad* hangovers showed up to breakfast this morning. Some of the boys overdid it last night at a local pub here in Superior. One of the guys passed out, fell off his bar stool, and had to be carried back to the boat. Geno was in high spirits this morning—he won over five hundred dollars at the casino last night, more than making up for his recent losses. John Sobeck wasn't so lucky. He lost again—big time. Maybe his brother Dick is right. Dick refused to go gambling with his younger brother recently, claiming, "John was born unlucky." Maybe so, Dick, maybe so. John's certainly taken a pounding the last few times he's visited a casino.

Saturday, November 9

Superior, Wisconsin

A quiet day on the *Calcite II.* The only visitors from the office were Dick Johns from personnel and Fred Jeffries, the port captain. Neither stuck around too long. When I wasn't preparing meals, I was cleaning and I'm not done yet. We're going to lose power to our big freezers tomorrow, so I want to get everything out of them tonight and into the small freezer in the night lunch refrigerator. I'm also going to spend some time cleaning the stove. That's something that can't be done during the day when it's hot. I'm going to fold some clothes, so I can quickly pack them. Since I'm going out with the *Speer* passengers tomorrow night, I'll have to pack my things Monday morning after breakfast. That shouldn't be a hassle, just as long as I don't have too much last-minute stuff to do in the galley on Monday. Breakfast will be the last meal we serve, as we've got the charter bus scheduled to be here to pick us up at 11:30 A.M. so we should be on the road by noon. That's going to get us home around midnight. I suspect I'll spend two or three days recovering from the ride. I can't believe I might have to do it again in a week's time, going in the other direction.

Showing the fatigue borne of a long shipping season, engine room personnel aboard the *Calcite II* wait for breakfast in the messroom during lay up. Left to right: Oiler Joe Fairbanks, Chief Engineer Bob Lijewski, First Assistant Engineer Tom "Bashful" Brege—with his back to the camera—Second Assistant Engineer Ignace "Iggy" Donajkowski, and Oiler John Sobeck. (Author's collection)

Dick Johns said today that the job on the *Blough* is probably only going to be for about two weeks, so I should be off in early December. That sounds good to me.

Fred Jeffries, the port captain, regularly works as second mate on the *Blough*, and he told me about the ship this morning. He said the boat's quite plush, as Great Lakes ships go. The rooms are large with a lot of finishing touches that are usually left out of freighters for the sake of economy. The ship is 858 feet long, but it's a full 105 feet wide, the same width as the thousand-footers. The *Blough* was built in the early 1970s, at the tail end of one of the industry's boom periods. The largest ship on the lakes at that times was just over 730 feet long, so the *Blough* should have become the Queen of the Lakes when she was launched. Unfortunately, before she could be completed there was a massive fire in her engine room. By the time the engine room was rebuilt and the ship was ready to go into service, Bethlehem Steel's 1,000-foot *Stewart J. Cort* had been launched, and the *Blough* went into the record books, not as the Queen of the Lakes, but as an also-ran, at least in terms of length and cargo capacity. The *Blough* was built in the classic Great Lakes style, with the pilothouse forward and the engine room aft. She was the last American ship built in that configuration, which had dominated the industry on the lakes since 1869. Unlike other traditional lakers, though, only the captain and mates are housed in the forward cabin. The space normally devoted to rooms for the unlicensed people in the deck department is taken up by elaborate passenger quarters. I'm anxious to spend some time on her.

Tuesday, November 12
Rogers City, Michigan

I didn't have a chance to make any entries in this log the last two days we were at the lay-up dock. Everything moved at a rapid pace from Sunday morning until Monday noon, when we packed our gear aboard a chartered bus and set off on the long trip home.

Sunday evening, I went out with Elliott Bayley, Anne Lewis, Joe Ehlers, Sarah Nelson, and Deb King, who had made the trip aboard the *Speer.* Anne and Elliott picked me up at the shipyard right after I finished serving supper to the crew, and we met the rest of the gang at a restaurant just north of Two Harbors. Deb's husband, Mark Johnson, didn't make it to the get-together, unfortunately. He'd played in a tennis tournament that day, and sore, tired, and probably a little disgusted at having finished second, he went home and soaked in a hot tub.

It was an enthusiastic reunion, and I fear our story-telling and laughter may have been distracting to the other guests in the restaurant. Joe told the best story of the evening. He collects pens, and for a number of years has been buying limited edition signature pens put out by a major manufacturer of fine writing instruments. When he and the other members of the *Speer* gang went into Chicago while we were unloading at Gary, Joe purchased the 1996 version, a pen with Alexander Dumas's signature on it. Dumas was the author of *The Three Musketeers*, among other works. Interestingly enough, the pen was recently recalled by the manufacturer. Joe received a letter advising him that the manufacturer had discovered that the signature on the barrel of the pen was not that of Alexander Dumas, the famed author, but that of his son, also named Alexander Dumas, who was a writer of little or no repute. They asked Joe to return the pen, and they would send him a new one with the correct signature on it. Joe, however, prefers to keep the pen he's got, and the rather amazing recall letter from the manufacturer. We all wondered how the error was discovered. Was there some collector out there who was such a Dumas fan that he realized that the pen had the wrong signature on it?

Our evening ended with lots of hugs, and the intention to try to get together again while I'm on the *Blough*, and hopefully have Captain Craig join us. It was almost 11:00 P.M. before Anne and Elliott got me back to the shipyard. I made the mistake of walking from the gate back to the boat. By the time I got to my room, I was wide awake from the combination of the brisk walk and the chill night air, and it took me quite awhile to fall asleep. Tommy Brege, the first assistant engineer, was packing his gear in the room next to mine and his banging around didn't help things. Neither did the realization that the engine room crew was going to work at 3:00 in the morning. By the time I awoke they'd have shut down the boiler that supplied hot water to our rooms. The chief had warned me, in fact, that someone might come into my room while I was sleeping to put antifreeze in my toilet, sink, and shower. Getting up without water the last day of lay up is pretty standard and I always hate it. I'm no good unless I can start my day with a hot shower. Last night, I filled a glass with water in the bathroom before I turned in, so I'd at least be able to brush my teeth when I got up, but I knew I'd feel miserable all day without my morning shower.

When my alarm went off at 5:30 A.M., I immediately hopped out of bed, went into the bathroom, and turned the hot water faucet on. To my amazement, water came out. Better yet, it was hot. Realizing that the stream of hot water could end at any moment, I jumped into the shower without shaving or brushing my teeth. Getting a hot shower on the last morning of lay up was a treat I wasn't going to miss.

Why the engineers had failed to shut down the boiler and drain the water lines was of no concern to me.

When I went into the galley a little later, I was surprised to find several of the guys sitting around drinking coffee. It turned out that the chief had changed his plans, and the engine room crew wasn't going to work at 3:00 A.M. as planned, but after they ate breakfast at 7:00 A.M. They were happy to have the extra sleep, and I was deeply thankful for my morning shower.

After a steak-and-eggs breakfast, a special lay-up treat, the guys set to work to finish laying up the boat. The boiler was knocked down and the water and steam lines drained. After Geno and I hurriedly finished the breakfast dishes, we filled one of the sinks in the galley with the last drops of hot water, as our dishwasher and the icemaker in the night-lunch refrigerator were shut off and drained. There wasn't much for us to do after that. We wiped everything down in the galley, carried out the garbage, mopped the deck one last time, bagged up the dirty linen the guys brought in, and then checked all the rooms in the after cabin to make sure they were clean. After that, I went to my room, finished packing, and dressed for the trip home.

Mike Meyer, one of the engineers, was the only member of the lay-up crew who wasn't from the Rogers City area. He lives in Duluth, so he had a short trip home. Chief Engineer Bob Lijewski had his truck at the shipyard and set off for Rogers City alone, planning to stop along the way to visit a relative. Tim Peacock's wife Val drove up on Saturday and they headed south in their minivan while the rest of us hauled our gear down to the dock. The bus we'd chartered arrived about 11:30 A.M., and the remaining ten of us boarded it for the 473-mile ride to Rogers City.

I considered renting a car and driving home to avoid a bus ride that I knew would be arduously long and uncomfortable, but we hadn't gotten very far out of Superior before I was glad someone else was driving. We had snow almost all the way home; it was so heavy at times that the visibility fell to near zero. Around Ironwood, in the western end of the Upper Peninsula, there was twenty inches of snow on the ground, and it was still coming down in buckets.

As bus trips go, the journey home from Superior wasn't bad, certainly better than the overnight trip I made with

With their ship laid up, crewmembers from the *Calcite II* stow their baggage aboard a bus chartered to take them from Fraser Shipyard in Superior, Wisconsin, to Rogers City, Michigan, where most of them live. From left to right are John Wysocki, Larry Post, and Butch Kierzek. The stern of the *Calcite II* is on the right. (Author's collection)

Jake Gajewski coming home from the *Speer*. Joe Fairbanks, Larry Post, John Sobeck, Andy McGinn, Geno, and I sat near the back of the bus, and talked or napped most of the way home. Joe Fairbanks was the only guy on the bus who brought any alcohol aboard. He picked up a twelve-pack of beer, downed six or seven in fairly short order, and promptly fell asleep for a few hours. We debated whether or not to wake Joe when we got home, or leave him on the bus for its return trip to Ironwood. We knew that would be a lousy thing to do to a shipmate, but it would have made for a good sea story next season. Joe saved himself from having to take two bus rides to get home when he finally woke up shortly after we crossed the Mackinac Bridge.

Tom Brege offered an ongoing diversion for the rest of us with a virtually epic display of his conversational abilities. Tom sat directly behind the bus driver when we left Superior and talked nonstop for the entire trip—about eleven hours. At one point, Joe Fairbanks and I tried to take bets from the other guys on when Tommy would finally run out of wind, but there were no takers. Knowing Tommy well, everyone was certain that he could keep up the chatter until we hit Rogers City. There was some interest, though, in placing bets on when the bus driver would get tired of listening to Tommy and throw him off the bus.

We stopped three times on the way home. The first was at an Indian reservation outside of Ashland, Wisconsin, where those of us who smoke stocked up on tax-free cigarettes. Butch Kierzek bought twelve cartons, which ought to last him darn near till fitout next year. The second stop was at Ironwood, Michigan, where we changed drivers. The third stop was at Escanaba, Michigan, in the early evening, where we picked up something to eat at a fast-food restaurant. Shortly before 11:00 P.M., we pulled into the snow-covered sailor's parking lot at Calcite. Quite a few of the wives were waiting, and the rest of us wandered around the lot in the dark until we found our cars. Mine wasn't parked even close to where I thought it was, and I actually just stumbled across it accidentally.

It didn't take but a few minutes for us to get our gear loaded up and head for home. After spending the past six and a half months together on the boat, there were no prolonged goodbyes in the parking lot. As guys scurried around, getting their baggage out from under the bus and loading it into their cars and pickups, there were a few parting handshakes, but nobody made a major production out of the fact that many of us wouldn't see each other until next season. When we hit that parking lot, our priorities changed. We weren't concerned about the shipping season or our shipmates any longer. All we wanted to do at that point was go home to our families. I was a little jealous of the other guys, all of whom had wives waiting for them, either there in the parking lot or at home. Going home to your mother is a lot less exciting. Despite that, I was glad to be home, and glad to know I would wake up the next morning and not have to worry about what kind of soup I was going to make.

While our season on the *Calcite II* was over, it's not the end of the sailing season for some of us. Of the ten of us on the bus, Andy McGinn, Iggy Donajkowski, John Sobeck, Joe Fairbanks, and Gene Schaedig are done for the 1996 season. Over the next week to ten days, though, the other five of us will haul our gear up the ladders of other ships. A

310

few of us will end up laying up a second ship before we're finally done for the season. If that's not dismal enough, some of us will even end up making another trip home on a chartered bus. Tommy may get another chance to talk the ears off a bus driver.

While some of us will move on, the season is over for the *Calcite II*. Her sixty-seventh season on the lakes was a short one. She left the fitout dock on May 1 and laid up on November 4, after just over six months in operation. Despite that, the *C-II* made sixty-three trips and carried a total of about 750,000 tons of cargo. That's a lot of rock, salt, stone, coal, and sand, but it pales in comparison to the tonnages hauled by the newer and larger ships. The AAA-class boats, like the *Callaway, Clarke,* and *Anderson* in our fleet, for example, will each probably haul around 1.5 million tons. Thousand-footers, like the *Speer,* may be expected to carry more than 3 million tons, even though they usually make only about fifty-five trips in a season that lasts almost ten months for them. Of course, they can't go places that the *Calcite II* can, so it's an apples-and-oranges comparison. There's a place in the industry right now for old clunkers like the *Calcite II;* barring unforeseen developments, she'll be back out on the lakes again in 1997. I wouldn't mind spending a little time on her.

Friday, November 22

M/V Roger Blough

Two Harbors, Minnesota

This is some boat! I've only been here on the *Blough* for a few hours, but I already know that it's something special. This will be an interesting two weeks.[24]

---

[24]Put into service on June 15, 1972, the *Blough* is 858 feet long and 105 feet wide, with twin diesel engines that produce 14,200 horsepower. It carries about 45,000 tons of iron ore each trip, compared to 60,000 that can be hauled on a thousand-footer. The *Blough* was named for the man

311

I "signed on the Articles" at about 3:30 this morning. I haven't had any sleep since 7:00 A.M. yesterday, so it's going to be one of those interminably long days. I'm also about three days late in getting aboard. I was originally scheduled to catch the boat on November 19, but last weekend the *Blough*, *Speer*, and *Gott* all got hung up at the Soo because of low water. We had several days of strong winds out of the south, and it pushed enough water out of Whitefish Bay that they couldn't get down to the locks. My brother saw them all anchored in a pack around Gros Cap, just inside Whitefish Bay, on Sunday. Fortunately, the winds finally went around to the north and the boats were able to head down the lake. We're going to take another delay loading today, too. The pellets sitting in the dock for the past few days got rained on and froze. The dock workers are using blowtorches to try to get the ore to come out of the hoppers.

---

who was chairman of the board and CEO of U.S. Steel when construction of the ship was authorized.

U.S. Steel certainly hasn't been very creative in naming their ships during the second half of the twentieth century. Most have been named for company officials or former company officials, men who aren't particularly well known outside the steel industry. The few exceptions to that naming scheme include the *Calcite II*, *Rogers City*, and *Cedarville*, all ships in the grey fleet that were named for their home port of Rogers City, the U.S. Steel quarry there, or the company's other stone quarry at Cedarville, Michigan.

Most other shipping companies on the lakes have been similarly unimaginative in naming their boats. The ships commonly outlive their namesakes, and most of the boats operating today bear the names of dead men. Other ships have been named for ports, including our *Calcite II*, American Steamship's *Indiana Harbor*, and Bethlehem's *Burns Harbor*, or for customers of the shipping companies, such as American Steamship's *American Republic*, honoring Republic Steel—now part of LTV Steel, and Oglebay Norton's *Armco*, named for Armco Steel. Columbia's Reserve was named for Reserve Mining, which was owned jointly by Armco and Republic Steel. That company went out of business in the 1980s, but its name remains on the freighter.

It's a little sad that so many magnificent ships have such boring names. You'd think that a company as progressive as Transtar would change that, maybe renaming the *Blough* the *Ultimate Laker*, because she was the last U.S. ship built in the traditional style, or calling the Speer the *Superior Shuttle*, because she loads on Lake Superior and has a shuttle boom. How about making the *Gott* the *Transtar Express*? Well, maybe my suggestions aren't so great, but just about anything would be better than *Roger Blough*, *Edgar B. Speer*, and *Edwin H. Gott*.

This could take awhile. But, what the heck, I'm not in any hurry to go anywhere.[25]

I had a nice ten-day vacation, although I didn't do anything very exciting. I put some time in editing earlier sections of this logbook—correcting spelling errors or adding clarifications where necessary. I had some things I wanted to do in Duluth before I got on the boat, so I drove up from Rogers City on Wednesday, and spent two nights— or one and a half nights, to be more accurate—in a motel. Wednesday evening, I met Joe Ehlers, who was one of the passengers on the *Speer* during the summer, and delivered some copies of my books and *Speer* sweatshirts I bought for all six of "the gang." On Friday, I spent a couple of hours at the fleet office, the first time I've been there since I came to work for this company. It was nice to see everyone in their environment for a change. Usually I only see them when they visit whatever boat I'm on. After stirring things up at the office, I spent the balance of the day wandering around Duluth, which is a wonderful city, combining shopping and sightseeing. In the late afternoon, I met Margy Kruger for drinks before we went to a restaurant in Superior, Wisconsin, called The Library, to eat. Margy, as you may recall, is the secretary to the president of the company, and she and two friends made a trip from Two Harbors to the Soo on the *Speer* when I was cooking over there. I had a great evening and we had a marvelous dinner of chateaubriand. I did make one mistake last night, however. Having had a wonderful meal, and enjoying Margy's company, I wanted to

---

[25]The Articles, or the Articles of Agreement, are signed by all crewmembers when they come aboard ship, and on the first of every month thereafter. They specify the terms of shipment and the length of the voyage that the sailor agrees to. The sailor also attests that he is sober and able to do the job for which he is being employed. The Articles are now largely a formality on ships, but they were initially required as a means to protect persons from being shanghaied for voyages they didn't want to go on. When you're on the Articles today, you're afforded a variety of rights under the Merchant Seamen's Act. Your employer, for example, is responsible to provide for your "maintenance and cure" if you're injured or become ill during the voyage. At the end of a voyage, you're given a discharge that indicates you completed the voyage. On the lakes, a "voyage" doesn't just mean a trip from Two Harbors to Gary and back. It could run from fitout until lay up, for example, if you didn't take any time off.

linger over a good cup of coffee. That was a bad decision. I react pretty strongly to caffeine, and when I got back to the motel and tried to get a couple hours' sleep before heading for Two Harbors, I had caffeine-induced insomnia. It had been such a nice evening, though, that I didn't even get too upset at not being able to sleep. Quite a few of the people in the office know Margy and I were going out last night, so I suspect she'll get a lot of grief today.

I'm here on the *Blough* as second cook. It's the first time I've worked as a second cook for three or four years. I think I'm a little rusty—I baked a German chocolate cake this morning that didn't get done in the center. Whoops! With a little creative trimming and a thick coating of coconut pecan frosting, no one knew the difference. Things will improve tomorrow, I'm sure, after I've had a good night's sleep.

The giant *Roger Blough* churns its way north on the Detroit River, heading for an iron ore loading dock on Lake Superior. The 858-foot-long ship, which went into service in 1972, was the last U.S. freighter built in the traditional fore-and-aft design that made its debut on the lakes in 1869. It has its pilothouse and quarters for some crewmembers in the cabin at the bow, while the galley and accommodations for the balance of the crew are located over the engine room at the vessel's stern. The last Canadian ship built in the classic style was Algoma Central Marine's *Algosoo*, launched in 1974. (Author's collection)

I had a chance to talk with Captain Bill Craig for a few minutes this morning. It was good to see him again. He's a fine gentleman with a wonderful sense of humor. I gave Captain Craig two *Roger Blough* sweatshirts that I had screen-printed in Rogers City, one for him and one for his wife Phylliss. They're attractive sweatshirts with a picture of the boat on them and I know the Craigs will enjoy them. They both dress casually much of the time and often wear sweatshirts.

Al Chesky, the cook here, is quite a character. All the stories I've heard about him are true. In fact, they may not even do justice to his unique personality. He's loud, rude, crude, and rants and raves constantly, but the crew doesn't seem to mind. Al's got a reputation as the best cook in the fleet and sailors are willing to put up with his lighthearted verbal abuse as long as they can eat well. He's probably a little extra wound up right now, because he's supposed to be getting off on vacation on December 1.

Saturday, November 23

Lake Superior, Downbound

We didn't leave the dock at Two Harbors until a little after 5:00 this morning, following a load that took more than twenty-four hours to finish. Another fiasco.

Both Al and Matt Sullivan, the porter, went up the street last night and neither moved too fast this morning. As soon as breakfast was over, they both disappeared, gone to their rooms, I presume, to try to heal a little before lunch.

I sat in the messroom until about 8:30 last night talking with Jim Abfalter, one of the engineers. Jim was in one of the classes at the Great Lakes Maritime Academy that I admitted when I was admissions officer there, and he took my History of Great Lakes Shipping course. It was that class, by the way, that led me to write *Steamboats and Sailors of the Great Lakes*. The genesis for the book were the copious notes I put together for the class. Jim's a true gourmand, and we spent most of the evening talking about contemporary cuisine, and how lacking it is on the boats. It's too bad he's working in the engine room. I'm sure he

315

would have made an excellent steward. He not only enjoys eating, but he does a lot of cooking when he's home in the winters. He cooks because he gets great enjoyment from it, and that's something that can't be said for most of the stewards out here.

If we don't have any further delays, and that's a big "if" this time of the year, we're now scheduled to be back in Superior to load late in the afternoon on Thanksgiving Day. That would be a great time for those of us in the galley. I'm not going to get my hopes up, though. We've got too much water to cross before we get to Superior, and we could just as easily get in there at midnight.

Sunday, November 24

Straits of Mackinac, Lake Michigan

We got to the Soo at about 6:00 this morning, and passed Mackinac Island and under the Mackinac Bridge at suppertime. The lake is so calm right now you could navigate it in a canoe. The gales of November are quiet, at least for now.

Speaking of quiet, this is one of the quietest boats I've been on. Most of the diesel-powered boats are noisy and vibrate constantly, but the *Blough* is as quiet and smooth as any steamboat I've ever been on. Given that this boat has as much power as many of the thousand-footers, it must be the hull form that creates the vibrations. They're much boxier than the *Blough*, which is built with the lines of a classic lake freighter that's on steroids. She has, however, a pointed bow and a rounded stern, while the footers are modeled after a shoe box that's slightly rounded at one end.[26]

One of the most striking features of the *Blough* is the size of its stern cabin. On the main deck level, the cabin extends the full 105-foot width of the ship, and it must run for about

---

[26] Al Chesky later told me that the *Blough* vibrated so badly when it first came out that the panels shook out of the dropped ceiling in the messroom, and some of the bulkheads developed cracks. They solved the problem by installing a skewed propeller. Instead of being rounded off at the top, the back edge of each propeller blade has sort of a fin extension.

150 feet fore and aft. The first 100 feet is dedicated to crew cabins, laundry room, and two recreation rooms—one for the officers and one for the unlicensed crewmembers. Aft of the living area is the self-unloading shuttle, which is transversely mounted so that it will extend out either side of the hull. It's similar to the shuttle on the *Speer*, except that hers is located in front of her cabin area on the main deck, while this one is tucked away into the stern.

On the poop deck, one deck up from the living quarters, are the galley, messroom, and a dining room for officers and passengers. For some unknown reason, the dining room is only used when there are passengers aboard. The rest of the time the officers eat in the messroom with the unlicensed personnel. They're waited on by the porter, so I can continue with my baking and other assignments during meal hours.

Despite the immense size of the stern cabin, some of the unlicensed crewmembers share rooms. I find that unbelievable. If the company and the naval architects had put a little more thought into the design, they could have easily produced a ship with private rooms for the entire crew. There are even some thousand-footers where crewmembers have to share rooms. That's true, for example, on Interlake's *James R. Barker* and *Mesabi Miner*. I worked on both as an unlicensed seaman and always shared a room with the other unlicensed person in the galley. Let me assure you, when you're my age there's no such thing as a good roommate. On two occasions, the other person was a woman, which made for an interesting, albeit extremely uncomfortable living situation. No one should have to put up with such nonsense. On the boat, my room is my home, for God's sake. If I want to lounge around in my underwear after work, play Elton John music at full volume on my stereo, or have complete silence, I should be able to do that. Anyone who spends seven to ten months a year on a ship should have privacy when they're not working. The sad thing is that there's enough room on this boat and on the thousand-footers to allow everyone a private room, but it wasn't a priority for the shipping company or the shipbuilders. That says volumes about their opinions of those of us who crew their ships year in and year out.

They commit other ludicrous acts, too. On the *Speer*, for example, all the guest rooms used by passengers have twin beds, yet most of the passengers are couples. How'd you like to take a romantic trip on the Great Lakes and sleep in twin beds? It reminds me of my days in married student housing at Lake Superior State University. They put twin beds in those apartments, too. We eventually concluded it was the conservative college president's birth-control program.

Tomorrow evening we'll be in Gary. We'll finish unloading by early Tuesday morning, then two and a half days back up the lake. We're scheduled to load at Burlington Northern Railway's dock in Superior, just a stone's throw from Margy's house. We should be in there in the late afternoon or early evening, on Thanksgiving. I hope I can see her for a little while, but Thanksgiving Day isn't a particularly good time to tear people away from their families. I can always talk to her on the phone. That's often all a sailor hopes for.

Monday, November 25
Lower Lake Michigan

I'm on my afternoon break now. We're just a couple hours from Gary, but there's quite a sea out of the north and Captain Craig isn't sure he's going to take the boat in. We would make it in okay, but the slip runs north and south and this sea could produce a powerful surge along the dock. That could move the boat around quite a bit, making it impossible for us to unload and even difficult to hold the boat alongside the dock. The captain thought it might be safer to anchor somewhere until the lake settles down. If we take much of a delay, it will put us up in Superior in the middle of the night. That would stink.

I spoke with Chief Engineer Joe Kolenda last night and discovered that he's married to Candace Peterson. Candace was a cadet at the Great Lakes Maritime Academy when I worked there in the early 1980s. She earned a deck license, but there were no jobs when she graduated, so she went back to school and got an engineer's license. Candace sailed awhile as an engineer, and then married Joe. Now she's a full-time mother. Maybe I'll get a chance to see her while I'm here.

Quite a few of the guys want copies of my books, so I called an order into Wayne State University Press this morning. I'll have them shipped to the Soo Warehouse, and we'll pick them up when we get groceries on our next trip down the lakes.

It's about 6:30 P.M. now and we're at anchor. The captain says the winds may increase and stay strong over the next eighteen hours, so we may be here awhile. My guess is that the captain will try to go in after dawn tomorrow. In the meantime, I've just thrown in a small load of laundry. All three of us in the galley worked an hour or so overtime tonight to begin our preparations for Thursday's Thanksgiving dinner. Thanksgiving is the major holiday of the year on the boats, at least in terms of fixing an elaborate dinner. In the old days ships almost always laid up before Christmas, so Thanksgiving was the season's last major holiday for the crew. The galley crew always did Thanksgiving dinner up special. That tradition continues today, even though many boats remain active well into January. After the meal hour ended today, Al and I mixed up a variety of candies, including almond bark, chocolate-covered pretzels, fudge, and fruit and nut clusters. Matt and I also ground cranberries and oranges for cranberry relish, while Al cooked cranberry sauce. Tomorrow evening we'll probably complete more prep work for the Thanksgiving meal. It will be nice to get the big Thanksgiving feast out of the way before we get up above; that way the three of us can relax and go up the street without the worry of putting together the biggest meal of the year the next day. It would have been lousy to be in Superior on Thanksgiving Eve, but worse if we had been forced to stay on the boat to get things ready for the big meal the next day. This is better, although what time we're going to be into Superior is now anyone's guess. I'll be more than a little disappointed if it's in the middle of the night. I'm going to be off here after the next trip, so it really isn't a big deal. In another ten to twelve days, my season will end and I'll be free to do just about anything I want.

319

Tuesday, November 26
Off Gary, Indiana

I awoke a little after 4:00 this morning to find the boat vigorously rolling from side to side. The watchman later told me there were twelve-foot seas. It's 9:30 A.M. now, and we're anchored four miles off Gary since we arrived here late yesterday afternoon. It was a good call on the captain's part. Since the seas are out of the north-northwest, I'm sure there's a powerful surge inside the harbor. If we tied up in there, there's no way our winches could hold the boat. We'd have been pushed and pulled up and down the dock all night long. Our *Speer* is midway down Lake Michigan, but they've apparently checked down, knowing that they won't get into Gary either. Since the *Blough* and the *Speer* can only unload into the hopper at Gary because of their shuttle booms, one of us will take a long delay. Word is that we could be here all day. There's no indication the wind will go down anytime soon. I'm glad I'm not on the *Calcite II*. In twelve-foot seas that little puddle jumper would bob around like a cork.

It's just before 6:00 P.M. now, and we're finally on our way into the dock at Gary. The wind died down rather abruptly at about 4:00 P.M., but the captain waited a couple of hours for the surge to slacken before starting in. This is reasonably good timing. If we don't take any more delays we'll be into Superior sometime early Friday afternoon. We're still scheduled to go to the Burlington Northern dock; it usually takes ten to twelve hours to load there, so we should all have time to get up the street. With this delay, though, everything may change before we get up above.

Wednesday, November 27
Lake Michigan, Upbound

It's almost 7:00 P.M., and I'm just getting out of the galley after a long day. Much of my time was spent prepping things for tomorrow's big Thanksgiving dinner. I made so much stuff today I can't remember all of it. I cooked off shrimp and made cocktail sauce for shrimp cocktail, cut up fruit for a fruit boat, made Waldorf salad, and baked four pies. In addition to that and my normal baking, I made the beds of all five engineers today, as it's linen-change day. Of all the jobs that a second cook has to do, making beds is my least favorite. I've still got to go back upstairs to put the pies in the refrigerator after they've cooled down, and chill a watermelon for the fruit boat. Other than that, I plan to spend the evening in a vertical position.

We received a fax from the office this afternoon stating that Al will get off when we get to Superior. I'll take over as steward until Lynn Sternberg gets here. He'll come here from the *Munson.* From the sounds of the fax, Lynn should be able to catch up to us in a day or two, either at the Soo or in Gary. While I'm steward, Matt will go second cook and we'll get by without a porter. That means a little overtime for both of us, which is fine with me. I usually work extra hours anyway, but now I'll be able to get paid for it.

We finished unloading about 5:30 this morning. That should put us into Superior between noon and 2:00 P.M. on Friday. We're in competition for the dock with Interlake's *George A. Stinson,* which is ahead of us at this point, but we've got a lot of water to cover before we get to the head of the lakes and the *Blough* is the faster boat. On a recent trip with a following sea, she made nineteen miles an hour. I doubt the *Stinson* does much over fifteen, so we ought to pass her somewhere along the way. Many of the guys on the *Stinson* are from the Duluth-Superior area, so they don't mind taking a big delay in their home port. We all feel that way.

Thursday, November 28

Thanksgiving Day

Lake Superior, Upbound

Our Thanksgiving feeding frenzy went off without a hitch. There was enough food to feed the entire Polish navy. Matt and I worked steadily from a few minutes before 6:00 this morning until about 5:15 P.M. Al came in an hour later

321

Captain Bill Craig, at the head of the table, presides over Thanksgiving dinner in the officers' dining room on the *Roger Blough*. The Thanksgiving meal is usually the most extravagant of the year aboard freighters on the lakes, a tradition dating back to the days when ships were generally laid up prior to Christmas. (Author's collection)

than we did. All three of us were ready to drop by the time we had fed the last man and straightened things up a little. We served from 1:00 until 3:00 P.M.—the crewmembers were on their own after that. The steam table was loaded to capacity when we left the galley, although I imagine that foraging crewmembers have already made quite a dent in it.

Here's a copy of our menu for our 1996 Thanksgiving dinner:

Appetizers
Chicken Dumpling Soup
Shrimp Cocktail
Steak Tartar
Marinated Shrimp & Olives
Ham Pinwheels
Deviled Eggs
Assorted Crackers with Meats and Cheeses
Cheese Ball
Stuffed Celery
BBQ Cocktail Franks

Waldorf Salad
Jello Salads
Fresh Fruit Salad
Fresh Vegetable Platter with Dips

Entrees
Roast Tom Turkey with Sage Dressing
Filet Mignon with Sauteed Fresh Mushrooms
Roast Duck or Pheasant with Wild Rice Stuffing

Side Dishes
Fresh Mashed Potatoes with Giblet Gravy
Stuffed Baked Potatoes
Acorn Squash
Candied Sweet Potatoes
Assorted Fresh Dinner Rolls
Fresh Baked Bread

Desserts
Dutch Apple Pie
Mincemeat Pie
Pumpkin Pie
Grannie's Fruit Cake
Dipped Pretzels
Fried Ice Cream with Choice of Toppings
Fresh Almond Bark
Fresh Peanut Fudge
Assorted Cookies and Dessert Bars

Beverages
Assorted Soda Pop
Apple or Cherry Cider
Milk
Coffee
Tea

In addition, each crewmember received a large pack of chewing gum, a small box of Russell Stover chocolates, a candy bar, a can of mixed nuts, and a paper cup full of assorted candies. In the old days they would have also received cigars and cigarettes, but that's no longer politically correct. Some ships would also have had beer or wine with their dinner, but that's illegal. Many fleets continued the practice long after regulations prohibited the consumption of alcohol on merchant ships, but enforcement of the ban on drinking is much stricter in the days since Captain Joe Hazlewood and the *Exxon Valdez*. That's okay with me.

About twenty-five years ago, a crewman fell overboard from one of the Cleveland Cliffs ships and drowned on Thanksgiving Day, after drinking too much. If you have alcoholic beverages on a ship, there are always those who will overdo it and that's dangerous.

After we finished serving and cleaning up, I ate a filet mignon and some Waldorf salad, and then napped for an hour. I've put a load of laundry in now, and I'm going to change my bed and clean my room a little. I'm still stuffed, so there'll be no turkey sandwich for me this evening.

Saturday, November 30
Lake Superior, Downbound

We got in to Superior at about 1:00 yesterday afternoon. I took supper off—for only the second time this season—and went out with Margy.

Al Chesky got off after supper last night to begin a thirty-day vacation. I'm steward until Lynn Sternberg catches the boat at the Soo or Gary. I made it through breakfast and lunch without any hassles, and even received quite a few compliments from the crew. It's good to have the run of a galley again, even if just for a day or two.

The galley seems as quiet as a morgue with Al gone, though. I suggested to Captain Craig that he call Al and ask him to send us a cassette tape of his ranting and raving, so we could play it at mealtimes for the crew. It'd make them feel more at home. The captain thought my suggestion was an excellent idea. I wouldn't be surprised if he calls Al.

I sat up well past my normal bedtime last night talking with Mike Hartley, the first assistant engineer. Mike wrote a book about baseball Hall of Famer Christie Mathewson and he's having some trouble finding a publisher. I suggested he send his manuscript to several successful baseball book authors for criticism. If one of them praises the book, ask the guy to recommend it to *his* publisher. Mike considers that a rather devious, but potentially effective tactic. We also talked at some length about the possibility of his self-publishing the book if he can't find a publishing house to take it. If no one had wanted to publish *Steamboats and Sailors,* I'd have forked over the money for at least one small printing. At least I could have given them to my friends and family members for Christmas, birthdays, wedding anniversaries, or bar mitzvahs. You get the picture. After all the agony of researching and writing the blasted book, it *was* going to be published in some form, even if I had to do it myself.

Captain Craig will get off with me in Two Harbors when we get back up above. He's only had a couple of weeks off all season and wants to spend at least a week or two at home before the holidays. The regular first mate, who's currently on vacation, will get back on in Gary as an observer, and then relieve Captain Craig at Two Harbors.

We'll be at the grub boat at the Soo at 2:00 or 3:00 tomorrow morning. Argh! It will be a short night for Matt and me.

Sunday, December 1
Lake Michigan

What a long day! I awoke at about 1:45 this morning as we went into the Poe Lock at the Soo; except for a thirty-minute nap this afternoon, I've been at it all day. Fortunately, I was tired enough last night that I went to bed around 7:00 P.M., so I had my usual six and a half hours of sleep by the time we reached the locks. Nonetheless, I've worked about fourteen hours today and I've a right to be tired. I actually feel rather invigorated right now. I've thrown in a load of laundry, so I'll be up for a couple of hours at least.

We got word from the office this morning that Lynn Sternberg won't get on until we return to the Soo in another two days. That's okay. I'd rather be the steward than second cook, even if we are shorthanded in the galley. Things are going just fine, so I'm happy to get the extra days as steward.

Jim Abfalter got off at the Soo this morning and was replaced by Jim Burke. Jim and I sailed together on the *George A. Sloan* for a short time last fall; it was good to see

325

him again. He had hip surgery earlier this year and hasn't worked much. Jim's the son of a former captain on the grey boats, and he lives in a farming area just west and south of Alpena. It's good to have someone else on board who's from northeast Michigan.

Jim Burke brought me up-to-date on the strike on the cement boats. It doesn't sound good. All of the parties involved in the dispute met with a federal mediator a week or so ago, but it sounds as though Inland Lakes will continue to run the boats with their crews of strikebreakers; there isn't much the strikers can do, except apply for their old jobs before the sailing season starts next spring. I doubt many will do that, and it's unlikely that many would be hired back in any case. It's more likely that most of the guys will ship out of the union hall to fill relief jobs next year, as many have done this season. That's the second unsuccessful attempt by the American Maritime Officers to unionize the cement fleet. It's not a very reassuring record.

At breakfast this morning Captain Craig commented

Her decks covered with a dusting of early winter snow, the 858-foot *Roger Blough* meets Interlake Steamship's 1,013-foot *Paul R. Tregurtha* in the St. Marys River. Since her launching in 1981, the *Tregurtha* has been "Queen of the Lakes," the longest ship operating on the Great Lakes. The *Tregurtha* and the 858-foot *Blough* are both 105 feet wide. (Author's collection)

about how much more difficult this boat is to handle than a 1,000-footer. I was surprised—I would have thought exactly the opposite was true, since this boat is shorter. What I didn't know before is that the *Blough* doesn't have twin screws. She's got two engines, but they drive a single shaft. The footers all have twin shafts and twin propellers that are used to help turn the ship.

One positive feature of this boat that I've forgotten to mention are the windows in the messroom and officers' dining room. They're placed low enough so that when you sit at the table, you can look outside. On all the other boats I've been on, the windows are higher up and you can't see out unless you stand up. This was particularly noticeable this morning, when I sat in the messroom drinking a cup of coffee while the ship passed Mackinac Island and slipped under the Mackinac Bridge. On another boat, I probably wouldn't even have noticed our location.

An envelope from my brother Gary was waiting for me at the Soo today. He sent me a copy of what's billed as "the world's easiest quiz." The first question is, "How long was the Hundred Years War?" Sounds simple enough, but the Hundred Years War actually lasted for 116 years. The last question was, "How long was the Thirty Years War?" The answer, of course, is thirty years. Tricky. While I scanned through the quiz, I also learned that most Panama hats are made in Ecuador, King George VI's real name was Albert, the Canary Islands are named after the Latin term for dogs, and purple finches are actually red. I stuck the quiz in an envelope to send along to Jerry Walls at the fleet office. I retitled it the Office Qualifying Exam and added a note to the effect that anyone who failed the quiz would immediately be reassigned to one of the ships in the fleet. I doubt they'll have much more luck than I did, but it'll give them something to do on the next slow day.

Monday, December 2

Gary, Indiana

We arrived here and started unloading shortly after 11:00 this morning. At this dock, they hook us up to a

327

shoreside telephone line so we can use the phone in the engine room to make calls using a telephone credit card. That's the only nice thing about coming into Gary, the "murder capital" of the country. It's very seldom anyone from the boats goes up the street here; if they do they usually try to take some company along for protection.

First Mate Dan Rentschler bought copies of both my books this morning, and flipped through *Steamboats and Sailors* in the messroom after breakfast, looking at the pictures. In one of the chapters there's a photo of the tanker *Saturn*. "I sailed on her," said Dan. "Did you ever sail on the *Jupiter?*" I asked. The *Jupiter*, the *Saturn*'s sistership, was destroyed when her cargo of gasoline exploded as she unloaded in the Saginaw River in 1990. There's a section on her in the shipwreck book I'm working on. "Ya, I sailed on her!" Dan exclaimed. "In fact, I was on her when she blew up." We spent a little time talking about the disaster, which claimed the life of one crewmember. I plan to talk to Dan at greater length when he comes in for supper after the 4-to-8 watch this evening. It'll be interesting to get a firsthand account from one of the survivors.

Tuesday, December 3
Lake Michigan, Upbound

We'll be at the Straits of Mackinac in a couple of hours, and expect to pull into the Soo about 1:00 in the morning. The office notified us by fax this morning that Lynn Sternberg won't get on until we get back to Two Harbors, so I'll stay as steward for the rest of the trip.

Nothing eventful happened today, but I did have a chance to talk to Dan Rentschler at length this morning about the explosion and fire on the *Jupiter*. The little tanker was unloading more than a million gallons of gasoline at a terminal on the north side of the Saginaw River when the incident occurred. The dock there was poorly maintained and the boat was moored to some old wooden pilings that were starting to disintegrate. While Dan was on watch, American Steamship's freighter *Buffalo* approached, on its way to a dock up the river. Dan saw the ship and called for the pumpman to stop discharging gasoline until the boat had gone by. He also told the watchman and wheelsman to stand by the winches, knowing it was likely that the *Buffalo* would suck them off the dock when it went by, even though it was going slow. As the *Buffalo* passed, the rush of water preceding the freighter pushed the *Jupiter* ahead, snapping one of the two stern mooring cables. When the tanker's forward movement stretched the mooring cables and hawsers tight, the ship recoiled and quickly moved astern, snapping the two steel mooring cables at the bow. At that point, Dan hurried toward the bow, intent on dropping one of the anchors in an effort to prevent the bow from breaking loose and drifting out into the river. It was then held only by a nylon hawser.

Even though Dan had slacked off on the tanker's discharge hose connected to an on-shore pipeline, the movement of the ship parted the hose and some electrical wires attached to it. The wires sparked, igniting fuel that spilled from the hose. As Dan ran toward the bow, he looked back and saw flames several feet high atop the manifold through which the fuel was discharged. The watchman had already left to get a fire extinguisher; he was in the process of trying to douse the fire when a drip pan under the manifold burst into flames that Dan estimated shot fifty feet into the air. In a matter of seconds, the fire spilled into the piping connecting the manifold to the gasoline-filled cargo holds of the ship and one of the tanks exploded. Fire quickly spread across the deck of the *Jupiter,* cutting Dan and the wheelsman off from the stern cabin area where the rest of the crew was. Dan didn't hear it, but the captain had sounded the general alarm, rousing the crew. They made a brief effort to fight the fire with the ship's foam extinguishing system, but the fire and explosions tore apart some of the piping for the fire-fighting system, and they quickly ran out of foam. It was obvious the ship was lost, and the captain gave the order to abandon ship.

As the ship's tanks continued to explode, hurling flames and debris high into the air, Dan and the wheelsman jumped over the starboard bow and began swimming toward shore. He estimates that it was only a matter of two or three minutes from the time the *Jupiter* was first sent hurtling down the dock until he and the wheelsman were forced into the water. It was a chilly, damp day, and both men were dressed in heavy clothing and rain gear. As Dan swam as hard as he could for shore, he heard the wheelsman behind him calling for help. In the finest tradition of the sea, Dan turned around and went back to save his faltering shipmate. Dan dragged the man toward shore, but the wheelsman was exhausted from the struggle and, with his clothing water-logged, it was like trying to carry an anchor. The wheelsman sank under the water. To save his own life, Dan was forced to let go and the man drowned. He was, amazingly, the only crewmember lost in the disaster.

Dan swam to a piling sticking up out of the water and managed to pull himself up on top of it. A few minutes later, two employees of the petroleum terminal rowed out and rescued him, despite the fact that the air was filled with chunks of metal being blown off the exploding ship. With Dan aboard, they circled the ship and began to pull other crewmen from the water. Others were rescued by pleasure boats and Coast Guard craft that arrived on the scene in a matter of minutes after the fire started.

It took several days to put the massive fire out. By then, the entire cargo hold area of the ship had been destroyed, warped and bent by the flames and heat like a child's plastic model someone had taken a blowtorch to. The stern cabin area of the *Jupiter* was largely intact, and Dan and the other crewmembers eventually got most of their personal gear back. They also each received a thousand-dollar "shipwreck payment" that's called for in our contract.

Coast Guard hearings and lawsuits followed. In the end, American Steamship was held to be 50 percent respon-sible for the incident. Cleveland Tankers, owners of the *Jupiter,* and the operators of the terminal were each found to be 25 percent responsible. While the *Buffalo* followed all appropriate procedures, its passing nonetheless trig-gered the disaster. The captain on the *Buffalo* at the time was John MacFalda from Rogers City, my brother's for-mer brother-in-law. John has a reputation as being an extremely prudent captain, always operating by the book. Cleveland Tankers was held partially responsible for the loss of their own ship, because flame arrestors in the pip-ing system intended to prevent fire from entering the cargo holds were defective. The operators of the petroleum terminal were faulted for the poor condition of their dock and pilings.

Wednesday, December 4
Lake Superior, Westbound

This is my last full day on the *Blough*. We should be docked at Two Harbors by about 2:00 in the morning and I'll get off. I have mixed emotions about leaving the *Blough*. It's a fine ship, with an exceptional crew who made me feel right at home. You don't always find a job as good as this one, and it's too bad it was for such a short time. On the other hand, it's been a long season, and I'm ready to get off.

This is probably my last full day on the lakes for the 1996 season and I leave it with mixed emotions. It has been the best season I've had as a steward, the best season since I've been sailing. That's probably due to the fact that I was able to spend so much time "at home" on the *Calcite II*, instead of bouncing from boat to boat every thirty days as an intinerant relief cook. "Have spatula, will travel" could easily be the motto of relief stewards. As ratty an old bucket as the *Calcite* is, staying there most of the season beat the hell out of packing up at the end of every month to go to a new boat, meet a new crew, get used to a new galley, find where the regular steward keeps his requisition forms, and so on, *ad infinitum*. Then too, much of the reason I was so comfortable on the *Calcite* was due to the crew. They were great shipmates. While I'm just getting to know the crew here on the *Blough*, they've also been a pleasant bunch. Many expressed their regret that I'm leaving so soon. It's always nice to go down the ladder with those sorts of comments ringing in your ears. Not every cook on the lakes is so lucky.

Despite all that, I'm glad to be getting off. I'm tired and I need a little recovery time before I start teaching at the union school in early January. Getting off now will give me about three weeks to get things organized for the school, which should be plenty of time, even with the holidays sandwiched in. The stint in Toledo will last at least nine weeks; by the time I'm done I'll probably only have a few weeks before

331

I'm called to go to work for the 1997 season. I have a lot I want to accomplish this winter, and little time to do it. I want to get this logbook off to my publisher, along with *Graveyard of the Lakes,* which is already more than six months overdue. Somewhere along the line, I'd also like to at least get started on my next writing project, a novel about an unemployed sailor who's trying to make a living as a writer. "Write what you know about," someone once told a young Ernest Hemingway. Given Hemingway's success, I'll follow that recommendation myself.

Time to go now. I've got to pack my sea bag, clean my room, and go back up into the galley and scrub down the stove before I try to get some sleep. I've definitely got a case of "channel fever," though. It may be difficult for me to relax enough to get any shuteye. I'll probably be a wreck tomorrow.

Saturday, December 7
St. Marys River, Downbound

As I've said before, the only thing certain in this industry is the uncertainty. I got off the *Blough* early Thursday morning, with the full expectation that the season was finally over for me. I spent Thursday night in Superior and got up early Friday morning to visit my brother while his boat loaded at the coal dock. When I went back to the motel to check out, the message light was blinking on my phone. Since Margy was the only one who knew where I was staying, I assumed it was a message from her, and I called the front desk. "You're supposed to call Bob Jackson at the Great Lakes Fleet," said the operator. "He's got a job for you." If the operator hadn't been on the line, I would have shouted a string of obscenities that would have shocked even the most hard-core sailor. I called Bob Jackson, our personnel supervisor, and he asked me if I could catch the *Edgar B. Speer* the following morning at the Soo. It seems that the second cook on the *Speer* had been fired for drinking. He's the same guy who got sent away to an alcohol rehab program when he got drunk while fitting out the *Calcite II* in the spring. I reluctantly agreed to take the job, though

332

I'm not sure why. So here I am, back on the run again for a couple of weeks. I got on at the Soo Warehouse at about 4:00 this afternoon, along with Elden Brege, who relieved the regular captain, and Mike Gapczynski, who's observing. Both are from Rogers City, but they also made the trip down from Duluth, having just gotten off the *Edwin H. Gott*.

There, that brings this logbook up-to-date. Now I've got to make my bed and try to get some sleep—4:30 A.M. is going to come very early tomorrow.

Sunday, December 8
Lake Michigan, Downbound

One day down, who knows how many to go. It was a tedious, boring day, without much activity on the boat. Most of the guys who weren't working were either napping or watching football games, except for the gang that started playing poker in the dining room after lunch and are still going strong at 7:00 P.M. We were bounced around quite a bit during the night and this morning; there were strong winds out of the northwest, but we're hugging the Wisconsin coast and riding quite nicely. We're checked down, though, so we won't get to Gary until sometime early tomorrow morning, instead of at midnight. I hope that doesn't screw up our schedule in Two Harbors.

There's nothing much to report today, so I'm going to curl up with a new book I picked up in the Soo. It's *Great Lakes Stories: Ashore After 50 Years*, by Ray McGrath, a retired captain. I'll let you know later if it's any good.

Monday, December 9
Gary, Indiana

Captain McGrath's book is quite good, although it could have used some careful editing. It rambles a lot and there are some factual errors, but most of the stories are wonderful. I'm about halfway through the book right now, so I'll reserve final judgment until I've finished it. I can say

333

it should be on the shelf of every Great Lakes boat buff. Interestingly, Bobby Bauer, who's the steward here on the *Speer*, sailed with McGrath at Kinsman, which is the fleet the captain retired from in 1985. According to Bobby, McGrath came to Kinsman after Columbia Transporation gave him the option of retiring or getting fired after he banged up a boat due to bad judgment. In the book, McGrath is quite critical of other captains who damaged their ships, including Dave Johnson, who captained the *Kinsman Independent* when it ran aground on Isle Royale several years ago. Dave was a first mate under McGrath at Kinsman, so maybe there's bad blood between the two. Dave's a pretty laid-back guy, and McGrath sounds as though he was a rather autocratic skipper. Anyway, I'm curious whether McGrath will explain the circumstances under which he left Columbia. We'll see.

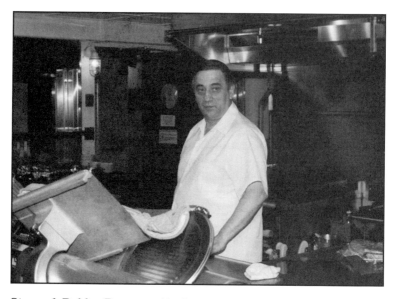

Steward Bobby Bauer waits for crewmembers to show up for lunch on the *Edgar B. Speer*. Personnel on the *Speer* and most of the ships built since the 1970s go through a cafeteria-type line to get their meals, while crewmembers on older vessels are generally served tableside by the porter or second cook. (Author's collection)

After we got into Gary around 11:00 this morning, I called Harry Crooks, director of our union's educational programs to find out when I should report to the school. Harry wants me down there on January 2 to complete all the final arrangements before classes begin on January 6. That means I could be out here over Christmas. The regular second cook is scheduled to come back sometime between December 23 and December 26. I'm hoping for the earlier date, but past history tells me that's unlikely. Guys don't like to go back to their boats a few days before Christmas, and the office is usually quite sympathetic. Ike Ross, the regular second cook, is likely to come back in Gary.

Despite the stories I've heard about Bobby Bauer, he's been excellent to work with the past couple of days. I was a little apprehensive, but he's treating me extremely well and we've had a lot of fun in the galley. The meals he puts out are different than what I'd do, but they've been varied and well-prepared. Having heard so many complaints about his cooking over the past couple of years, I find that interesting and a little puzzling.

Tuesday, December 10
Lake Michigan, Upbound

I had trouble getting to sleep last night. The unloading elevator that raises the cargo from the belt under the cargo hold to the hopper that feeds the deck boom is just on the other side of the wall of my room, so it's rather noisy in here during an unload. In my bathroom, you can actually feel the vibration of the unloading elevator as it races past my room carrying hundreds of tons of iron ore. Vibrating toilets are novel, but based on my experience I don't think they'll catch on.

I finished Captain Ray McGrath's book last night. (No, he didn't mention that Columbia supposedly gave him the choice of quitting or getting fired after he damaged one of their boats.) The parts of the book about his career are interesting and entertaining, and he discusses many of the dramatic changes that took place during his career on the lakes, from 1935 to 1985. The book is not well-organized,

Classified as a self-discharging ship, the *Speer* has a shuttle-type unloading boom mounted transversely on her main deck, just ahead of the cabin. The boom can extend about 40 feet out either side of the vessel to discharge cargo. Here the ship is unloading into a shoreside hopper at Conneaut, Ohio. The only other port the vessel can unload at is Gary, Indiana. (Author's collection)

however, and it jumps around chronologically, which can be confusing. He also intersperses the vignettes about his own career and his childhood with short pieces about various ships that sailed on the lakes that have no relationship to the book's primary focus. The pieces about the ships are accompanied by Captain McGrath's drawings, which aren't particularly good. An aggressive editor could have turned this good book into an outstanding one. Despite the shortcomings, however, it's well worth the modest cover price, as it contains a lot of valuable information about the evolution of the boats that operate on the lakes. It also paints an interesting picture of a Great Lakes captain who, by the way, is typical of many captains who worked on the lakes over the years.

McGrath comes across as a macho captain who bordered on being tyrannical aboard his ships. He also devotes considerable space in the book to patting himself on the back for his shiphandling talents, his willingness to come to the aid of pleasure boaters in distress, and the soft spot in his heart for many of the sailors who shipped with him. A number of his stories are about how he rewarded sailors for helping him out by putting them down for overtime pay they didn't earn. Bobby Bauer said that McGrath's wife occasionally boarded the boat at the Soo, and a crewmember would get off and drive her car to the head of the lakes. The sailor continued to get paid while he was off the boat, and he got overtime on top of it. McGrath's generosity was, of course, being paid for by the shipping company he worked for. The character profile we piece together from McGrath's stories has plenty of blemishes, but it's typical of many captains who've sailed the lakes . . . and many of the captains who currently reign as masters of their small domains. I don't think he's a captain I'd have enjoyed serving under. I've worked for quite a few guys just like him. They're not too hard to find, unfortunately.

In the end, I finished the book feeling sorry for McGrath's wife and two sons. He makes much of the fact that there were only two years when he got off the boat during the sailing season, to attend the funerals of his father and his mother-in-law. For much of his career, McGrath sailed during the winter months on the railroad ferries that operated then on Lake Michigan, rather than spend the winters at home with his family. He obviously equated being a husband and father with providing a substantial income for his family, rather than spending time with them. That's sad, but fairly common in the sailing community. I suppose it's no different than the corporate executive who puts his job ahead of his family.

My heart's not in being second cook. Right now, I just don't want to be out on the boats. I'll struggle through, though. There are only about two weeks to go.

Wednesday, December 11
Lake Superior, Upbound

We went through the Soo Locks just before breakfast this morning, and should be into Two Harbors by 8:00 A.M.

tomorrow. That's a bad time, unless Margy managed to get the day off. We could be there until about 8:00 P.M., which would be great, but you can't count on that. If we happen to get a fast load, we could be on our way by 2:00 in the afternoon.

Quite a few crewmembers complained about Bobby's supper tonight, the first widespread complaints I've heard since I've been on here. Bobby cooked fifteen pounds of shell-on shrimp, which are always popular on the boat, but he let them sit in the hot water for more than an hour after they were cooked. They were, shall we say, well done. He also cooked some breaded shrimp, and he overcooked them, too. I don't know why, but Bobby seems to overcook everything he deep-fries. The guys complained about that on the *Calcite II* after he'd been there in the fall. The chief said he once deep-fried salmon patties until they were so hard you could throw them against the bulkhead and they wouldn't break. My guess is that he once deep-fried some frozen shrimp or scallops and didn't get them cooked thoroughly in the center. Now he's overcompensating. All in all, though, Bobby's cooking has been reasonably good. It's "steamboat cuisine" without any contemporary dishes, but he's done a nice variety since I've been here. And, he's certainly easy to work with.

The crew on this boat is definitely more temperamental than those on the *Calcite II* or *Blough*. There are guys in both the engine and deck departments who are sullen, moody, and argumentative. I haven't said much since I've been here, except to the few guys I consider to be friendly. I went through the crew list today and calculated that there are thirteen crewmembers I feel comfortable talking to out of a total of twenty-six. In other words, 50 percent of the crew are hospitable. There are a couple of other guys I'll talk to, but only if they initiate the conversation. They're moody— sometimes they're friendly, sometimes they're not. Bobby said "Good morning" to one of them the other day, and didn't get *any* response.

Some of the guys who aren't too friendly are "anti-Rogers City." They don't like sailors from Rogers City, and they're generally pretty open about it. With the current captain being from Rogers, however, they've been noticeably quieter than usual. Geez, we're such lovable guys. How could they not like us? Once Elden gets off, I'm sure the Rogers City–haters will become much more vocal. I try not to pay attention to them, but when you're drinking coffee at one end of the messroom table and the jackals are sitting at the other end badmouthing Rogers City, I get the distinct feeling they're trying to send *me* a message. Okay, message received. One of these days they're going to catch me in a bad mood, and then they'll get an earful. As you already know, I'm proud of my hometown and the generations of sailors it has produced.

Thursday, December 12
Two Harbors, Minnesota

We arrived a little after 8:00 this morning, and after a lot of breakdowns on the dock, it now appears that we may not be out of here until midnight. If we don't lose any more time on the run, that's going to put us back in here about 4:00 A.M. next Wednesday. That would be a *terrible* time, so I hope we get stuck in boat traffic at the Soo, or take a little weather delay.

One of the crewmembers talked to the regular second cook on the phone today, and his present intention is to come back in Gary the trip following this one. Without delays, that would have me getting off in Gary on December 21. Even if we lose a couple days along the way, that should still get me off here before Christmas.

Saturday, December 14
Lake Michigan, Downbound

We made an uneventful passage across Lake Superior yesterday, and I was up at 3:00 this morning to stow groceries going through the Soo. I had about a thirty-minute nap after lunch, but I'm still whipped. On top of getting up in the middle of the night, it was "bed day" and I had to change the beds of all six of the engine officers, while the porter did the four deck officers. I think it was somewhere

339

in the midst of that unsavory task that I decided this would be my last second cook's job . . . ever. I don't like making beds, I don't like playing second fiddle in a galley, and I don't like sleeping in a twin bed. (Unlicensed personnel have twin beds, while officers have double beds. The officers' contract actually requires their rooms to have a double bed, desk and a recliner.) I'm far enough up on the steward's seniority list now that I should be able to get in all the work I want in subsequent seasons without taking any jobs as a second cook.

Sunday, December 15
Lake Michigan, Downbound

We've run into a bit of dicey weather that's going to delay our arrival at Gary. We're battling forty-mile-an-hour winds out of the south and eleven-foot seas. Sometime during the night, they shut one engine down and reduced speed, so we won't be down to Gary until around 5:00 P.M. (It's now almost 10:00 A.M. and we're just south of Muskegon, Michigan.) Even when we get to Gary, we don't know whether we'll be able to get into the harbor to unload. At this point, I cringe at every delay, because it means that much more time on the boat for me. If this keeps up, with delays at both ends of the lake, I could end up spending Christmas on the *Speer,* and that wouldn't make me very happy. I'm psychologically geared up to be home for Christmas, and I'll be extremely disappointed if I'm not.

We're so cut off out here that it's hard to get too excited about Christmas. If it wasn't for the scraggly imitation tree in the corner of the messroom, Christmas could almost pass without notice. This is a difficult time for us to be away from our families and loved ones. I don't think anyone on the boat is really caught up in the Christmas spirit. There's more to Christmas than just giving and receiving gifts. There's a special ambiance to Christmas that's created by decorating the Christmas tree, listening to Christmas music on the radio and in stores, baking Christmas cookies, being around so many people who are in unusually joyful moods, and enjoying all the lights and decorations.

340

The consoles and electrical panels in the engine control room deep within the hull of the *Edgar B. Speer* contain hundreds of dials, gauges, and lights that engineering personnel rely on to monitor the operation of the ship's powerful diesel engines and myriad other critical equipment. The twin-screw *Speer* is driven by two sixteen-cylinder diesel engines that produce more than 19,000 horsepower. (Author's collection)

We miss all that. Our routines go on, just as they have since fitout last spring, except that most crewmembers are a little grumpier than usual. It's been at least eight years since I've really enjoyed a Christmas. Over those years, I've usually been out here on the lakes for Christmas, and that's been the pits. I've found that spending the holidays on the boats is far worse than the Christmas I spent on a crowded troop ship on my way to Germany, or the year when I spent Christmas in Vietnam. On the troop ship, there was the anticipation of our arrival in a foreign land on December 28. In Vietnam we spent the day guarding the Bob Hope troupe—including Raquel Welch, who gave each of us a hug and kiss—and followed it up by cooking hamburgers on a grill in front of our hootch, the only cookout we had that entire year. We even had a Christmas tree of sorts—a single bulb someone had gotten from home hanging on a small palm tree. So there'd be no mistake about what day it was amid the red clay and incessant dust of Vietnam, I hand-lettered a sign: "Christmas 1967, Long Binh, Vietnam," and bordered it with dark green holly and brilliant red berries. I was a short-timer by then, and my family kept their Christmas tree up until I got home on January 11, and there were still plenty of presents to be opened.

Out here on the boats, however, there's simply nothing to make the day special for most of us. Christmas becomes a sad day rather than a joyous one. We're filled, not with peace and happiness, but with loneliness and longing.

Until the 1970s, most of the ships on the Great Lakes were laid-up by Christmas and most of the crews were home with their families. In the 1970s the shipping companies began experimenting with extending the shipping season. There were a couple of years when a few ships actually ran all winter, but that proved too costly. In the end the companies and government maritime agencies such as the Coast Guard and Corps of Engineers decided it was feasible to keep the boats running through the second or third weeks of January, and that's the situation today. Many sailors don't get home until the first of February, and they're on their way back to fitout around the middle of March. That makes for a short winter and an awfully long shipping season. If we weren't entitled to thirty days off for every sixty days we work during the season, it would be unbearable.

There's a rumor circulating that Interlake Steamship is going to have their *J. L. Mauthe* converted to a tug-barge. To do that they remove most of the equipment from the ship's engine room, and then cut a "notch" in the stern for the bow of the tug to fit into. The tug pushes the barge most of the time rather than pulling it at the end of a towing hawser, because it's more maneuverable that way. The *Mauthe* is a straight-decker, with no self-unloading system, and she hasn't operated for a few years now. When she last ran, the *Mauthe* was in the grain trade between Superior-Duluth and Buffalo. She's one of the AAA-class boats, built during the Korean War in the early 1950s. Of the surviving boats from the class, the *Mauthe* is the only one that hasn't been lengthened and converted to a self-unloader. Those who told me of the planned conversion

342

didn't know if she was simultaneously going to be converted to a self-unloader. If she's not, then it's likely that Interlake intends to put her back into the grain trade, as there's no market on the lakes for straight-deckers in the ore, coal, or stone trades anymore. Only about 647 feet long, the *Mauthe* is one of only a handful of U.S. ships on the lakes that are small enough to go up the river at Buffalo to the grain terminals. It'll be interesting to see what Interlake is planning to do. They'll be the first of the major Great Lakes shipping companies to convert a freighter into a tug-barge. I hope that doesn't start a trend, at least not while I'm still out here sailing. I worked on the *Mauthe* during the 1990 season.

Monday, December 16
Gary, Indiana

I woke up at 4:00 this morning when we lifted the anchor to head into U.S. Steel's Gary plant. We had been at anchor offshore since yesterday evening, waiting for the wind to go down. Absent any delays, this is going to put us back up in Two Harbors at about 11:00 P.M. Wednesday. That's a terrible time. We could be loaded and gone before the sun comes up Thursday morning.

We got "official" word from the fleet's personnel office yesterday afternoon that Ike Ross, the regular second cook here on the *Speer*, will be coming back the next time we get to Gary, which will probably be on December 23. We already knew that unofficially, but it was good to get the formal notice from the office. I can't believe Ike's actually coming back to the boat two days before Christmas, but I'm certainly glad he is. Now I can try to firm up my plans to get home from Gary. With all the gear I'm carrying, I'd like to avoid flying, if that's at all possible. Just getting from the boat to O'Hare Airport in Chicago is a major hassle. It involves finding someone here at the steel plant to pick me up at the dock and give me a ride out to the gate, taking a cab to the Tri-State bus terminal in nearby Hammond, Indiana, riding the bus from Hammond to O'Hare, flying to Detroit, changing planes—and airlines—there, fly-

343

ing to Alpena on a small commuter airplane—"kamikaze" airlines, I call it—and then having my brother or someone pick me up at the airport there and drive me to Rogers City. I could probably get to Timbuktu with fewer hassles. It's seldom easy to get to and from the docks we call at around the lakes.

We finished unloading and left Gary just before 6:00 P.M., which will put us into Two Harbors shortly after midnight Wednesday. There's a storm brewing up on Lake Superior, though, so we may get delayed a little.

Tuesday, December 17
Lake Michigan, Upbound

Finally, again, my last trip of the year. This time next week I'll be on dry land. I'm sure the time will fly by. I should be off the *Speer* next Sunday or Monday. Like most of the guys on the boat, I'm ready to wrap things up for 1996. By this point in the season, we're all a little ragged. We've been fortunate this year, though, as the weather has been unusually moderate. We haven't had any of the brutal cold yet that's so common on the northern lakes in December.

The way things stand right now, the *Speer* will lay up around January 10. After I get off, they're scheduled to make only two more trips. Building in some time for delays, they should unload at Gary for the last time around January 7, and then race north for the lay-up dock at Duluth. The *Blough* is on a similar schedule, while the *Gott*, the fleet's other 1,000-footer, has one additional trip to make. The tug-barge *Presque Isle*, which our fleet manages for Litton Great Lakes, should be laying up during the first days of January. The *Munson, Callaway, Clarke,* and *Anderson* are all supposed to be finished by the end of December, while the *Sloan*, the only one of the little grey boats still running, should be going in sometime this week. The Soo Locks will close on January 15, which will bring the season to an end for most of the shipping companies. I think this is probably the earliest end to the season in the last seven or eight years. There've been far fewer delays this year than during 1995, so the fleets were able to carry all the tonnage they

344

were contracted to haul in a shorter season. They have a sign at the entrance to the docks at Two Harbors that compares the number of ships loaded this year to 1995, and I was surprised at how many more boats were loaded there this season. I'm sure the companies are happy. Cutting a few weeks off the season saves a lot of wear and tear on the boats, reduces operating costs, and undoubtedly increases profits.

We had a fire-and-boat drill after dinner tonight, but the weather was too bad for us to go out on deck. Instead, we went down to the CO_2 room in the engine room, and First Mate Scott Moore explained how the system works. When activated, the system floods the engine room spaces with CO_2 to smother a fire. Of course, if any crewmembers are in the engine room at the time, the carbon dioxide would probably kill them. There's an alarm that sounds when the system is activated, and anyone working in the engine spaces has eighty seconds to evacuate before the CO_2 is released. That's not a lot of time. The engine room is five stories high.

After our little class down in the engine room, we all went back up to the galley deck with our survival suits and dumped them out of their storage bags so the mates could make sure the signal lights were working. When I turned the bag with my suit upside down to shake the suit out, the first thing that clattered onto the deck was an empty whiskey bottle, a souvenir, no doubt, of the prior occupant of my room—the second cook who got fired for being drunk. That got a laugh out of the rest of the crew, and led to some lighthearted ribbing.

Wednesday, December 18

Lake Superior, Upbound

It's 2:00 P.M., and we're doing some rocking and rolling. There's a stout sea running out here on Lake Superior, so we've deviated from the normal course and will head for the shelter of the north shore. That'll add a little time to our trip, and put us in at Two Harbors at a slightly saner time tomorrow. I'm thankful I'm on a 1,000-footer. If we were out here on a smaller boat, we'd get one merry ride. There are a couple more drawbacks to sailing: you get seasick from the boat rolling back and forth in high seas or your boat may break up and you might drown! After making a trip on the Great Lakes in the last century, British author Charles Dickens said something to the effect that being on a steamboat was much like being in jail, with the added possibility of drowning. That's still accurate today.

I just went into the messroom to get a cup of coffee, and Ray, the jovial 4-to-8 watchman, asked whether I'd replaced the empty whiskey bottle in my survival suit bag with a full one. He thinks "bring the booze" should be added to my abandon-ship assignments on the station bill, along with "provide first aid kit and extra blankets."[27]

Friday, December 20
Lake Superior, Downbound

This should be my last full day on the lakes this season. When we were at Two Harbors yesterday, I talked Dick John from personnel into letting me get off when the boat gets back to the Soo, instead of waiting until Gary. That will save me a lot of hassles getting home. We should be at the supply boat at the Soo around 1:00 tomorrow morning, and I'll get off the *Speer* and catch a bus to Rogers City. With luck, I should be home by around 9:00 tomorrow morning.

Today will be a long and busy one. Since Bobby and the porter will run short-handed between the Soo and Gary, I'm going to not only do my baking for today, but I'll prepare some stuff they can use on their trip down Lake Michigan tomorrow. I'll also try to get some of the engineers' beds made up today, a day ahead of schedule. The porter or Ike can finish them up Saturday or Sunday. This evening, I'll

---

[27]The "station bill," posted in a number of locations throughout the ship, specifies the duties of each crewmember in case of a fire, or if we should have to abandon ship. In either scenario, having a bottle of booze handy might greatly improve the general outlook of the crew.

do a load of laundry, so I don't have to haul a bag of dirty clothes home, pack my bags, and touch up the room a little bit. That's how my last day on the *Speer*—and my last day of the 1996 shipping season—will shape up. Busy, but not too exciting.

As I look back, it's been quite a year. For being at the bottom of the fleet's relief list, I got in a lot more sailing days than I'd anticipated. This is probably due to the fact that I got called early to finish fitting out the *Calcite II*, and the fact that cooks in the fleet with more seniority than I have avoided the old girl like the plague. They're all from the Duluth-Superior area, and they stayed away from the *Calcite* because she doesn't go up to Lake Superior. Despite the fact that the *C-2* isn't air conditioned, and it's got a tiny galley with equipment that's older than I am, she quickly became a "home" for me.

One of the best aspects of being on the *Calcite II* was that she called at a lot of places I'd never been before— Green Bay, Saginaw, Lake Charlevoix, Ludington, Drummond Island, Brevort, Menominee, Goderich, and a number of different docks on the Cuyahoga River at Cleveland. It kept things interesting, and broadened my knowledge of the Great Lakes shipping industry.

While the little *Calcite* became my "home," I also enjoyed the opportunities I had to relieve on the *Speer, Munson,* and *Blough.* All three are magnificent ships, among the finest ever built on the lakes. Working in their modern, well-equipped galleys certainly made my job easier.

The work in the galley is seldom easy, at least not if you're doing your job right. No matter how many hours you work, there always seems to be something else that needs to be done. During the 155 days I worked as a steward this season, I prepared and served about 3,030 meals. To feed the hungry crews on the four boats, I made about 230 gallons of soup, or slightly over 4 barrels, and roasted, fried, stewed, broiled, and grilled in excess of 4,000 pounds of meat. The hard-drinking sailors also consumed more than 600 gallons of milk—about 10 barrels—along with similarly copious quantities of *Kool-Aid* and fruit juices. Yes, keeping the crew fed and the galley clean will definitely keep you busy, sometimes busier than you want to be, but it's still the best job I've ever had.

347

In the final analysis it wasn't the ships I sailed on, the cargoes we carried, the ports we called at, or even the working conditions in the galleys that made the 1996 season such an outstanding one for me. This has been the most enjoyable season I've ever put in on the lakes *because of the crews I sailed with.* I've never had better shipmates, especially my gang on the *Calcite II.*

When you go aboard a ship for the first time, most of the faces are new and it's quite a task just to match names with faces. Amazingly, though, whether you're on the boat for a week, a month, or a season, you always manage to develop some close friendships—friendships that usually endure. In that respect, this season has been quite extraordinary. Never before have I made so many good friends in a single season.

This is how the season of 1996 will end for me, not with the rush of excitement that was generated by that unexpected call to go and fitout the *Calcite II* back on April 23, but with mundane housekeeping chores I've done so many times before this year—doing laundry, cleaning my room, packing my bags. When I pick up my discharge tonight it will be with the calm assurance that I made the best of the season of 1996: I visited many new ports, served on some marvelous ships, and met a lot of interesting people. Most importantly, when I get off the boat tomorrow morning, I'll be leaving behind not just shipmates, but friends.

Going down the ladder for the last time during the 1996 season doesn't signal a finale, but merely an intermission. As happy as I am to be getting off the boat now, I'm already looking forward to shipping out again in 1997. When the ice starts to break up on the lakes in the spring, I'll be eager to pack my old, worn sea bag and report to a ship, as countless generations of sailors have done on the Great Lakes over the past three hundred years.

TITLES IN THE GREAT LAKES BOOKS SERIES

Michigan Lumbertowns: Lumbermen and Laborers in Saginaw, Bay City, and Muskegon, 1870–1905, by Jeremy W. Kilar, 1990

Detroit Kids Catalog: The Hometown Tourist by Ellyce Field, 1990

Waiting for the News, by Leo Litwak, 1990 (reprint)

Detroit Perspectives, edited by Wilma Wood Henrickson, 1991

Life on the Great Lakes: A Wheelsman's Story, by Fred W. Dutton, edited by William Donohue Ellis, 1991

Copper Country Journal: The Diary of Schoolmaster Henry Hobart, 1863–1864, by Henry Hobart, edited by Philip P. Mason, 1991

John Jacob Astor: Business and Finance in the Early Republic, by John Denis Haeger, 1991

Survival and Regeneration: Detroit's American Indian Community, by Edmund J. Danziger, Jr., 1991

Steamboats and Sailors of the Great Lakes, by Mark L. Thompson, 1991

Cobb Would Have Caught It: The Golden Age of Baseball in Detroit, by Richard Bak, 1991

Michigan in Literature, by Clarence Andrews, 1992

Under the Influence of Water: Poems, Essays, and Stories, by Michael Delp, 1992

The Country Kitchen, by Della T. Lutes, 1992 (reprint)

The Making of a Mining District: Keweenaw Native Copper 1500–1870, by David J. Krause, 1992

Kids Catalog of Michigan Adventures, by Ellyce Field, 1993

Henry's Lieutenants, by Ford R. Bryan, 1993

Historic Highway Bridges of Michigan, by Charles K. Hyde, 1993

Lake Erie and Lake St. Clair Handbook, by Stanley J. Bolsenga and Charles E. Herndendorf, 1993

Queen of the Lakes, by Mark Thompson, 1994

Iron Fleet: The Great Lakes in World War II, by George J. Joachim, 1994

Turkey Stearnes and the Detroit Stars: The Negro Leagues in Detroit, 1919–1933, by Richard Bak, 1994

Pontiac and the Indian Uprising, by Howard H. Peckham, 1994 (reprint)

Charting the Inland Seas: A History of the U.S. Lake Survey, by Arthur M. Woodford, 1994 (reprint)

Ojibwa Narratives of Charles and Charlotte Kawbawgam and Jacques LePique, 1893–1895. Recorded with Notes by Homer H. Kidder, edited by Arthur P. Bourgeois, 1994, co-published with the Marquette County Historical Society

Strangers and Sojourners: A History of Michigan's Keweenaw Peninsula, by Arthur W. Thurner, 1994

Win Some, Lose Some: G. Mennen Williams and the New Democrats, by Helen Washburn Berthelot, 1995

Sarkis, by Gordon and Elizabeth Orear, 1995

The Northern Lights: Lighthouses of the Upper Great Lakes, by Charles K. Hyde, 1995 (reprint)

Kids Catalog of Michigan Adventures, second edition, by Ellyce Field, 1995

Rumrunning and the Roaring Twenties: Prohibition on the Michigan-Ontario Waterway, by Philip P. Mason, 1995

In the Wilderness with the Red Indians, by E. R. Baierlein, translated by Anita Z. Boldt, edited by Harold W. Moll, 1996

Elmwood Endures: History of a Detroit Cemetery, by Michael Franck, 1996

Master of Precision: Henry M. Leland, by Mrs. Wilfred C. Leland with Minnie Dubbs Millbrook, 1996 (reprint)

Haul-Out: New and Selected Poems, by Stephen Tudor, 1996

Kids Catalog of Michigan Adventures, third edition, by Ellyce Field, 1997

Beyond the Model T: The Other Ventures of Henry Ford, revised edition, by Ford R. Bryan, 1997

Young Henry Ford: A Picture History of the First Forty Years, by Sidney Olson, 1997 (reprint)

The Coast of Nowhere: Meditations on Rivers, Lakes and Streams, by Michael Delp, 1997

From Saginaw Valley to Tin Pan Alley: Saginaw's Contribution to American Popular Music, 1890–1955, by R. Grant Smith, 1998

The Long Winter Ends, by Newton G. Thomas, 1998 (reprint)

Bridging the River of Hatred: The Pioneering Efforts of Detroit Police Commissioner George Edwards, 1962–1963, by Mary M. Stolberg, 1998

Toast of the Town: The Life and Times of Sunnie Wilson, by Sunnie Wilson with John Cohassey, 1998

These Men Have Seen Hard Service: The First Michigan Sharpshooters in the Civil War, by Raymond J. Herek, 1998

A Place for Summer: One Hundred Years at Michigan and Trumbull, by Richard Bak, 1998

Early Midwestern Travel Narratives: An Annotated Bibliography, 1634–1850, by Robert R. Hubach, 1998 (reprint)

All-American Anarchist: Joseph A. Labadie and the Labor Movement, by Carlotta R. Anderson, 1998

Michigan in the Novel, 1816–1996: An Annotated Bibliography, by Robert Beasecker, 1998

"Time by Moments Steals Away": The 1848 Journal of Ruth Douglass, by Robert L. Root, Jr., 1998

The Detroit Tigers: A Pictorial Celebration of the Greatest Players and Moments in Tigers' History, updated edition, by William M. Anderson, 1999

A Sailor's Logbook: A Season aboard Great Lakes Freighters, by Mark L. Thompson, 1999

For an updated listing of books in this series, please visit our Web site at http://wsupress.wayne.edu